Advance Praise for *Healing Wounds*

"Diane Carlson Evans' book chronicles an amazing journey; a tale of passion, mission, and tenacity. It was a journey that took far longer than it should have and, beyond being incredibly inspiring, it is instructive about the bureaucracy of Washington, the pettiness and self-interests that had to be overcome to recognize the contributions of women so overlooked and understated. Having been to The Wall and the Statue many times now, and moved by it each time, I appreciate even more Diane's well-told story of 'leadership, persistence, resilience, industriousness...' (her daughter's words). I admit to a personal connection to this story; son of an Army Nurse, cared for by Army Nurses in Vietnam; part of Army Medicine where nurses shaped me professionally; serving at the VA where we were challenged to get women veterans to identify and to be welcoming and responsive to their needs; and having served with Diane and her husband at Brooke Army Medical Center. *Healing Wounds* is a must read and a reminder that one person can make all the difference!"

—James B. Peake, MD, Lieutenant General, USA (Ret), 6th Secretary of Veterans Affairs

"A powerful book. A necessary book. Within the first dozen pages, tears were flowing. Diane took on three heroic tasks in her life: serving as a combat nurse in Vietnam; despite ferocious opposition, leading the battle for a monument on the Mall to women who served in Vietnam; and telling her story in this book of the emotional price paid when she was shamefully rejected and reviled by fellow Americans. Diane recovered from the war and its aftermath by acting, doing, and salvaging the memories of the women who served. We owe her an incalculable debt."

—Theodore Roosevelt IV, Underwater Demolition Team 11, Vietnam two tours: 1966 and 1967

"Evans' book is a soulful accounting of her long-fought journey to recognize the immense contributions and sacrifices of women during the Vietnam War."

—Chuck Hagel, 24th Secretary of Defense,
United States Senator, and Vietnam Veteran

"A fascinating, yet heart-rending chronicle of Diane Carlson Evans' heroic journey and her decade-long struggle to honor the women who served during the Vietnam War. Every Brother and Sister veteran, their families, and those who haven't served, should read *Healing Wounds*."

—John Finley Sommer, Combat Medic, 3/12th
Infantry, 4th Infantry Division, Vietnam, 1968 and
Executive Director, The American Legion, 1991–2009

"Diane Carlson Evans went from working as a combat nurse to becoming a national advocate for all the women who served during the Vietnam War. What makes *Healing Wounds* different from other nurses' wartime memoirs is the aftermath. Evans came home with the awful inventory of battle in her memory. She married and became the mother of four, yet the loss and sacrifice she witnessed in her fellow nurses and patients never left her. This emptiness, combined with the country's indifference to the women's war efforts, drove her into the political world to push for a statue to honor those females who served, next to the statue of the Three Soldiers at the Vietnam Veterans Memorial. One powerful Washington D.C. committee vetoed the idea and said if there was a statue dedicated to women, the next statue might have to be for the dogs who served in the K-9 units. It is this compelling story of perseverance that will make you angry, proud, and inspired."

—Elizabeth M. Norman, PhD, RN author of
*Women at War: The Story of Fifty Military Nurses
Who Served in Vietnam* and *We Band of Angels: The
Untold Story of American Women Trapped on Bataan*

"'The sun is shining on us,' Diane Carlson Evans said on a radiant fall day as she opened the ceremony to dedicate the Vietnam Women's Memorial on November 11, 1993. I was among 25,000 others who celebrated in a triumphant moment for our nation, for all women who served in Vietnam, and for Diane, whose dignity, decency, and courage are of the highest caliber I know. I was in Vietnam as a twenty-two-year-old reporter. Diane, a twenty-one-year-old nurse. We thought we were all grown up. *Healing Wounds* affirms what I have long believed: the best Vietnam war stories are love stories. Diane's love of her country, her patients, and her fellow nurses, carried her through the mud and blood of Vietnam. Her love carried her over every obstacle placed in her path in the ten years, ten years, it took her to spearhead her vision into reality. Don't be fooled by her Minnesota nice. Diane is a woman warrior who fights with love and the courage of her convictions instead of bullets. *Healing Wounds* is exquisitely painful, heartbreakingly beautiful, and ultimately, triumphant. Finally, the sun is shining on Diane Carlson Evans."

—Laura Palmer, Author, *Shrapnel in the Heart*, Co-author, *War Torn: Stories of War from the Women Reporters who covered Vietnam*

"I was Lieutenant Sharon Lane's Head Nurse when she was killed by a rocket while on duty in our hospital in Vietnam. She is remembered with her name etched on the Wall in Washington, D.C. Diane Carlson Evans' long journey fighting for us has helped heal my deep emotional wounds and those of thousands of sister veterans who lived through that war and who are honored and forever remembered by the Vietnam Women's Memorial."

—Colonel Jane Carson, USA (Ret), Vietnam, 1969–70

"Diane Carlson Evans helped to unleash the stories of thousands of women who served in the Vietnam era when she bravely walked into her own past. She led the charge for a sacred space to commemorate the courage, healing, and community of this generation of women. As a result of her courageous leadership, the Vietnam Women's Memorial is an icon of healing and hope—not just for those touched by the Vietnam War—but for those serving in current conflicts and the generations that will follow. I am in awe of how in claiming her own narrative, she has allowed others to believe they can do the same."

—Dr. Marsha Guenzler-Stevens, PhD,
University of Maryland

HEALING WOUNDS

A Vietnam War Combat Nurse's
10-Year Fight to Win Women a
Place of Honor in Washington, D.C.

DIANE CARLSON EVANS
with Bob Welch

PERMUTED
PRESS

A PERMUTED PRESS BOOK

ISBN: 978-1-68261-912-4
ISBN (eBook): 978-1-68261-913-1

Permuted Press, LLC
New York • Nashville
permutedpress.com

Published in the United States of America

For my husband Mike
Our children Guy, Luke, Carrie, Jon-Erik
Our grandchildren
and
My sister and brother veterans of the Vietnam War

First they ignore you, then they laugh at you,
then they fight you, then you win.

—Mahatma Gandhi

CONTENTS

FOREWORD

BY JOSEPH GALLOWAY

I read Diane Carlson Evans's *Healing Wounds* through a veil of scalding tears and burning memories of a war of our younger days that gripped our hearts and simply would not let go.

I first met Diane on the speakers' platform at Memorial Day and Veterans Day events at the Wall in Washington, D.C. When I looked into her eyes, I saw something I recognized: the same hidden pain I saw when I looked into the mirror each morning. Mine grew out of four tours as a war correspondent in Vietnam in some of the bloodiest battles of the war. I had carried and held young Americans terribly wounded. To some I whispered, "You will be all right," even as I watched the life drain from their eyes. I had seen a few; Diane had seen literally hundreds—this combat nurse holding their hands while they died. Her pain was deeper and wider by far.

From that first meeting, I believed in her and her cause to establish a memorial for women who had been part of the Vietnam War. I watched as she overcame every obstacle and silenced every foe with polite determination, but an iron will.

On November 11, 1993, I marched in a veterans' parade that wended its way down Pennsylvania Avenue past the White House and on to the Vietnam Veterans Memorial. Up above the Wall, in a small grove of trees, Diane and the women would later dedicate their memorial—a glorious bronze statue of three women and a wounded soldier, larger than life. One woman cradles the soldier, one looks skyward, searching for a Dustoff helicopter or perhaps God. A third holds the soldier's helmet.

That statue is a reminder that Diane Carlson Evans and her hard-fighting group had finally gotten the job done. America owes them a great debt of gratitude for opening our eyes and our hearts to those who also served and suffered in that war of our youth.

—Joseph L. Galloway

Galloway was a Vietnam war correspondent from 1965–66, and in 1971, 1973, and 1975. He is co-author of We Were Soldiers Once…and Young, We Are Soldiers Still, *and* They Were Soldiers: The Sacrifices and Contributions of Our Vietnam Veterans.

PREFACE

It's been fifty years since I returned home from Vietnam. My story has been burning inside of me ever since. Why didn't I tell it sooner? I wasn't ready to pour it out to the world. A part of me still feels like that young combat nurse getting off the plane at Travis Air Force Base in August 1969—afraid to face the public hostility rooted in riots and protests against the war and *us* for having served our country.

I could endure rocket attacks, but I couldn't endure mean-spirited words telling me that my generation and I were not worthy. I had been warned to not wear my uniform home. But I did. I was proud of the Army Nurse Corps uniform and of our contribution to the war. In Vietnam, I became numb and felt little fear of rocket and mortar attacks or the ominous vibration of helicopters bringing in another load of casualties. I had no fear of knowing what to do when yet another young soldier with chest injuries needed a ventilator. There, I had overcome my worst fears. But back in the U.S., fear kept me from finding the courage to tell my story; it would lay me open to more criticism, more speculation, more sleepless nights. Who would believe me? Who would care?

Beyond that, a huge part of my Vietnam story—the one involving the memorial for women—had yet to come to fruition.

As in Vietnam, it took time to become brave, to face what was in front of us. I found my courage again. Part of that comes from the inspiration of so many extraordinary women veterans who have preceded me.

I salute them, women such as Florence Nightingale of the Crimean War, Clara Barton of the Civil War, and countless others whose names and contributions regrettably haven't made history books.

On a more personal level, there is Vera Brittain, an English woman who served as a volunteer nurse in World War I in the British Empire. When I read of her wartime experiences in her memoir *Testament of Youth*, I was stunned to realize how deeply I related to her. Even though she served over a century ago, her feelings about the experience of caring for wounded soldiers, and war's aftermath for her generation, were so close to mine. I honor her by using quotes from her book at the beginning of each of my book's five parts.

We wouldn't know of these women if they hadn't shared their stories. Now, I share mine.

This is not the definitive story of women and the Vietnam War. It's simply one woman's story about military service—and the unexpected journey that followed. I hope it's an inspiration for all women who serve our nation, a reminder that their stories are important, too.

—Diane Carlson Evans
August 2019

PART I: FACING THE PAST

Only, I felt, by some such attempt to write history in terms of personal life could I rescue something that might be of value, some element of truth and hope and usefulness, from the smashing up of my own youth by the War. It is true that to do it meant looking back into a past of which many of us, preferring to contemplate tomorrow rather than yesterday, believe ourselves to be tired. But it is only in the light of the past that we, the depleted generation now coming into the control of public affairs, the generation which has to make the present and endeavor to mould the future, can understand ourselves or hope to be understood by our successors.

—Vera Brittain, *Testament of Youth*

1

The Wall

November 1982

The boots. I remember the jungle boots.

A cool breeze swept across the National Mall as I joined a growing crowd. The throng gently pushed me along the path, people unaccustomed to such gatherings but loosely tied in purpose. Though cocooned in this pack of people, I felt a quiet solitude as I neared the names etched in granite on the Vietnam Veterans Memorial that was being dedicated on this day.

Earlier, at the parade, before my focus had narrowed and my heart had started marching double-time, the scene was overwhelming: a parade of vets, myself included, locked in a bewildering sense of reunion and pride—thousands of mainly thirty- and forty-something people whose common thread was having served in a war that most of America hated as much as we did—all of us together for the first time.

We were a rag-tag bunch, mostly men, faces creased too early in life from the never-ending weight of war; smiles uncertain; and tears falling unabashed, breeching dams mortared with a stoicism that, on this day, could simply not hold back the emotions. Everywhere, hugs and hellos.

Flags and field jackets. Combat boots and boonie hats. Bands played one patriotic song after another for this gathering, coming, as it were, long after a war that was not won, but lost. Lost by politicians who had their own complicated agendas and egos. Not us.

"You were at Củ Chi?" you'd hear someone ask. "Damn, just missed ya. Arrived in August sixty-seven. Tunnel rat. Glad you made it home, buddy. Too many didn't."

Along the parade route, people on the banks of this human river stretched out their hands for slaps and bear hugs. Never mind that most of us had been back more than a decade, a few people shouted, "Welcome home!" and, "Thanks for serving!" It felt strangely good.

From the triangle peak of two extended fire-truck ladders, a huge American flag wafted in the November breeze. Children in stocking caps sat atop their parents' shoulders, wildly waving miniature flags. Whoops and hollers punctuated the sky from both sides of the street.

Some messages were more sobering. "We killed, We bled, We Died, For Worse Than Nothing," read the sign of one vet. "No more Vietnams!" said one giant banner. "Fuck Jane Fonda" said another. A vet struck a match and torched an effigy of the anti-war actress; her trip to Hanoi in the 1970s was seen by many as an act of betrayal. Behind a truck: one "float" with a lone man, representing our prisoners of war in Vietnam, bent over in a jail made of thin bamboo slats.

Some vets in the parade propelled themselves in wheelchairs. Walked with crutches. Limped. A few were missing limbs. Others, escorted by family or friends, were blind or carried other visible wounds of war. And, of course, many of us carried wounds that couldn't be seen.

Now, as I approached the Wall, and the nearly fifty-eight thousand names of the dead carved in its black granite, any revelry or pride I'd momentarily felt had morphed to numbness. The noise of the parade had given way to a deep quietness within myself. It was news of the names on the Wall that had summoned me to this place, but I still feared the memorial's power and meaning.

A kind of gravity pulled me along the path, down a slope, toward the names. But I kept my head down. I looked at the man's boots in front of me, and other people's shoes. It gave me a good excuse to avoid eye contact.

I stopped when realizing the granite plates of 1968–1969 loomed before me. Was I ready for this? To look up at the names etched on this wall? Since August 1969, when I'd returned home, I'd look up, instinctively, every time a helicopter flew overhead. But otherwise, in the aftermath of Vietnam, it was safer to keep your head down in moments the war might be discussed. Safer, when meeting someone, to say I'd been a nurse in Washington and Texas instead of Vũng Tàu and Pleiku. Safer to not make eye contact, to not reveal more than I'd want to. Safer to rationalize that the soldiers who came to my dreams on stretchers, especially a kid named Eddie, would go away on their own. Safer to keep busy, losing my life in the comings and goings of my husband and children. Safer to scrub the kitchen floor every night, finish folding the clothes at midnight, and get up early in the morning to make the peanut-butter-and-jelly sandwiches for lunches that day.

The result? I'd never shed a tear over my time in Vietnam. I had no tears. They didn't solve problems; they only made them worse. Tears would be a copout, proving the experience had actually affected me, which was easier to not believe. As the years rolled by, hunkered down in survival mode, I'd tried my best to forget Vietnam. It was less painful to live in the present if you could pretend you had no past. I sought to convince myself that I was never there (and convince my husband that he should never bring it up).

So, yes, even though I'd come to the Wall as if on a pre-ordained mission, now that I was here, I kept my head down. I was here, but in some ways didn't want to be, as if to do so was violating my unwritten self-promise to not look back. I looked at the tennis shoes, penny loafers, flats, sandals, and literally hundreds of jungle boots of the people around me.

Right in front of the Wall, the shoes stopped moving. Some shoes turned toward other shoes and I knew the people in those shoes were embracing. I heard muffled sobs, reminding me of my patients—my *guys*—who'd tried so hard to stifle their pain. I heard gasps from men startled when seeing a name on the Wall they recognized. I heard outright sobbing. Uncontrollable sobbing. I was terrified I might do the same and break down—in public. My worst fear. No one would ever see me do that. Ever.

I had a fleeting thought that I'd been wrong to not invite my husband, Mike. We had met in 1970 at Brooke Army Medical Center in San Antonio, Texas, where he had just finished his internship and was doing a general surgery residency, so he was no stranger to military life. But though he'd volunteered to serve in Vietnam, the war had ended before he got called. Maybe to protect me, maybe to protect him, I'd always kept him at arm's length from my war, thinking he could never understand what I understood because he hadn't been there. Now, I felt a loneliness that suggested perhaps I was wrong. I suddenly missed him.

I followed the shuffling of boots. Had I once started an IV on the guy in the boots to my left? Had I cleansed the sucking chest wounds of the guy in the boots to my right? Had any of them been my patients, guys whose names I never knew but had never really left me? As opposed, of course, to the guys who took their last breath in front of me—the reminders of war who came in the night, jolting me out of sleep as if I were still in my Pleiku hootch? And those names on the Wall—which among them were my guys? The Wall knew 57,939. I needed to see, up close, two specifically—one a soldier I had cared for at the 36th Evacuation Hospital in Vũng Tàu, one a nurse whose death haunted me in the night.

Instead of my boots, I'd brought only one thing with me from Vietnam to the Wall; my boonie hat, with patches from the 44th Medical Brigade and the 71st Evacuation Hospital. I hadn't thrown that into my Vietnam footlocker that I hadn't seen for years and wasn't sure still existed.

The crowd around me had thinned a bit. I was in the front row, standing before the names. I pushed back the boonie and, against all instinct, looked up.

Oh. My. God.

Names. So. Many. Names.

The death. So much death.

The names stretched left and right, like a blood-stained horizon, seemingly forever. The Wall took my breath away, the names as thick as late-night stars over the Minnesota farm of my childhood. *Who of you died on my watch? I'm so sorry we couldn't save you. I'm so sorry for your heartbroken families. We tried. We all tried. Why?*

Then, while the emotion temporarily ebbed, I had a revelation: the memorial itself, created amid much controversy, was powerful. It was perfect.

The two names I now began looking for were those of Eddie Lee Evenson, Panel 28W, Line 17, and Sharon Lane, Panel 23W, Line 112. I looked again at the locations I'd scrawled on a piece of paper, then back at the panel where I thought they'd be. First Eddie's. I threaded my way through the thick crowd until I came to Panel 28W. My gaze climbed up the panel. There he was. Blond hair, youthful face, lean body. Smiling. Innocent. He had been one of mine. I had touched his body—dressed his wounds and removed his stitches. And now, I was touching him again.

The emotion jolted me out of my trance. I reached to touch his name, but as I did so, a hand lightly tapped my shoulder. I turned. It belonged to a thirty-something man wearing a faded field jacket. His eyes riveted to me as if he knew me—or thought he did.

"Ma'am, were you a nurse in Vietnam?"

It startled me. It wasn't a question I'd ever been asked. With a touch of hesitation, I nodded yes.

He gulped. He looked as if gathering his thoughts, or rehearsing, or both. He looked nervous.

"I've waited fourteen years," he said, voice quivering, "to say this…to a nurse…but I never came across one. Until now."

He paused. I felt a twinge of uncertainty as his eyes pooled with tears. He took a deep breath and exhaled, then said two words I'd never heard since getting off the plane at Travis Air Force Base in California.

"Thank you."

I nodded, feeling anxious. Unused to being in this position. Unsure of this emotional expression.

"I can never thank you nurses enough. I love you. Thank you for being there for us. You're all we had."

He buried me in a smoldering hug that felt like no other I'd been given. Just as I never wrote down a name, and remembered only one from the long list of my patients in Vietnam, I did not get his. He was as nameless to me as all the others. But like the others, he was "mine" in that moment. I don't remember ever being hugged in Vietnam by a patient. And now, a desperate, wounded warrior was unabashedly hugging me with gratitude. The ice was melting. Yes, along with doctors and medics, some nurse had helped save this man's life, and, because of it, he was looking at the names on the Wall instead of *being* a name on the Wall. I felt his genuine warmth and desire to simply say thanks. He needed me to accept it. And until I heard those words—"thank you"—I never realized how much I needed to hear them.

It was called healing, an act, I would learn, far more powerful than we might imagine. And one that had everything to do with so many of us feeling we were, after all these years, still far from home.

The soldier nodded and moved along. I just stood there, transfixed, feeling blessed, full, and empty, all at the same time. A new feeling emerged. I *belonged*. I actually belonged here, to these people. To this place. This place was also my place. If he belonged here, so did I. If Eddie belonged here, so did I.

Gathering myself, I reached again for Eddie's name and slid my finger left to right. I wondered if I'd been the first to touch his name. Had he lived, he would've been thirty-four. To me, he was still twenty-one, the age he was when he came in by stretcher to the 36th Evacuation Hospital in Vũng Tàu. Injuries among the wounded were a blur to me. I didn't remember his specific injury except that he had a DPC—delayed primary closure for his wound. We had administered pain meds, irrigated and dressed the wound several times a day, and loaded him with antibiotics. And he started to improve.

But there was never any certainty in Vietnam. A soldier who got better was often instructed to get his boots back on, grab his rifle, and get back to the fight. Such was the case for Eddie.

Now, in D.C, I took a deep breath and moved toward Panel 23W, Line 112. I was shaken, but amid the crowd of others, was hardly alone in struggling to keep my composure. I had not known 1st Lt. Sharon Ann Lane, but we nurses felt we did know her, bound by a common cause. We'd all volunteered to serve as nurses in the military and many of us would go to war in Vietnam. Lane, twenty-five, of Canton, Ohio, was one of eight female nurses whose names were on The Wall. She was killed in Chu Lai on June 8, 1969—two months before I'd left Vietnam for home.

As my fingers swept across her name, something inside me shattered like broken glass. For the first time since Vietnam, I cried. Years of contained tears flowed for Sharon, for Eddie, and for the soldier I'd just met who embraced me. I cried for the men I'd been privileged to save and for the countless others I had not. I cried for the dying soldier hooked to a ventilator who begged me not to leave, just before the chopper whisked me away from the madness.

Try as I might, I could no longer hold back thirteen years of tears. I'd been terrified of crying—afraid that once I started, I wouldn't stop. But now, it felt liberating. They weren't simply tears of loss. They were tears of anger, injustice, futility. They were tears of the betrayals of war by presidents, their cabinets, and others who had no clue what fear looked like in the eyes of a nineteen-year-old kid whose entrails were half in, half out.

For the first time since returning from Vietnam, I felt no shame whatsoever.

I didn't lose the war, nor did the men who fought it. The high command lost the war. And after the war was over, they didn't stand up for us. Veterans had to build their own memorial—with their own initiative, time, and money. Congress had to pass a bill so we could have this memorial; all they had to do was lift a pen to their fingers. But almost three million men and women who served in Vietnam lifted things far heavier—and carried those things every day, long after the war was over.

On November 13, 1982, I left the Wall drained and weary. In those magical and mysterious moments, touching the names of Eddie Evenson and

Sharon Lane, and being hugged by a stranger, I had, for the first time, given myself permission to *feel*. And nothing felt so good and bad at the same time. In the years, and decades, to come, I would return to this place many times, but for reasons beyond honoring Eddie and Sharon. I would return because on that day, I understood, for the first time, the power that honor plays in the process of healing.

As any nurse knows, to survive, sometimes a patient must first go through hell and back. In a sense, I was, at age thirty-six, that patient. And I was about to embark on a decade-long journey that's as close to hell-and-back as I'd experienced in Vietnam. Not just to help get myself well again. But to help every woman who'd served during the Vietnam War on that path to wellness.

I'd already enlisted in one war, but I was about to enlist in a second: the battle for women like me to find our way home in the aftermath of war.

2

The Footlocker

My visit to the Wall stirred something deep within me. Soon thereafter, the soldiers from my wards started appearing at night in my dreams, more frequently than usual. I'm covering the face—or what's left of that face—of a twenty-two-year-old chopper pilot with a sheet. I'm opening the door to a ward full of South Vietnamese kids who've been seared by napalm. I'm leaving a young soldier—my year in Vietnam is over—who pleads for me to stay.

My life started unraveling. Many nights I was back in Vietnam, but I couldn't grab my helmet and get to work. I'd wake with a jolt, trying to run to my ward, only to realize I was in my own bed, my legs frozen in place next to Mike's. My heart raced with the adrenaline I had grown addicted to. Now it was working adversely; I was shaking, sweating, and agitated. As it had been in Vietnam, my sleep was fitful. I was always half-ready for the next chopper to drop in with its load of wounded. I was exhausted. Depressed.

11

"Your anger turned inward," a counselor told me, "is depression." And that, clearly, was where my anger was turned. Because for thirteen years I'd been denying the whole Vietnam experience.

I enlisted my ever-willing mother, Dorothy, then sixty-six, to start helping out with the kids; my folks' farm in Minnesota was only a ninety-minute drive from our house in Wisconsin and she had since retired as a nurse. Mike, a surgeon at the local River Falls Hospital, hung with me day after day, week after week; a less understanding husband probably would have left me after realizing I was now one of those crazy Vietnam vets everyone was talking about. Except he knew I wasn't crazy, and neither were the rest of my fellow veterans. He knew we were wounded. Wounded by war, wounded by the betrayal of our nation. Wounded twice, once in Vietnam, and again at home.

Mom understood. She noticed the difference in me since I'd returned from the Vietnam Veterans Memorial dedication. As a nurse, she had seen emotional wounds, too. My mother was not afraid; she'd seen carnage in the emergency room—she'd seen pain—and knew I was resilient. Dad, meanwhile, worried about me, but wasn't about to express such feelings.

If my visit to the Wall had loosened my emotions, it hadn't fixed anything. In remodeling-speak, it was the tear-down before the re-build. My default format was still, "Tell nobody. Feel nothing. Risk nothing." When my older brother, Chester, had been dying of cancer at thirty-eight a couple years before, I'd administered his last shot of morphine. But as others wept, I had not. Nor had I cried at his funeral. I loved him and his death was untimely and tragic, but I had no tears left for the dying. I was emotionally frozen—and if the Wall experience was a breakthrough in that regard, it wasn't "all better now." Just a single candle in the night. A touch of hope. But I was still groping in the dark.

Finally, I went to a Vet Center in Minneapolis-St. Paul that initially didn't know quite what to do with me. A woman seeking counseling at a center that served almost exclusively men? But as we talked further, they welcomed me.

Therapy didn't come easily for me. Sometimes I'd sit outside in my car, paralyzed, wanting to roll up into a ball and hide forever. But gradually I began attending, the lone woman with nine men in group therapy. I was appreciatively surprised at the warm welcome I got. They made me feel as if I belonged. And I realized something: I wasn't alone. Everyone else had a sadness in the pit of their stomach, had nightmares, got edgy.

My counselor, a wounded combat vet, was frank with me.

"Diane, the only way you can heal is to face the past," he said. "You're going to have to think about it, write about it, talk about it."

Slowly, I did, but it was two steps forward, one step back. Somehow, I got through the Christmas of 1982. In late January, a couple of months after the Wall dedication, we were at Mom and Dad's in Buffalo, Minnesota, in the 1868-built farmhouse where I'd grown up. It sat atop a hill where the kitchen afforded a lighthouse view of our sea of 160 acres. It was just me and Mom in the kitchen, enjoying the smell of fresh cinnamon rolls we'd soon surprise the kids with. Mike and our four children—ages four to ten—were off sledding and riding snowmobiles.

As was our habit, my mother and I sipped our coffee and glanced out the window where several feet of snow lined the fallowed fields like her famous whipped egg white frosting. She had always been, and still was, my heroine. I was a nurse because she was a nurse. I was attuned to the suffering of others because she was attuned to the suffering of others. I was stubborn because she was stubborn. When they tried to shuffle her off to an administration position when she was in her fifties, she wouldn't have it.

"Dorothy, it's a day job," the nursing director, Agnes Feckler, told her.

"And I'm the evening nurse-in-charge," Mom said. "Which is exactly where I'll be staying, thank you."

She had beautiful red hair—her mother was Scotch-Irish, her father Danish (a calm disposition that was rarely rankled)—and an absolute commitment to her job and to her six kids. In many ways, I was my mother's daughter, even if my hair was a darker shade of auburn. But here's where we differed: even if my mother wasn't the one who'd break into a smile at the sight of a camera and my father could be ill-tempered, she'd weathered many storms and maintained a peaceful, calm nature. She hadn't changed. Me? I had. I'd been happy before going to Vietnam.

As a light snow began to fall outside, she suddenly brought her coffee cup down to its saucer with a touch of urgency. The men and the kids would be coming back in soon.

"Diane," she said, "perhaps it's time for you to go up in the attic and get your stuff."

"My stuff?"

"Your footlocker. Your duffel bag. The things you brought back from—"

"Mom, you saved that all these years? Why?"

"It's yours. It's part of you. And you told me to save it for you. You sent it with explicit instructions, 'DO NOT OPEN.' I haven't. But maybe you should."

Was part of me. And that was then; this is now.

"Thanks, Mom. Maybe I'll take a look later."

I was enjoying having some rare quiet time with her.

She got up from the table and started to get busy. Always busy. Always something to do.

"Diane, I'll take care of supper—you go on up."

She went to the water-heater closet and found the flashlight on top, its usual place. There was hell to pay from Dad for anyone who moved it.

"Here," she said, "you'll need this."

Mom had a way of getting you to do things, an intuition for which she could ever-so-gently get buy-in. And so, I trudged up to the attic, chilled by its cold and dark—and more so by what I thought I might find. I would have dismissed her suggestion altogether if I hadn't been curious about one thing: the boots. Was it possible that they were in that footlocker?

Once in the attic, I dawdled at nearly every object I found, anything to postpone my real purpose for being there: The trunk that came from Sweden with the original Carlson homesteaders. The white pair of ice skates on which I'd twirled on the surrounding lakes of my youth. And, of course, the books. I opened a copy of one of my Little House on the Prairie favorites, *On the Banks of Plum Creek*, and smelled the musty pages, thinking of how Pa had suddenly appeared after four days in that blizzard, alive, and I—Laura Ingalls herself, of course—had buried my head in his damp, cold chest.

I fanned through a 1963 Buffalo High yearbook, in which beneath a class photo of Charles Streiff was written "intelligent...tenor...able writer." What were the chances that a few years later, after I landed in a Dustoff medevac chopper in Vietnam, I'd see a wounded soldier coming in by land ambulance—Charley, it turned out. Two kids from Buffalo, Minnesota, together for a few moments in a place that could not be farther from home.

Even when I wasn't looking for Vietnam, I found it. I set the yearbook down and pointed the flashlight into a corner. My stomach lurched when I saw it: the duffel bag, full of memories I'd tried hard to ignore. When I touched its collar, it was as if I were twenty-two again and standing at the baggage carousel at Minneapolis-St. Paul International Airport, just back from Vietnam.

"Lemme help you with that, Lieutenant," said a uniformed young enlisted soldier who started to reach for it.

Across the carousel, a college-aged kid in a "Make Love Not War" t-shirt couldn't resist. "Why don't you let soldier girl carry her own goddamn bag; she's in a man's arm—"

"Diane," Mom yelled from downstairs. "Did you find it?"

I hesitated for a just a moment. "Yes, Mom. Thanks."

I looked at the scuffed olive-green footlocker. Wood handles, left and right. My name stenciled in faded black on the lower front—"Carlson"—with my Army Nurse Corps number. I cradled the padlock in the palm of my hand. Thirteen years had passed, but I still remembered the three-digit combination. It was the same lock I had used on my door in the hootch. When it slipped open and I lifted the lid, I knew I wasn't just opening a footlocker. I was opening Pandora's Box.

The Wall was ours, a memorial to our war dead. The footlocker was mine, a memento of my personal war. A war that I was trying to leave behind, not make room for in a house already too tight with a husband, four kids, a dog—and wounded soldiers in the night.

My stethoscope. Two bandage scissors, one large and one small. A rubber tourniquet. All still hanging in the buttonholes of my jungle fatigue blouse. Two black U.S. government-issued pens in the blouse's shoulder pocket. Unit patches gifted to me from patients: 1st Cavalry Division, 1st Infantry Division, 101st Airborne Division, 25th Infantry Division, 4th Infantry Division, 9th Infantry Division, U.S. Army Ranger tab, and a Dustoff unit patch. A Viet Cong flag that a patient insisted I have. A rabbit's foot, the good-luck charm of a soldier for whom it had not been. And a copper peace symbol I'd worn around my neck on a leather shoelace, given to me by a medic who'd made it for me. I tried to see him now; what did he look like? Why can't I remember him? A Green Beret. Yes, I remembered the face of the confident U.S. Army Special Forces lieutenant who had given this to me as he limped out of the hospital and back to his unit in the Central Highlands.

I opened a box that said "DO NOT OPEN" in my own handwriting, sent from Vũng Tàu. I found the Saint Christopher medal given to me by a West Point lieutenant who got the million-dollar wound and left for home. I felt his hand reaching out to me now, giving it to me as I helped him roll over onto the gurney for his evac out, taking the medal off his neck and hearing him say, "Put it on, ma'am, wear it. It will keep you safe."

As he watched, I clasped it around my neck. Not that I was Catholic or, for that matter, particularly religious. Maybe someday I'd return to my Lutheran roots, but not now. God, I was convinced, had gone AWOL in Vietnam.

Finally, I saw them: my boots. Still coated with the reddish-orange dust of Pleiku and the splatters of soldiers' blood. I turned them over and gaped at their soles. They were worn thin with large holes. I hadn't noticed that in Vietnam. How could I have walked in those? Why hadn't I requested a replacement? They were my second skin. I'd lived in them every day.

I closed my eyes and smelled the monsoon rain, my moldy room, burned flesh, jungle rot, and pseudomonas. I had no recollection of good smells in Vietnam beyond coffee, the cinnamon rolls I made in Pleiku, and the perfume some of us wore.

It's true. I'd really been there.

Then came a thought that I hadn't expected: I missed Vietnam. Despite so much tragedy, there were elements that I genuinely missed. I missed the GIs, the intensity of every day, every minute. I missed the adrenaline. I missed my medics and my patients and getting up every day to go to work to do something worthwhile. I missed being valued, being someone important to hundreds of lives. I missed the rush. The thinking on your feet. The responsibility. The risk. The doing something few could do, as if part of a secret, if dark, world.

Maybe I should talk to somebody to process this. But who could possibly understand the apocalypse that Vietnam was, the dichotomy Vietnam was?

It was the best year of my life. It was the worst year of my life. I wanted it all back and I didn't want any part of it. I missed my hootch-mates, the women who lived with me in our compact wood-built quarters. I missed the docs and medics, and my ward masters. I missed the noisy skies filled with assault helicopters, the Dustoffs—choppers that plucked the wounded from the ground—and supply planes. I missed seeing the convoys of mud-crusted, sweating GIs. I missed the daring chopper pilots we loved. I missed defying orders by the "lifers"—some of the high-ranking officers we loathed. I never turned down the offer to fly in a chopper or plane—and not caring that I wasn't on approved orders because, as we joked, what could they do to us—send us to Vietnam?

We were defiant, we became good at what we did. No, *great* at what we did; even now, my Vietnam inferiority complex coerced "good" into "great." The country didn't welcome us home, but our patients knew that we mattered. A soldier who signed his name simply "Peter" attested to as much. I slowly unfolded the sheet of paper, yellowed by time, and blotted here and there with smudges of Pleiku dirt. In a poem "for Miss Carlson" called "Who Shall Answer?" he'd written:

> As the flower greets
> the sun with an
> open blossom
> So does your charming

smile aid the fallen man
With the tenderness of
dripping dew you calm
his fear and rest his worries
With petal soft hands
you wipe his brow
and rid his pain
And when he sees
your caring eyes
Tears wet his face
and you learn your
reason why for
what he whispers
is…thank you, nurse…

"Diane, everything okay up there?" Mom called up the stairs.

I wiped the tears even though she wasn't with me in the attic to see them. Instinct. Thirteen years of it. Self-preservation. Keep your head down.

"I'm okay, Mom. Everything's fine."

That was life more than a decade after Vietnam: continually assuring the people I loved that everything was fine, even when it wasn't.

3

The Ball of Clay

September 1983

A small yet vocal subset of people, including some veterans, deeply dis-
liked Maya Lin's design for the Wall. While viewed now as an extraordinary and truly visionary memorial, it was remarkably controversial
at the time. At times, racism infused the dissent aimed at Lin, then a
twenty-one-year-old Asian-American Yale undergraduate student who
won a design contest for the memorial. Tom Carhart, a Vietnam vet,
lawyer, and author, called it a "black gash of shame and sorrow, hacked
into the national visage that is the Mall." (Another time, he said the
inscription should read, "designed by a gook.") The dissent wasn't univer-
sal, but there was enough of it to trigger political action from the Reagan
Administration—none of whose senior administrators attended the dedication of the Wall. The memorial honored the dead, went the thinking,
but where was the memorial to honor the men who lived, those who
served in Vietnam but came home with breath in their lungs?

To appease the Tom Carharts and their outspoken dissatisfaction,
contrary though they may have been, plans were afoot in the spring of
1983—six months after the dedication—to place a sculpture portraying

three Vietnam War soldiers—men—opposite the Wall. If the names in the black granite represented the dead, the Three Servicemen (also known as the "Three Soldiers") would represent the living. Secretary of the Interior James Watt spearheaded this, before ultimately resigning after referring to the members of a department panel as "a black, a woman, two Jews, and a cripple."

When the addition was approved—Watt overruling the Commission of Fine Arts that opposed it—Lin was furious, calling artist Frederick Hart's Three Servicemen "a coup." Hart had been a vocal critic of Lin's design, calling it "intentionally not meaningful" and "elitist." (Never mind that he demanded $330,000 to design and sculpt his three-man bronze monument.)

Amid this fiasco—and as photos of the prototype for the sculpture began showing up in newspapers and magazines here and there—I couldn't help but feel something was missing: a woman or women.

In 1984, I had come to Washington, D.C., for the dedication of the Three Servicemen sculpture. In his remarks, not once did President Ronald Reagan mention anything about women having served. Actually, about 10,000 women, more than eighty percent of them nurses, were stationed in Vietnam during the war. Meanwhile, some 265,000 military women served their country during the Vietnam War around the world. Amid what I saw as a blatant oversight of much-due recognition, something emerged deep within me: a quiet calling. A little focus to my fuzzy feeling that suggested I needed to turn my bitterness about the war into something better. I needed to crawl out of my shell and move forward.

Only later would I realize I needed to follow a sense of destiny that I suspected was calling not only to me, but to thousands of other women who'd shared my Vietnam story. I sensed the need to find my voice and help other women find theirs. By late summer 1983, however, I had no idea how that might happen. But I was open to ideas. I was listening for whispers of direction, looking for clues, waiting for orders.

Meanwhile, there were sporadic dark times when I thought about ending it all.

Inspired by the Vietnam Veterans Memorial and its welcome-home parade in 1982, a number of U.S. cities put on similar events—a sort of better-late-than-never nod to Vietnam War veterans. One of the first such parades was to be held in Minneapolis on September 25: the Minnesota Salute to Vietnam Veterans. I committed to going, even though shortly beforehand I'd wound up in the hospital with life-threatening encephalitis. The pain was excruciating, and I remember moments of feeling close to death. It was almost as if it were a physical expression of my deep-seeded mental exhaustion. I lapsed in and out of consciousness as the analgesics alleviated the pain.

"Were you in Vietnam?" my nurse, a lovely woman named Paula, asked me one morning.

"I was," I said, a tad surprised at my vulnerability. "Why do you ask?"

"My husband was in Nam and was wounded." I couldn't read her. Friend or foe? She looked me in the eye, then looked away, deep in thought. "Nurses like you saved his life."

Beyond the vet at the Wall, I'd never heard anyone say that to me.

"Oh, thank you. I hope he's OK now."

"He's better."

I nodded and paused. "So, how did you know I'd been in Vietnam?"

"You said some things last night while you were delirious. I could just tell."

"Like what?"

"You mumbled something about choppers and ventilators."

I sighed. Trying to hide my experience in Vietnam was like trying to hide a fear of flying on a two-hundred-passenger plane.

"It's OK," she said, smiling. "I've been through a lot with my husband. I get it."

I had spent nearly a week in the hospital, slipping into, and out of, waves of pain and nausea. In the roughest moments, I wanted to die. Dying, I'd thought, was the easy way out. Beyond the physical challenges, I was mentally drained. I was that soldier without his ventilator, only my ventilator—the thing that kept me going despite my wounds—was the break-neck pace of life. I was the workaholic super mom. As long as I could get lost, and stay lost, in raising kids and getting them to school, playing host to sleepovers, helping with eleventh-hour homework assignments, and keeping the household running smoothly with a husband who spent time in the operating room day and night, I would be all right.

I could conveniently forget soldiers crying out for their mothers in their final breaths. I was blessed to have these four wonderful children who brought me unconditional love and a happiness I had never known. They were the single most important part of my life. They were my sanity. They gave me a reason to live. Mike knew he came in second—after the kids. I think he intuitively understood why they came first. But when he said, "Get a sitter, we're going out," he meant it.

I could conveniently forget senior officers insisting, in casualty reports, that we not say a soldier was wounded in Cambodia when the soldier, when I asked where he'd been hit, had told me, "Cambodia, ma'am." Meanwhile, our president was conveniently lying to the American people that we did not have troops in Cambodia.

I could conveniently forget how my younger sister, Nola, when I'd returned, had said, "You're not the same sister I had when you left. You're not fun anymore."

Yes, stay busy, stay in the now, and you never had to remember the *then*.

And keep it to yourself, which I did wonderfully well until my armor of secrecy would shatter in some spontaneous outpouring to Mike.

I hated being a patient instead of a nurse. I felt utterly hopeless. My head felt as if it were in a giant pair of vice grips. For a week in the hospital I'd been in virtual isolation. Alone. Just me and my thoughts. At first, dark thoughts. Death thoughts. I didn't want to leave Mike and the kids and yet, at times, the idea of death comforted me. Death would wash away the betrayals by our country, the sadness that followed me wherever I went, and, foremost, the guilt.

Yes, guilt. It overwhelmed me. Not guilt about saving soldiers and children; I never worked so hard in my life as I did in my year in Vietnam. But, once I'd returned, the guilt of camouflaging the chaos in my life. Of having so much—an understanding, loving husband who worked hard

and provided a comfortable living for me and the kids—and yet considering taking my own life. And perhaps most importantly, of having all this
fire in me over Vietnam but never translating that energy into anything
beyond self-pity.

As a fellow nurse in Vietnam liked to say, trying to get over Vietnam
was like being operated on by a rusty knife; try as you might, the wound
just kept festering.

At the hospital that week, my body battling the encephalitis, each day
bled into another. Reading was hard; my head throbbed. So, all I could
do was think. And by week's end, thoughts of futility gave way, somewhat
surprisingly, to thoughts of the future. Yes, our government had failed us
in Vietnam. And, in some ways, I had failed us. By denying my involvement in Vietnam, hadn't I (in essence) denied my sister and brother veterans? Hadn't I denied *myself*, someone who'd returned home sickened
by war, yes, but privileged to have saved the lives of those warriors? And
hadn't I denied my country by, once home, slinking into the shadows
instead of looking for ways to recognize and honor those who served?

In Pleiku, when a heavy-lift, twin-engine Chinook had landed that
night with more than two dozen sick and near-death soldiers, it mattered
not that it was just me and a single corpsman working in a mandatory
blacked-out ward with him shining a flashlight. Despite this, I'd started
IVs on twenty-eight dehydrated soldiers in less than four hours. Where,
I wondered, was that fearless, roll-up-the-sleeves reaction now?

Such thinking marinated in my soul day after day, gradually spiked
with a subtle sense of clarity and purpose, as if perhaps I was meant to
somehow transfer this angst into honor. Honor for the women who had
served in Vietnam.

Finally, the vision became clearer. It was time.

"Paula," I said one day from my hospital bed, "I need your help."

"What can I get you, darling? Juice? Newspaper?"

"No, I need you to help get me out of this place."

"What?"

"I have to leave."

"But you're sick and—"

"I'm getting better, and my husband's a doctor; he'll know what to do if there's a problem. I'll be fine."

"But, Diane, my hands are tied."

"I understand. I don't want to get you in trouble."

The event in Minneapolis to welcome home Vietnam vets was only two days away. I tried to get a doctor's release. When that failed, I did what I had to do: I signed myself out and had Mike pick me up. He knew before he married me that I had a mind of my own and it didn't do any good to try to change it. My neurologist hadn't signed my papers, but neither had he thrown himself across my path as I left. He knew Mike was a doc.

Once home, I began laying out clothes for the next morning's trip. It was a weekend—Mike was the only surgeon in the county and would be busy. I'd arranged for Mom to watch our two youngest children. And I'd take the two oldest boys with me.

The even-keeled Mike was not having it.

"Honey, you shouldn't even be home, much less driving to Minneapolis for a parade."

"It's not any parade," I said. "It's *our* parade. Finally."

"But, Di—"

"I'm sorry," I said. "I'm going."

"But—"

"Dear, *please*. Don't argue with me."

He deserved better, but my nerves were tinder-dry, my head still throbbing, my stomach still queasy. For now, I had no "better" to offer. The next morning, I showered and dressed before Mike was even out of bed. I stashed my boonie hat in my purse, put on my Vietnam fatigue blouse retrieved from the footlocker in the attic, and told Guy, now ten, and Luke, eight, to be ready; we were heading out. They wanted to march in the parade with me. It was the first time they would see their mother as a Vietnam veteran. I gave Mike a kiss goodbye.

"Sure about this?" he asked.

"I love you, honey, but yes, I am. It's just something I have to do."

He offered the slightest nod. He'd been patient with all my Vietnam baggage since we'd married in 1971. Still, I couldn't tell him my deepest secret—that somewhere between seeing the Wall last November and going AWOL from the hospital this summer I'd begun to sense that something deep was at work and I was to be part of it, even if I didn't yet understand what that something was or how I was to be involved.

In retrospect, I felt the same kind of tug my dad's horse, Pal, responded with when he neared the barn. Once, in fact, he dumped me in our alfalfa field in his single-minded pursuit of his straw-filled home. Now, it was as if I were being pulled toward the home I'd never felt since returning from Vietnam—not my physical home in Wisconsin at that time but something deeper, the home I'd left but found missing when I returned from the war. And the way back to that home now was tugging me to a parade in Minneapolis, though I was pretty sure this was only one stop on a much longer journey.

I wasn't going to Minneapolis to be feted in a parade. Whatever mission I was on, it wasn't about smiling at folks while we marched down the street. It was about something more. But as if I was on some sort of scavenger hunt, I had to get to Minneapolis to find the next clue.

"Hi, I'm Leanne Combs!" said a woman with Navy insignia, throwing her arms around me soon after the boys and I arrived. "Looking for women vets, too?"

We walked the parade together like long-lost friends. Perhaps because it was a smaller, and cozier, parade than the one in D.C., the spirit in Minneapolis was warmer, friendlier, more upbeat. We laughed. We cried. In the Midwest, at winter's end, there comes this one day that dawns with buttery sunshine when you dare to take off your sweater and feel the warmth on your skin and realize, for the first time in as long as you can remember, that you are no longer shivering. That there is hope. That winter isn't forever. That spring might actually come. This parade was exactly that for me. The ice was thawing. Our generation of vets was re-emerging into a warmth that we might have to create ourselves, but we would create.

"If I don't stop hugging you," a male veteran said to me, "I'm gonna have to marry you."

"Sorry," I said, smiling, "you're too late."

For the first time since the interminable loneliness of the previous years, I felt I had a toehold on the future, however small. But it was nebulous; I had no idea what this future looked like. I only sensed that I was on the brink of something. And I was about to find out what that something was.

After the parade, at the Curtis Hotel, the boys and I wandered into an exhibit of beautiful sculptures done by an artist named Rodger Brodin. A Minnesota native, he specialized in sculptures of soldiers, cops, and firefighters. Brodin, forty-three, had been commissioned to design a memorial honoring Vietnam servicemen on the grounds of the capitol in St. Paul, Minnesota. Some of his other work was on display at the hotel. It was striking—and far better suited for my young sons than the giant photograph of a headless U.S. soldier we'd seen in another exhibit.

"It's beautiful," I said to a man who seemed to be hosting the exhibit. "Are you Rodger?"

"No, he just left."

The man handed me a brochure, on which he'd scrawled Brodin's phone number. That night, back home, I couldn't sleep. I was too wired. Too curious about Rodger Brodin. Too enthralled with the possibility that, in this scavenger hunt, he was my next clue. And too exhausted. But as soon as the kids were en route to school Monday morning, I was on the phone to the sculptor.

"Mr. Brodin, I'm Diane Carlson Evans and I was a combat nurse in Vietnam. I saw your exhibit yesterday and I just want to thank you."

"Well, thanks," he responded in a gravelly voice.

"Your piece, 'The Squad,' reminded me of the men I saw in Vietnam. All the men in it look fit and strong, which rings true to what I saw— beyond the hospital, of course."

"I'm a Marine myself. Vietnam era."

"I'm not surprised. So, Mr. Brodin—"

"Rodger."

"Yes, Rodger. So, what I wanted to know is—I mean, would you— have you ever thought of doing a sculpture of a female veteran?"

I immediately liked Rodger Brodin's down-to-earth sensibility. He'd come to his craft as a sculptor after a career doing body work on cars. Many of his sculptures had military, law-enforcement, and fire-fighting themes, in part inspired by his two brothers who were police officers.

He invited me to visit him at his studio in Minneapolis. I went the next day. His studio/workshop was, like him, unpretentious. It was a working-man's workshop, reminding me of a blacksmith.

"To answer your question," he said, "yes, I've thought about doing a sculpture of a military woman, but nobody's come to me wanting one."

"Until now," I said.

"What do you have in mind?"

"You're aware that they're adding a statue of three soldiers across from the Wall in D.C.?"

"Sure. Buncha vets got upset because the names on the Wall only honored the dead, not the living, right? And the whole design was too dark, too bleak."

"Right, thus the addition of a new statue—all men, of course."

"Well, soldiers do tend to be men, yes."

"Right, but the nurses who patched up the casualties—three hundred thousand casualties, by the way—were mostly women. That's a lot of involvement in the war by women."

He tilted his head with a look that suggested, "tell-me-more" instead of, "Lady, you're wasting my time." Good sign. I took a deep breath and kept going.

"Women were there when those soldiers first arrived fresh from the chopper, mutilated and bloody," I said. "They started the soldiers' IVs, cleansed their wounds, bandaged those wounds, and breathed hope in them—kept some alive who would have died. And were often the last human being a man would see before he died."

Rodger leaned forward. "And you want a memorial for them?"

I nodded yes. "Unlike the men, these women all volunteered. None were drafted. And none of them have ever been thanked. So, yes, I think a memorial would be appropriate. Right across from the Wall. Down from the Three Servicemen. All together in one place."

"And where are you in the process of getting the go-ahead from the bigwigs on adding such a statue?"

"Nowhere at all. You're my first stop."

"Diane, what did you say the name of your organization was again?"

"I didn't," I said, taking a moment to breathe deeply. "I mean, there is no organization. At this point it's just, well, me. And maybe you."

He nodded a confused sort of nod. But as we talked more, I realized Rodger hadn't totally dismissed me, or the idea, on the spot. Quite the opposite. He seemed all the more intrigued, as if daring me to prove that this was all realistic. Meanwhile, he made me feel at ease, as if we already had some sort of seat-of-our-pants partnership going. As if the default format was yes. As if he were taking me seriously, something men didn't always do.

"Do me a favor," he said. "Come back with some stuff you had with you in Vietnam."

"Stuff?"

"I don't know. The dress you wore. Medical stuff. Anything."

"We wore fatigues. And I've got a stethoscope and scissors that we used to cut uniforms off or bandages and tape. Sure."

"Perfect."

A few days later, I returned with the stuff from my footlocker, including my boots.

"Great," he said, "these will help me create a miniature clay rendition of a sculpture. Now, help me understand the life of a nurse. I need to catch the vision of what nurses did in Nam, what it was like. Tell me, Diane, about nurses in Vietnam."

His comment caught me off guard. It was now the fall of 1983, fourteen years since I'd arrived home. And I couldn't remember a single time when anyone, even family, had asked me to tell them about the experience—beyond a cursory, "How was it?" with feigned interest in the response.

"Really?"

"Yes, really," he said. "Look, a poet creates with letters and words. I create with clay, then bronze. And my sculpture, like a painting, must say in an instant," he snapped his fingers, "what needs to be said. So, what needs to be said? Diane, I wasn't there. I can't see or hear or smell or feel what you did. So, tell me."

Immediately I felt overwhelmed. Maybe he thought what I was doing was selfish, self-aggrandizing. "Rodger, this isn't a memorial to me. It's for my sister veterans."

"OK," he said. "So, tell me about them, then. What did they do? Who were they? Where did they come from? How old were they?"

I talked for close to an hour, then saw my first warning sign. Rodger yawned.

"Am I boring you?"

"No, you're intriguing me," he said. "But—"

"What?"

He shook his head in exasperation. "Diane, no offense, but you're talking like an encyclopedia. I don't want a World Book account of your experience in Vietnam. I don't want a 'this-happened-on-that-date' account. I want a personal account. I'm an artist. I need to feel what you felt. As a nurse at war."

"But, Rodger, as I said, the memorial is not about me. It's to symbolize, to honor, all the women who served in Vietnam. I will *not* be your model."

"I get that, Diane, but for now, you're all I've got. So, with all due respect, stop telling me about all these generic nurses and tell me about one: you. Diane Carlson Evans. Tell me about your experience in Vietnam."

My heart quickened—with dread. It was one thing to listen to a veteran talking about a land mine he had stepped on; that was someone else's experience, not mine. Or to open a footlocker; that was my experience but had taken place in the cocoon of an attic with no obligation on my part to share it with anyone else. This was different. This was opening myself to, well, everyone, like undressing in front of a window. This was nothing I'd prepared for. This was—

"Here, let's try this," he said. Beneath his work bench, he pulled out a chunk of orangish clay that reminded me of the mud of Pleiku. He rolled it in his hands with the strength and dexterity of the craftsman he was. He began shaping it.

"Ah, like Silly Putty," I said. "Brings back memories as a kid."

"And that's exactly what I hope it will do."

"What?"

"Bring back memories. Look, I have a homework assignment for you."

I wasn't sure I liked this. What was I getting myself into?

"When I start a life-size sculpture, I start small," he said. "With clay. And a vision. I need to catch that vision. Your vision."

He handed me the softball-size clump of clay. His eyes widened and his head nodded slightly.

"What can you make of this?" he asked.

"I'm no artist," I said. "I have no idea what this should look like. That's your job. I'm just a mom. And a wife. And a former nurse."

"Diane," he said, "take the clay home and bring it back next week. Mold it. Shape it. Tell me your story."

PART II: SURVIVING VIETNAM

Personally, after seeing some of the dreadful things I have to see here, I feel I shall never be the same person again, and wonder if, when the War does end, I shall have forgotten how to laugh.

—Vera Brittain, *Testament of Youth*

4

❧ ❧ ❧

Innocence on the Farm

1946–1965

In Buffalo, Minnesota, Wright County's six-bed hospital sat above Wagner's Drug Store on Main Street. I should know. Not only was I born there on November 10, 1946, but my mother was one of two registered nurses who worked there with two fresh-from-med-school general practitioners: Dr. Catlin and Dr. Sandeen.

Dorothy Carlson was more than my mother. She was my North Star, the woman who set me on my course to becoming a nurse. She didn't pressure me to follow in the footsteps of her white leather nursing shoes. She was the consummate professional just doing her job. But she did that job while showing so much dedication, compassion, and proficiency that I couldn't help but want to grow up and be just like her. Once when I lamented that she had to go to work, she said, "Don't feel sad for me Diane, I love my work." Still, it was hard having a working mom. My siblings and I missed her. We needed her at home for her comfort and attention. The advantage? We learned to take responsibility for our lives at a young age.

"Mother, please can I go with you to work?" I'd ask as a young girl. "I really, *really* want to."

Finally, she'd give in; as the only nurse on her shift, she was the boss. I'd sit under a desk—I couldn't, of course, go in the examination or patients' rooms—and watch her white-stockinged legs go this way and that, always with purpose, always with pride, until my father, Newell, would stop whatever farm work he had going to come into town and retrieve me in his pickup.

Our farmhouse sat atop a hill, having been built at this location in 1868 by homesteader John C. Carlson, a new emigrant from Värmland, Sweden. White clapboard siding put up in 1893 hid the house's original log cabin made of tamarack cut from the homestead.

The house often smelled of homemade bread and cinnamon rolls, my mother's favorite things to bake. And soon mine.

In a post–World War II America marked by the rise of suburbia, we were more *Little House on the Prairie* than *Leave It to Beaver*. I was nine years old before we had a bathroom and running water. Meanwhile, it was my job to empty the "winter pots" that the family used on cold nights instead of the outhouse. I carried them out to a nearby field. Everything on our farm seemed to be recycled.

One by one, the Carlson kids arrived: Chester, 1942; Ronald, 1945; me, 1946; Nola, 1952; Maynard, 1954; and Ward, 1958. The first three were distinguished by red hair, myself included.

Dad and the four boys milked cows, scooped manure, pitched hay, and drove tractors. He fertilized our garden with the same thing he put on the fields: cow manure. Mom, Nola, and I worked the garden, did laundry, cleaned house, and cooked and baked. When Dad and the boys took a break, I'd bring them a gallon of iced tea with fresh lemon slices. When it was dinner time, I'd wave a white dish towel and my father and his blue 1946 Ford tractor would soon arrive from the field.

Work was endless. I don't remember us complaining about the chores. That was simply life as we knew it. We each knew what our jobs were. Since I liked being outside more than inside, I had a reason to get my work done fast and escape outdoors. Early on, I figured out that being

Above: My parents, Newell and Dorothy Andersen Carlson, married, 1939. (Courtesy Diane Carlson Evans)

Right: My dad and our horse, Pal, with my brother Ronald, 1950. (Courtesy Diane Carlson Evans)

Above: Our growing family in 1964. L to R: Nola, Ronald, Chester, Newell, Maynard. Seated: Diane, Ward, Dorothy. (Courtesy Diane Carlson Evans)

Left: My mother received her RN degree at St. Luke's Hospital in Fargo, ND, 1937. (Courtesy Diane Carlson Evans)

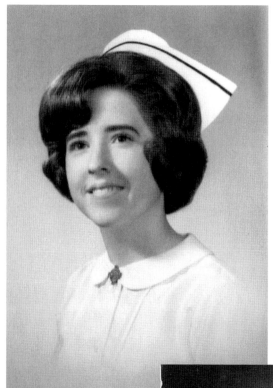

Graduation from St. Barnabas Hospital School of Nursing, Minneapolis, MN, 1967. (Courtesy Diane Carlson Evans)

I had this photo taken in my military "Dress Blues" uniform for my parents the month before leaving for Vietnam, 1968. (Courtesy, Diane Carlson Evans)

Above: 1st Lt. Ann Cunningham, wearing her "Dress Blues" uniform, and me in my hospital white uniform representing the Army Nurse Corps in a parade during Charlottesville Dogwood Festival, April, 1968. (Courtesy Diane Carlson Evans)

Below: I am head nurse on this forty-five-bed surgical unit, 71st Evacuation Hospital, Pleiku, 1969. (Courtesy Diane Carlson Evans)

Right: Visiting Mike's mother in Lehi, Utah. Engaged to be married, 1970. (Courtesy Diane Carlson Evans)

Below: Jon-Erik, Carrie, Guy, Luke (L to R) all under the age of ten when I began the Vietnam Women's Memorial effort. River Falls, Wisconsin. (Courtesy Diane Carlson Evans)

Not all women wore
love beads in the sixties.

VIETNAM WOMEN'S MEMORIAL PROJECT

A collage of military women encircled in dog tags: "Not All Women Wore Love Beads in the Sixties" was a promotional poster used by the Vietnam Women's Memorial Project to publicize that women also wore the metal identification tag in the combat theater. "Love Beads" in the United States were worn to protest the Vietnam war. (Courtesy Vietnam Women's Memorial Foundation/Eastern National)

Left: Prototype 36" bronze statue for a Vietnam Women's Memorial designed by Rodger Brodin, Minneapolis, MN, 1984. Titled "The Nurse". (Courtesy Vietnam Women's Memorial Foundation/Eastern National)

Below: Edie McCoy Meeks, my former hootchmate from the 71st Evacuation Hospital, Pleiku, and me together at the Vietnam Veterans Memorial, Washington D.C., 2012. (Courtesy Diane Carlson Evans)

Left: Lt. Col. Evangeline Jamison, USA (Ret.) and me following a congressional hearing in Washington, D.C.,1989. (Courtesy Diane Carlson Evans)

Below: I appeared on the television series China Beach's "Vets" Episode in 1989. Dana Delany (on the right) became an ardent supporter of the Vietnam Women's Memorial effort. (Courtesy Vietnam Women's Memorial Foundation/ Eastern National)

Above: I am testifying at the National Capital Planning Commission hearing,1991, Washington, D.C., contemplating commissioner's remarks. (Courtesy Vietnam Women's Memorial Foundation/Eastern National)

Below: Col. Jane Carson, USA (Ret.), in uniform, and me at the Plaque Unveiling Ceremony, November 12, 1992, Vietnam Women's Memorial future site, announcing its forthcoming dedication date. (Courtesy Vietnam Women's Memorial Foundation/Eastern National. Photo credit: USAF Photo SSGT Jeffrey G. George)

Sculptor Glenna Goodacre puts the finishing touches on the larger-than-life clay sculpture in her Santa Fe, NM studio before the statue is sent to Art Castings of Loveland, CO, to be cast in bronze. (Courtesy Goodacre Studio. Photo credit: Daniel Anthony)

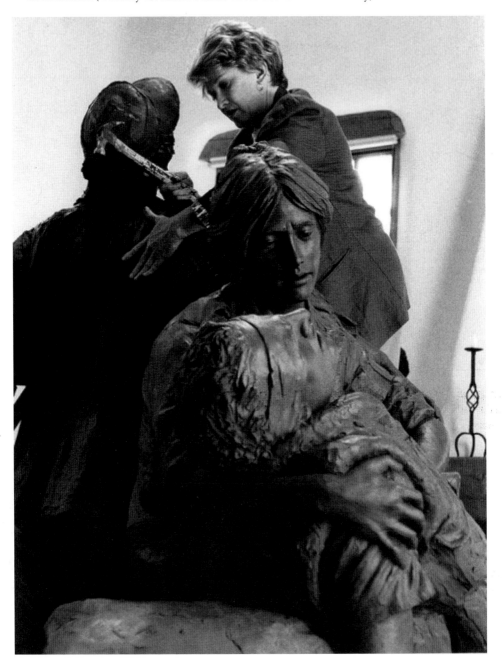

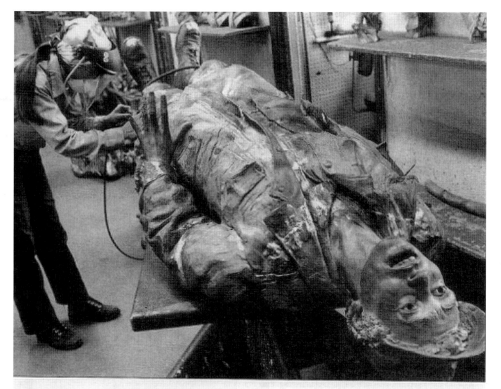

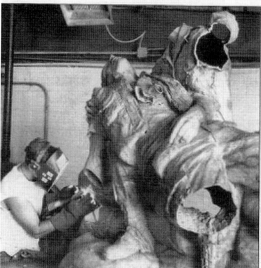

(Top) Metal worker Jeanne Toussaint at Art Castings of Colorado retextures a weld on the bronze standing figure. (Left) Welder Chris Buford assembles the bronze Memorial. (Right) After one year of sculpting, Glenna signs the finished clay original. Daniel Anthony photos.

Welding and assembling the monument. After one year of sculpting, Glenna Goodacre signs the finished clay original, 1993. (Courtesy Goodacre Studio. Photo credit: Daniel Anthony)

Above: Glenna Goodacre and me on site at the Vietnam Veterans Memorial with a maquette of the future memorial. Veterans Day, 1992. (Courtesy Goodacre Studio. Photo credit: Daniel Anthony)

Below: Senators sponsor luncheon in Statuary Hall celebrating the success of the Vietnam Women's Memorial. Back, left to right: Senator John Kerry, Senator Ted Kennedy. Seated, left to right: Glenna Goodacre, Senator John Warner, and me, 1993. (Courtesy Vietnam Women's Memorial Foundation/Eastern National)

Above: I am posing with the three women who modeled for the bronze monument, May 1993. (Courtesy Vietnam Women's Memorial Foundation/Eastern National. Photo credit: Dirck Halstead)

Below: Breaking ground for the placement of the Vietnam Women's Memorial, July 29, 1993. L to R: Doris Troth Lippman, Jan Scruggs, Senator John Warner, George Dickie, National Park Service representative, me, Kevin Foley, General Colin Powell, Glenna Goodacre, Lynda Van Devanter, Senator Paul Wellstone, Senator John Kerry. (Courtesy Vietnam Women's Memorial Foundation/Eastern National. Photo Credit: Bill Snead / Getty Images/*Washington Post*)

Above: I am conducting the Celebration of Patriotism and Courage dedication ceremony, Veteran's Day, 1993. (Courtesy Vietnam Women's Memorial Foundation/Eastern National)

Below: The Vietnam Women's Memorial, located 300 feet behind the apex of the Wall at the Vietnam Veterans Memorial—surrounded by eight trees, one for each of the women whose name is on the Wall. Vietnam Women's Memorial, Washington, D.C. © 1993, Eastern National, Glenna Goodacre, Sculptor. (Photo credit: Greg Staley)

Women veterans attending the dedication are reflected in the Wall of the Vietnam Veterans Memorial, November 11,1993, as Lt. Sharon Lane's name is touched by a sister veteran. (Courtesy Vietnam Women's Memorial Foundation/Eastern National)

Celebrating the 20th Anniversary of the Vietnam Women's Memorial, Veterans Day, 2013 with our children. L to R: Guy, me, Carrie, Jon-Erik, Luke, Mike. (Courtesy Diane Carlson Evans. Photo credit: Jika Gqiba-Knight)

efficient was to my benefit. Since I was sandwiched in between two older siblings and three younger ones, a lot of work fell on me. I changed a lot of diapers and cooked many meals. I loved working in the kitchen, especially when we got running water. Before that, we pumped water from the well outside, carrying it to the kitchen in buckets. We dumped it into a big wood-handled copper boiler and heated it on a nineteenth-century wood stove. The 1950s brought a welcomed modernization to our kitchen and the farm.

Among the most profound lessons this cycle of work taught me was that meeting basic needs required finishing what you started. There's a process, and each detail is important. You grab your shovel and dig the holes. You plop a potato in the ground. You fertilize. It rains. You wait. And then, when ready, you dig up new potatoes and store them in gunny sacks in the basement for winter. It was a lesson that I would employ my entire life, particularly when I sensed that women who served in Vietnam had been forgotten and deserved a memorial all their own. The process would take hard work and not giving up.

Another lesson: nothing comes easy. Farm families are constantly in motion. You take care of the farm animals and the fields; they, in turn, take care of you. In another context, you make a mistake, you pay the price. Mom told me to never get my hands close to the wringer on the old Maytag washing machine that squeezed water out of the laundry. I wasn't paying attention once when I put a sheet into it and screamed that my arm was in the wringer! Thankfully, Mom was nearby and saved me from my shoulder being yanked out of its socket.

"Next time, remember what I tell you," Mom said.

Once one of my brothers got caught drinking and driving. When the sheriff called to tell Dad he could pick up his son and bring him home, which was three miles from town, he didn't miss a beat.

"Let him walk," I heard Dad say on the telephone.

And he did.

One final lesson: "Don't ever expect gratitude. It will never come." Those words came from Mother, who was right about nearly everything but this. For women who served in Vietnam, gratitude would finally come. It would just take far longer than any of us imagined—and would involve a process far more complicated than growing potatoes.

I loved life on the farm. It wasn't all about work. In 1952, my dad bought the very first television in the township. I watched every *Lassie* program on CBS. Though I didn't go to many movies or dances like the town kids did, I rode horses and my bicycle and walked endlessly in our fields, woods, and pasture. In summer, I swam in nearby lakes and in winter, ice-skated on those lakes. In those years, Minnesota supplied an abundance of snow and ice and below-zero weather. We loved a good blizzard and the rule was it had to be forty below zero before school could be canceled.

My brothers and my sister and I spent hours sledding down the hill from our house on Yankee Clippers. Later when snowmobiles came on the scene, Dad was quick to buy one and winter took on a new meaning for my siblings.

Our parents gave us wide swaths of freedom to be outdoors and visit neighboring farm families. My younger sister, Nola, followed me wherever I went (or tried to). My friends called her my shadow. With four brothers around, I adored her. There wasn't time for frivolous games or even school-sponsored sports. Our play was in our work. My brothers hunted and fished, meaning pheasant or sunfish or walleye for supper. Nola and I cleaned the bounty. We never took fun trips just to "play." Dairy cows need attention twice a day. On the rare times we traveled, it was to North Dakota to visit Mom's relatives.

We loved going to the city and county fairs. There'd be a parade and my father would ride his palomino while carrying the American flag. Mom seemed to know everybody in Buffalo (pop. 2,500) because she'd delivered their babies or helped with their gallbladder or appendicitis surgery.

During the school year, I'd walk across a field with my lunch bucket to a one-room clapboard schoolhouse built by the Carlson immigrants. I had the same teacher, Mrs. Gerard, for seven of those years, and one year with Mrs. Wodtke. They were strict, excellent teachers. Mrs. Gerard, always in a dress with her upswept gray hair, used the ruler on the hands of any disobedient student, but was never abusive in any other way.

While I was attending, the school never had more than seventeen students. I had only one classmate, Jimmy Anderson, during those eight years. Jimmy, whose hand was slapped by the ruler many a time, could be a bully. Once, I'd had it. I kicked him in the shin in self-defense.

"Stop being mean!" I told him.

I read every one of the Laura Ingalls Wilder books and many of the classics—Charles Dickens, Charlotte Brontë, Jane Austen, Thomas Hardy, Willa Cather, and the Cherry Ames Nursing Series. I read Vilhelm Moberg's *The Emigrants* series on Swedes who came to America, and history books about the Lakota, books that galvanized me with a deep sense of respect for the past.

I spent much time alone on that beautiful homestead but was seldom lonely. Our country school was limited in books and extracurricular activities compared to the town schools, but I was prepared for high school academically. I won spelling bees. But I wasn't prepared for ninety-two classmates. I was overwhelmed. I found friends who were also country girls. We had more in common than the city girls who had never done the types of things we had done, like chopping the heads off chickens and gutting them (a task that remarkably didn't bother me as a young girl).

I knew and appreciated our family's stories. I came to understand that the reason my mother was kind, hard-working, and compassionate was because she grew up on an 800-acre farm in North Dakota and her folks died within a year of each other, when she was still in her teens. At fifteen years old, Mom was now the mother figure for her younger siblings. The tragic, and early, deaths of her parents instilled in her the desire to become a nurse. As such, she was forever thinking of—and doing something for—those around her.

And I came to understand the reason my father, Newell, was often crabby and depressed was because of the emotional wounds of abandonment. His unwed mother had abandoned him at the Carlson farm when he was four years old, in the year 1919. He remembers being called a "doorstep baby" and a "bastard." He and mom met in 1938 in Buffalo, Minnesota.

In his younger years, I remember my father as hard-working, stoic, and strong. He rarely drank alcohol. After a hot, humid day of putting up hay, he would drink one beer. He never went into a bar. Alcohol wasn't the excuse for my dad's sporadic hostile behavior for which my mother and us kids took the brunt. Once, she threatened to leave him, though she never did. But the threat worked. He calmed down after that, and there were fewer terrifying days.

I never dreamed of any knights in shining armor coming to whisk me away, nor of a house with a white picket fence. I dreamed of being a nurse. During my teen years, Mother worked the three-to-eleven-at-night shift at Buffalo Memorial Hospital. In the 1950s it evolved from a few rooms above a drug store with two RNs to a brand-new facility of fifty beds, fully staffed on a hill overlooking Buffalo Lake. Only one nurse had scored higher than her on the North Dakota state nursing boards. She was the head nurse on her shift. Few were respected in Buffalo as much as she.

Mother looked for the best in people. She would occasionally talk about her work but never name names. I saw Mom as the quintessential professional nurse. Co-workers, doctors, and patients loved her. She was confident, competent, compassionate, and kind to everyone. She was firm and stood up to the doctors and the hospital administrator. I know, because I witnessed it.

Starting at age fifteen, I worked at the hospital after classes and on weekends until graduation, then put in three more years as a student nurse while studying at St. Barnabas in nearby Minneapolis. I spent six years working with Mom, each paycheck deposited in the Buffalo National Bank to help pay for college.

"Diane," Mom once said, "follow me. I'm going to have to deliver this baby on my own." The doctor wasn't going to get there in time. Watching Mom in action at a hospital was like watching some prized pianist who never missed a key. I was in awe of her. How did she stay so calm under pressure?

I saw new life come into the world and I saw tragedy end life in the Buffalo Memorial emergency room. Mom spared me nothing, including the rainy night five teenagers were in a gruesome car accident. All five were dying. When the doctors arrived, Mom had already started IVs and told them which one to attend to first. Chaos ensued.

"You are *not* in charge here!" one doctor screamed at her.

In a firm, measured voice, Mother said, "If you don't stop screaming, I will leave this room." She was the calm in the storm and soon they were a team pulling together to do the sad, hard work of medical professionals. I went home and cried that night. We didn't save them all. But I learned a lesson. Your job as a nurse wasn't to save lives, just to do *everything possible* to save lives.

Mom's sister, my Aunt Ruth, had served in the army in World War II. When she returned home, she used the GI Bill and earned her doctorate degree at Columbia University. She taught college the rest of her life. I admired her greatly, in particular the way she carved out her own space in the world instead of simply going with the flow expected of women at the time. She had learned, like my mother, that women need an education. The two sisters, and another younger sister, Florence, had, after all, lost their parents as young girls and had to navigate the world on their own. Their brother, Ernest, also served in the U.S. Army. I grew up believing that serving one's country was an honorable thing to do.

I was never one to follow the crowd. I wasn't very interested in boys. Who had time? I had three jobs and homework after school. In addition to working at the hospital, I also worked as a telephone operator for Northwestern Bell my junior and senior year in high school, making $1.25 an hour, and babysitting for twenty-five cents an hour—sometimes for up to six children. I was assuming my own independence, intent on becoming a nurse, and fearful of only one thing: not letting anyone down, most notably myself.

By the time I graduated from Buffalo High in 1964, in a class of ninety-three, I was aware that there was a war underway in Southeast Asia— in a place called Vietnam. Some of my male classmates—a lot of farm boys—were enlisting in the service or being drafted. By 1968, three

Buffalo High School students—friends of my brother Ronnie—had been killed in Vietnam, along with Corporal Daniel Roger Bodin, a 4-H buddy whose family's farm was close to ours.

My family attended Danny's service at Zion Lutheran Church in Buffalo, and Dad said there wasn't a sadder day. By the late 1960s, I was well-aware that people my age were burning flags, flipping off the establishment, and protesting the war. What I didn't know was that in March 1962, the first contingent of ten Army nurses arrived in the Republic of Vietnam, assigned to the 8th Field Hospital, Nha Trang. And that by June 1966, 390 army nurses were serving in Vietnam, a figure that would triple by 1968. And that more were needed. I also didn't know that in February 1966, two female army nurses had been killed in Vietnam, the first of eight military nurses to die there.

In June 1966, gas was thirty-two cents a gallon. A black civil rights protestor, James Meredith, was gunned down in Mississippi. Surveyor 1 scanned the moon and proved it was flat enough to accommodate a landing craft. And the Vietnam War was playing out every night on the six o'clock news with Walter Cronkite (CBS) or the Huntley-Brinkley news team (NBC), bringing updates to living rooms across America.

In the nurses' lounge at St. Barnabas Hospital's School of Nursing in Minneapolis, where I was a junior, I watched the carnage in living color. I was glued to the TV nearly every night, fascinated, and troubled, by what was happening in Vietnam. Everywhere: helicopters, body bags, bombs. Men in battle. Men on our side. Men on their side. Men. Men. Men. But where, I wondered, were the women? Was it possible some were part of this war, too?

A few weeks later I heard an army recruiter officer on WCCO radio say that nurses were needed in Vietnam. That's all I needed. *Could I help?* I was co-winner with Cliff Eng of Buffalo High's American Legion Citizenship Award when I graduated in 1964. When I was fifteen years old, I had visited my brother Chester, who was in the army at Fort Lee, Virginia. It was a beautiful Army post. I liked what I saw. If skills like mine were needed, why not experience some adventure and go? Not only go, but be right there, where the fighting was?

By now I had six years of experience at the Buffalo Hospital and was working a three-month internship at the Veterans Administration Hospital in Minneapolis, finding a special place in my heart for these vets whose stories I loved to hear. I was in my second year of nursing school. And I'd grown up on a farm; I wasn't squeamish around gore. Beyond cutting chicken's heads off, I'd helped calves be born and witnessed cows die from lightning strikes and milk fever. I watched Dad take out his pocketknife and stab a bloated cow in one of her four stomachs to relieve the gas pressure and save her life.

"How can I sign up for the Army Nurse Corps?" I asked a recruiter, Captain Sarah Balkema, at an office in downtown Minneapolis.

"You're in luck," she said. "The government recently passed a bill that will pay for student nurses to finish up their schooling—tuition, books, uniforms, the works—and then you'll only be obligated for two years with the Army Nurse Corps."

The financial benefit was huge since I was paying for my own schooling. Captain Balkema handed me a brochure that said something like, "Be an army nurse and travel the world." On every page was a photo of a female nurse in a nice, clean uniform, smiling glamorously.

A large poster adorned the wall. It was of a gorgeous woman in uniform, with the inscription: "The Most Beautiful Girl in The World. A U.S. Army Nurse." I mentally scoffed. Being in the Army couldn't possibly make me beautiful. *I wish.* And, on the news, I'd been watching the body bags and villages being bombed and children running around naked and burning and screaming. I knew propaganda when I saw it and felt deceived. They didn't have to whitewash it to convince me to join.

My interest in joining the military came with no illusions of taking temperatures of soldiers in Paris or Italy who'd sprained an ankle while barhopping on bicycles. I had read about nurses' experiences in the Civil War, in particular Clara Barton, the "Angel of the Battlefield," who tended to the wounded at Antietam and Fredericksburg and went on to found the American Red Cross. I was intrigued with the perils of wartime nursing. After all, the legendary, courageous Florence Nightingale paved the way for us nurses following her time in the Crimean War.

In fact, the grit and gore were more draw than deterrent. Mother dealt with this stuff every day: farmers who'd had legs severed after clothes being tangled in their tractor's power-takeoff shaft, drunks who'd run their Chevy and Ford pickups into trees after binges at the local bar, women whose husbands had beaten them unconscious. Someone had to be there for the victims, the people who couldn't help themselves. My mother was that someone who could stay calm amid the chaos. I wondered if I could be that someone, too. I wanted a challenge.

"Diane, the military's no place for you," said Chester, my older brother, who'd been in the Army's 101st Airborne, though not in Vietnam. "I've seen how women are treated."

In my naiveté, I didn't understand what he meant.

Another brother, Ronnie, had been drafted in 1965 and pointedly told me he didn't want his sister in the army. He was just back from basic training, though he would wind up in South Korea on the DMZ, not fighting in Vietnam.

"I could handle the discipline, the grueling forced marching in the heat, and obstacle courses," he said. "But all they do is teach you to kill people. Kill, kill, kill. And to dehumanize the enemy as 'gooks' and 'dinks.' I hated it."

But killing wouldn't be my role. I would be there to save lives, not take lives.

On December 30, 1965, I signed an agreement to give the U.S. Army Nurse Corps two years of my life after I finished nursing school. Back home in the kitchen, I told my folks. My father clenched his fist and slammed it on the table like an ax chopping wood. He looked at me, dropped his head and walked out the door to the barn.

Only my mother seemed to understand.

5

Prelude to Vietnam

1965–1968

The U.S. military wouldn't have been training hundreds of nurses if we weren't going to be needed. That said, the Army Medical Service Officer Basic Course at Fort Sam Houston in San Antonio, Texas, didn't prepare us much for combat wounds. We covered battle indoctrination, chemical warfare (no mention of something called Agent Orange), code of conduct, Geneva Convention stuff, survival escape and evasion, and weapons familiarization in arms. In some ways, it seemed like a vacation.

Because of overcrowding on the base, we were put up in motels with swimming pools for six weeks. Learned how to salute and march. Easy. Classroom stuff. I learned how to carry a litter. And, while off-duty, how drinking something called a Singapore Sling on my 21st birthday might not be a good idea as an indoctrination into the world of alcohol. Beyond that, the six weeks seemed unlikely to truly prepare me for the graphic images I was seeing on the evening news each night. When the training was over, we had an opportunity to visit with an officer to talk about where we wanted to go from there.

"How about it, Lt. Carlson?" said the officer. "What are your top three choices for assignment?"

I tilted my head ever so slightly and shrugged my shoulders to suggest the inevitability of my choices.

"Vietnam. Vietnam. Vietnam."

Moderately surprised, he asked, "And stateside, in preparation for your deployment?"

"Kenner Army Hospital in Fort Lee, Virginia?" I had visited Chester there six years ago and it looked like a cool place.

"I'll put in your request. No promises. You go where you're needed."

I received my orders and spent nine months at Fort Lee. Among the first people I was introduced to was Colonel Sears, who had been a chief nurse in the 36th Evacuation Hospital in Vũng Tàu, Vietnam. She was, others had told me, someone to be feared. Old—meaning from my twenty-one-year-old perspective, probably forty-something. And tough as horse leather. Very much the colonel that she was. I liked her immediately.

"I hear you want to go to Vietnam," she said. "Why would you want to do a thing like that?"

"They need nurses, don't they?"

"Yes, they do. I just came back. I know what it's like. Not easy, Lieutenant. But I'm sending you to orthopedics so you can get some experience."

This was my first taste of the wounds of war in Vietnam. Thirty beds, all full. Casts. A trapeze on every bed, hand bars, and pulleys. And young soldiers in pain, none of whom wanted to talk about the war. Their bodies were broken, and their spirits warped by war.

Once, I had to wake a soldier to give him his meds and he lunged at me as if he were going to kill me.

"Don't ever do that again!" he shouted.

"I'm sorry!"

"And you damn well better be. I could've killed you."

"I understand," I said. "Now, take this pill and try to get back to sleep."

The wounded all had a hard time sleeping. It was as if they were waiting for something. Something bad to happen.

I didn't win back any points when, days later, I dropped a metal bed pan on the night shift. The shouting from a couple of them woke all of them. But then something interesting happened: I started earning my patients' respect. And they earned mine when some of the doctors hit on me.

"They're too old for you," the patients would say. "Steer clear."

They were right. I was barely twenty-one, and not interested, for now, in romance or a relationship, even less so after I met Ann Cunningham. She arrived as my new roommate at the base BOQ (Bachelor Officer Quarters). Operating Room nurse. Twenty-three years old, a southern California girl, fresh from Vietnam. Friendly. Fun. We hit it off.

"How do you like Kenner?" she asked.

"I'm loving it. I'm in orthopedics. The guys are helping me prepare for Vietnam."

"Nothing prepares you for Vietnam."

She stared off in the distance, then changed the subject.

"Ever been to a polo game?" she asked.

"I grew up among horses. Had my own. But no polo."

"You'll love it."

Upon arriving in Virginia, she'd bought a car, so we drove to a polo match. Later, another. On our days off, we drove to old Civil War battlefields—she had a keen interest in such places—and checked out horse barns and the beautiful Shenandoah Valley. As a farm girl, I hadn't had lots of friends—everyone lived miles away—and it was fun to build this new friendship, particularly with someone who shared an interest in nursing and in a place where she'd been and I was going: Vietnam.

On Memorial Day 1968, she suggested we go to a military service at a local ceremony. Make that *strongly* suggested. I was glad to do so but was a bit surprised at how insistent she was. I didn't want to sound unpatriotic, but something deeper seemed to be going on inside her.

"Ann, can I ask…why is this is so important to you?"

She nibbled her bottom lip for a few seconds, again looking off in space.

"I need to do it for Gary."

"Gary? Who's Gary?"

"Who *was* Gary," she said. "Guy who died in Nam. First Lieutenant Gary Jones. He was a Wolfhound."

"What's that?"

"Second Battalion, Twenty-Seventh Infantry Regiment with the Twenty-Fifth Infantry Division, Cù Chi," she said.

"I'm so sorry. Someone you knew?"

"You could say that," she said. I waited for the other shoe—and when it dropped, I felt horrible. "We were engaged. He died on the battlefield and they brought him in to the Twelfth Evac Hospital on February Ninth, where we received casualties from the Twenty-Fifth Infantry Division. They were hit hard during the Tet Offensive."

I put my arm around her. "Oh, I am so, so sorry, Annie."

She seemed numb. No tears, her face like stone, fixed in resignation.

"I escorted his body home to Georgia. He was his parents' only son. I need to go to the service, to remember—to honor—Gary."

"Of course."

I got up to get ready.

"Diane," she said, "let me give you one bit of advice: don't get close to anyone over there in Nam. They'll only die on you."

I nodded, though hadn't begun to fully understand the warning. At the service, she didn't cry. In fact, I never saw her cry. She was stoic. She wasn't going to fall apart. She went to see Gary's folks—and didn't break down. In Ann Cunningham, I saw what a combat nurse looks like when she returns from war.

A few days later, on April 4, we learned of the tragic assassination of Martin Luther King Jr. We just looked at each other, incredulous at so much killing in Vietnam and right here at home as American citizens fought for racial and gender equality—and protested a war they believed was wrong.

When Colonel Sears suggested Ann and I ride in the Charlottesville Dogwood Festival that spring, wearing our uniforms, Ann was all for it. She was proud of the Army Nurse Corps. So, in April 1968 Ann and I rode in a convertible in the parade with Army Nurse Corps emblems on the doors. This wasn't Washington, D.C., or Los Angeles or Chicago, where anti-war protests had exploded or were brewing. This was the home of former presidents James Monroe and Thomas Jefferson in a state full of military-oriented colleges. People waved and cheered and blew us kisses, some veterans wearing their uniforms. It felt good. I was proud of Ann. She deserved the accolades. She was a Vietnam veteran.

It would be nearly twenty-five years—1993—before Ann or I felt this honored again. And that honor would not come easily.

The goodbye with my family came outside the barn. It was July and the day was hot and humid. The smell of hay and manure wafted in the sticky air. I had come home to Buffalo, Minnesota, to see Mom and Dad and my siblings. And to take care of some necessary matters that I don't imagine many twenty-one-year-old women were doing in 1968. I made out a will. I wrote a handwritten letter to my mother and father telling them how much I loved them and how thankful I was for them. I told them I was doing what I wanted to do and, stupid though it might have sounded, said they should try not to miss me if I didn't make it home alive. I left the will and the letter in a lock box at Buffalo National Bank, giving a key to mom, telling her to save it for me until I returned. She knew what I meant—*in case I didn't return.* I left them with a new color photograph of me in my dress blues uniform.

Mom and Nola were going to drive me to the Minneapolis-St. Paul International Airport.

"I'll write you every day," said Nola.

To be honest, I was excited for the adventure ahead. I hadn't been a parent yet; I didn't have the context of what it's like to see a son or daughter go off to war. One by one, I said goodbye to my siblings. Then it was just me and Dad, a guy never known for hugs and emotion. I understood why he couldn't take me to the airport. A farmer had to get the hay put up before it rained.

Wearing the Sears overalls in which he was seemingly born, he looked at me. I saw sadness in his eyes and smoldering emotions. In the distance, thunder rolled; it was going to be another hot, sultry Midwestern day.

"Four sons," he said, then took a huge breath. "I have four sons. And—and I send my daughter off to war."

With that, he uncharacteristically shed tears and took me into his arms. I didn't cry. The tears would come later. Many years later.

Of the 257 people on the Continental flight to Vietnam, exactly four were women. All nurses. I remember my seat mate, Lieutenant Colleen O'Keefe. I hoped that the Army's insistence that we wear our Class A uniforms—a green cord jacket and skirt accompanied by heels, nylon stockings, and a purse—was the last ridiculous order we'd get, and not the first of many to come. I couldn't have been more uncomfortable on that flight if they'd duct-taped me in a gunny sack. Back then we had to wear *girdles* or garter belts to hold up the nylons. It was ludicrous, going off to war like that.

When we rose out of San Francisco for the Far East, I glanced back at America. A few weeks back, when I'd flown from Washington, D.C., to Minneapolis to say goodbye to my folks, the flames and smoke of protests had blotted the D.C. sky. This was not a war America wanted to be fighting, but torching cars and setting off bombs on college campuses probably wasn't going to bring our boys back any sooner. And, in the meantime, the wounded in Vietnam needed nurses.

The highlight of the trip was mid-air word from the pilot that because of mechanical concerns we were going to have to land in Honolulu, Hawaii, and maybe spend a couple of nights. The cabin erupted into cheers. It would prove to be a final gasp of air before we all took a dive into deep, dark waters. I visited the USS Arizona Memorial at Pearl Harbor, built just six years before, and read the names on the marble wall of those who had died on the Arizona twenty-seven years earlier. I felt a stab of sadness as I departed for another war across those same waters.

As we approached Vietnam—since Minneapolis, on two planes, I'd been in the air for some thirty hours—the cabin grew quiet except for the steady thrum of the engines. Between memories of home, hangovers, churning stomachs, and tautened nerves, we were all in our own worlds. Though I was charged with anticipation, I'd be lying if I said fear wasn't part of my feelings during those hours in flight. Not fear of dying. I had that false sense of youthful immortality and couldn't see myself dead. Instead, I was feeling a sense of dread that I wouldn't know what to do when faced with the wounded and the dead. Learning how to carry a stretcher wasn't going to hack it. And what good would my "Overall Excellence in Nursing" award from the sterile halls of St. Barnabas Hospital be in a combat zone?

I wasn't afraid of blood and amputated limbs, but I had 365 days in front of me and had no idea what lay ahead, beyond what I'd seen on the nightly news about thousands of American boys injured and dying. The previous January and February, the Tet Offensive—a series of major attacks by communist forces—had escalated the war severely. And what about all those old women and men wearing conical hats clutching young, terrified children?

The jet bounced on the Bien Hoa Air Base runway, avoiding mortar-exploded holes, and eventually lurched to a stop in the darkness of the night, July 31, 1968.

"Women first!" yelled a male officer up front. I wondered why we would be singled out.

The door popped open and like a tongue of fire, a blast of humidity and heat hit us, accompanied by the stench of sewage and jet fuel. We worked our way down the passenger stairs to a runway pocked with shell holes. A grim-faced soldier in fatigues awaited at the bottom. He was holding an M16 rifle, a bandolier of bullets wrapped around his torso. He pointed to several buses that had their windows painted black and were covered with wire mesh that looked like chicken wire, the paint to visually hide the human cargo inside, the mesh used to deflect rocket-propelled grenades and exploded shrapnel.

"Keep your heads down, ladies," he said.

It was the last time that year that I was called a lady. Then, best as we could in skirts and heels, we ran furiously for the bus—and whatever lay beyond.

6

Vũng Tàu

August–October 1968

After three days at the 90th Replacement Battalion at Long Binh, and having traded my skirt, nylons and heels for jungle fatigues and combat boots, I choppered to my ultimate destination, the 36th Evacuation Hospital in Vũng Tàu, a seaside resort town with a backdrop of small mountains about seventy-seven miles east of Saigon.

Once a French colonial town called Cap Saint-Jacques, it was situated at the tip of a small peninsula in southern Vietnam. As the door gunner locked his eyes on the ground, I noticed the red crosses signifying U.S. military hospitals. Even if the Viet Cong weren't great respecters of the off-limits status of hospitals featuring such designations, Vũng Tàu was considered one of the safer hospital locations relative to the twenty-three or so other U.S. Army medical outposts in Vietnam. Trips off the compound to visit downtown were allowed and fairly safe. White surf folded on beaches that hemmed the South China Sea. Soldiers on R&R swam, drank beer, and tossed footballs back and forth.

That said, you quickly learned that even the relatively heavenly places in Vietnam could be tinted with a certain hell. On my first day in the sixty-bed unit the inside temperature was 105 degrees and we had no air conditioning. I wasn't worried about me; I'd grown up in the hot, humid summers of Minnesota. I also knew what sub-zero temperatures felt like. I welcomed the heat. But I couldn't imagine what it was like for wounded soldiers already going through enough misery.

Vũng Tàu was a 400-bed evacuation hospital providing care to patients evac'ed from other in-country hospitals and casualties directly out of the field. It provided intensive care for the VSI (Very Seriously Ill) and recovery units for the wounded; many were sent back to their units after suture removal. They wound up here for one of myriad medical or surgical reasons: bullets, shrapnel, booby-trapped grenades tripped by wires and fragmentation mines detonated by enemy guerrillas, Bouncing Betty mines, snake bites, punji-stick wounds, helicopter and vehicular crashes, leeches, fevers, water buffalo attacks, rat bites, monkey bites, burns, malaria, dysentery, and dozens of diseases we'd never heard of before we arrived. Half of all deaths of U.S. soldiers would come from small-arms fire, a third from artillery, a tenth from booby traps, and others.

The Bouncing Betty land mines were among the worst; they were designed so that when a soldier stepped on one, the charge would blast three to four feet upward, waist high, and basically blow off his genitals. That would sicken, and suck the morale out of, the soldier and his unit. It also would require extensive medical resources, both in the field and in a hospital.

Vietnam during wartime, I soon found, was a dirty place—which complicated our medical care. North Vietnamese forces invented cheap, clever ways to immobilize our troops with lethal homemade booby traps. They would lace punji sticks with human feces so when a U.S. soldier stepped on it, he would suffer debilitating pain and guaranteed infection. Most wounds required DPCs—delayed primary closures. Our skilled medics irrigated the wound and packed it with fresh dressings daily. On the third day, the surgeons could close the wound. Meanwhile, the soldier would be given tons of antibiotics. When the wound was sufficiently healed, we nurses and medics would remove the sutures and the soldier would go back to his unit—or home, if the injury was bad enough.

I was temporarily assigned to the malaria ward, which was dou-ble-bunked and overflowing with incapacitated suffering GIs. In the fall of 1968, the 36th Evacuation Hospital was usually filled to capacity.

I was often the only nurse on the night shift, along with two medics. We were from all parts of the U.S. Most of us were between twenty-one and twenty-five. I was twenty-one, slightly older than the average age of the soldiers themselves, who were about seven years younger than the average U.S. soldier in World War II.

Almost a third of our nurses were male. We reflected the fabric of our society at the time: mainly Caucasian, but also Native American, African-American, Asian-American, Hispanic, and Jewish.

We had a few gay male nurses and a few lesbian nurses, but those preferences were far more secretive than they would be today. They had to be. If discovered, they were discharged, and their military career ruined. Many of them were my friends; they were outstanding nurses.

Although there had been talk the previous year about nurses at Vũng Tàu wearing white dress uniforms, mainly to inspire morale and paint the stereotype of a true nurse (female, no less), that idea was blessedly nixed. We wore what was practical in Vietnam: lightweight jungle fatigues, which protected the arms and legs from mosquito bites, didn't require the laundry attention whites would in such a dirty place, and didn't require any "bending-over" worries. Above all, they didn't require the awful con-striction of a belted waist and those dreadful nylon stockings.

The wounded soldiers we saw at Vũng Tàu were with us between a few days and a couple of weeks or more. For all the horror involved, the reality was that if a wounded soldier could just get on a helicopter and then to a hospital within an hour, he had a ninety-eight percent chance of surviving. The next few hours in the ER and OR often determined whether he stayed in Vietnam or was handed off to Air Force flight nurses and personnel for the trip along the air-evac chain to determine the next best place for recovery.

I was assigned to a surgical unit, all pre-op and post-op. I did my share of nights but preferred the day shift, when I could interact more with the patients.

We sometimes ate dinner downtown in the village. I recall four male sergeants unexpectedly giving us female nurses leis to wear around our necks and pink champagne. They snapped photos of us eating together. They walked out, handed us the Polaroid, and paid the bill for the whole thing. Two MPs (Military Police) followed us until we were safely back to our billets.

Because we also took care of the local Vietnamese, we nurses saw things we'd never been trained to treat. On Christmas Eve 1968, I was working a burn unit when some fifty children were admitted after being seared by napalm when their village was bombed.

I cared for these innocent children, blackened by man's inhumanity to man. The juxtaposition of innocence and horror was like nothing I'd ever seen; most were crying for parents who were dead, wounded, or searching frantically for their missing child miles and miles away.

Napalm, a jellied-fuel firebomb mixture, sticks to its target when ignited. And even if people weren't the intended target, it burned them deep down to the bone. Like a lot of wounds in Vietnam, I'd never seen anything like it before; we were inadequately prepared for what we were going to face. But there wasn't time to bemoan that; instead, we simply figured it out what to do on the fly and from each other. Doctors gave the orders and we followed them.

We got the children into beds, some two to a bed—the unit was overflowing—and started IVs on those we could. For days, we applied topical Sulfamylon on the burn area, which would help prevent a pseudomonas infection, and later debrided the necrotic tissue. Our physical therapists worked their magic with whirlpool baths. For us, it was tedious work with slow progress; for the children, endless days of excruciating pain.

Was it that night, seeing a ward full of burned children, when I stopped being the idealistic farm girl from Buffalo, Minnesota, who, just like her mom, could whip up a batch of cinnamon rolls and put a smile on the faces of all who enjoyed them?

Or was it the agonizing ritual of placing the white sheets over the faces of dead young men before they'd be put in black body bags, then flag-draped coffins and shipped home to mothers and fathers?

Or was it hearing of the spooked soldier whose machete whacked off the head of a prostitute outside her hut?

Or was it when the soldier walked into my ward, an agitated grunt with a red bandana wrapped around his head and a necklace made of the dried ears of Viet Cong dead, his eyes either crazed by the horrors of war or his latest hit of heroin? He had arrived, apparently, to see a wounded buddy.

"Please, you need to park your weapon at the door," I said.

He retorted with a look suggesting he wasn't keen on taking orders from a female 1st Lieutenant even if she was wearing a flak jacket and a helmet, but he grudgingly complied and returned.

"And, please, lose the necklace," I said.

If looks could kill, I'd have been in a body bag. But he left and came back without the ears, apparently having stuffed them in a pocket.

In Vietnam, it was impossible to prepare for the sinister threats about to destroy the bloom of our youth. It happened gradually. And though I clung to whatever soul I still had left, I was discovering that the carnage threatened to suck the life, hope, and dignity out of each one of us—if not now, then when we got home.

The weirdness of Vietnam was that even the silver linings had hidden clouds. You could walk the beautiful beaches of the South China Sea, sure, but did you ever feel totally safe as you might back home? No. You could stroll the villages of friendly Vietnamese holding their endearing children, yes, but in a time of war, did you ever trust them or feel totally safe? No.

As my time in Vietnam continued, I saw the best of America in our hospital beds while working side by side with hundreds of our brave men and women. Fate chose this battleground for my generation. It did not distinguish between combatants and noncombatants or innocent children who were machine-gunned, bombed, or tortured. Our fate, I was starting to realize, was being determined by the stroke of a pen by senators and congressmen in Washington, D.C., most of them who knew nothing of war.

Our civic action program was ostensibly designed to "win the hearts and minds" of the people whose freedom we were there to defend. Docs, medics, and nurses would go into the villages or orphanages with supplies to treat a variety of illnesses. We set up temporary field clinics to provide dental and medical treatment to the local population. The South Vietnamese civilians seemed to appreciate our visits and were fascinated by our presence.

I did this on my days off from the 36th Evacuation Hospital, falling in love with the sweet little kids. But while relief from a toothache and removing parasites helped them immensely, we continued to bomb their villages and inadvertently kill their innocent families, creating a hypocritical monster in the process that couldn't be ignored. Those villages harbored the enemy, the Viet Cong. And the VC, "Victor Charlie," were killing and torturing our men.

In a perfect world, there would be no war. In a perfect world, the combat theater could separate the enemy from the innocent. But the lines between perfect and imperfect were blurred badly in Vietnam; like it or not, our job was to clean up the mess left by our government's decisions.

Both sides played the game. The U.S. paid our "mama sans," South Vietnamese women, to scrub floors in the hospital wards, to do our laundry, to help free us up so we could devote ourselves to our jobs as nurses. Meanwhile, though, in their own economic desperation, some stole our underwear, bras, perfume, and clothing. Because they had access in the hospital areas to clean, it was not uncommon for us to learn of stolen drugs, at times stuffed up the women's vaginas to avoid detection. IV bottles and surgical supplies also sometimes went missing.

We were women on different sides of the war. Were they friend or foe? Were the supplies going to a nearby underground hospital for the North Vietnamese Army and Viet Cong or to their husbands serving with the South Vietnamese Army? They received our government's money for their duties. They would do anything to save their husbands, brothers, fathers, and sons—whatever side their loved one was on.

At the time, I couldn't feel empathy for these women, probably because I was trying to save the lives of our soldiers who would pay the price for a turncoat's efforts.

Some on our medical staff dealt with the misery through booze, drugs, and sex. War time produces "geographic bachelors" who might have wives and children at home, but who had apparently forgotten them for now. One of our nurses fell in love with a Navy pilot and the two talked of marrying when they returned to the states; both survived, but when she went to look him up in the U.S., she realized he'd given her a fake address. Later, she found he had a wife and kids.

Some, not all, of the hospital pharmacies dispensed birth-control pills and condoms, something I didn't know at the time but later learned from a hootchmate, Edie.

"You living under a rock, Carlson?" she said.

"Hey, we can't even get tampons at the PX," I said, "because the GIs are buying them to clean their weapons."

I knew of nurses who'd gotten pregnant in Vietnam and had abortions performed by our doctors (abortion was legal in our military hospitals in Vietnam at the time) or flew to Japan for the procedure. I knew of nurses who fell in love with corpsmen or chopper pilots who helped get the wounded to us—only to learn his helicopter hit the side of a mountain or he had his head blown off from a grenade.

I wasn't interested in having a serious boyfriend in Vietnam. I remembered what Ann Cunningham had told me. But I had suitors— lots of male friends. Soldiers called us "round eyes"; we were reminders of home. We were surrounded by tens of thousands of men, most of whom would've given anything to date a female nurse or American woman serving in Vietnam. We reminded them of home. And in a time when many were convalescing from painful wounds, we represented comfort.

Frankly, female nurses in Vietnam embodied a complicated role. Beyond caring for a soldier's physical wounds, the unspoken assumption was that we were also to provide morale. But where was the line between morale and romance? And where was the line between sex and unwanted sex?

While we don't know the exact numbers, we know that many American women serving in Vietnam were sexually harassed, and some raped, but afraid to report it to higher military authorities for fear of retribution. We were vulnerable and knew the Army Nurse Corps could not, or in some cases would not, protect us. Women who did report were often transferred, lost promotions, or were marked as troublemakers. Our surviving Vietnam meant keeping secrets and watching our backs.

Some of us worried more about being raped than about being hit by enemy mortar rockets. We were young. And wartime provides a highly charged environment of testosterone and bravado. Men were miles away from home, had prying eyes, and, with the numbers imbalance of males to females, we became prime targets.

Pilots—the older senior officers, in particular—could be a lot of fun. Many were my father's age. Most were good decent guys who simply wanted to have some female company over a steak dinner, a setup their air base offered every Friday night. Others were in the predator category; they frightened the hell out of me. I sensed I could trust the younger helicopter pilots who were more my age and often protective of us. Many of them flew Dustoffs, choppers that dove quickly to snatch the wounded. I admired them. They were fearless, flying hundreds of hours into enemy territory on terrifying rescue missions.

I was caring for a badly burned Dustoff pilot who'd been recovering on my ward for more than two weeks. His record showed that day he was turning twenty.

"Can this be right?" I said to him. "You were nineteen, flying choppers?"

"Yes, Ma'am."

"How does this happen?"

"Simple. You lie about your age. No, really I graduated from high school when I was eighteen, went to Fort Wolters, Texas, for nine months of helicopter training, and here I am."

I was incredulous—a nineteen-year-old Dustoff pilot. He wanted me to go on R&R with him. He wanted me to be his girlfriend. Ultimately, it turned out, he wanted to marry me.

"I'm staying away from you guys," I said. "You'll just die on me."

"Hey, I haven't died."

"No. And let's keep it that way. Now take your meds and get some sleep."

When it came to drugs, Vietnam was like a vending machine that only took dimes and nickels. Pot, opium, hashish, and heroin—all were easily, and cheaply, obtained.

None, I determined, would become my way of escape; I was afraid of them. I wasn't a goody-two-shoes and it wasn't my job to judge the choices of others; to each his or her own. But I hadn't been experimenting back in the States and didn't want to take the risk in Vietnam. I understood how, amid the insanity of war, there's a tendency to look for comfort any way you can get it. I wasn't some sort of social outcast; I went to parties or to the officer's club. But, no, I cared too much about my job and I didn't want anything to rob me of the precious little sleep I was already getting.

So, I looked for other distractions. I wanted to learn about this place where I'd be spending a year. I worked at the orphanage. I'd commandeer a Jeep from a willing and smiling GI to take me for a ride off the hospital compound. The guys were careful; they knew we could get into trouble traveling around without orders. I accepted offers from pilots flying a variety of aircraft.

One pilot gave me a fascinating tour along the coast of the South China Sea. I looked down and saw the stark beauty; it all looked so peaceful, except for the craters pocketing the ground from bombs. My biggest thrill was a ride in the U.S. Air Force's Jolly Green Giant, a search-and-rescue helicopter. Armed with two machine guns, it could lift twenty-five passengers or fifteen litters with casualties. The crew of four flew often under lethal operating conditions. They flew me over a junkyard.

"The only time I felt sick out there was going by the junked helicopters and planes," I wrote home in September. "Nothing but tangled, distorted heaps of metal. Really grotesque shapes and forms. Not so much the sadness of junked helicopters, but the lives which they cost."

I wrote lots of letters home, each addressed to "Mr. and Mrs. Newell Carlson & Family, Route 3, Buffalo, Minnesota." Sometimes with a zip code, sometimes not; they got there either way.

"Please send hand lotion, bath powder, candles, Clairol Hair So New Cream rinse, fudge, and fruit cake," said a November 20, 1968 letter. "Have you heard yet about the Cardinal boy's death over here? Ronnie knows him. He's from Montrose. The bombing halt hasn't made any difference that I can see."

I sometimes wrote to my sister and brothers, including Ward, who was only eleven. I drew pictures of what the Vietnamese children looked like and how they rode bicycles and carried water. "You'd love them," I told Ward.

At the 36th, I made friends with roommates and colleagues, Lt. Mary Jane Haughney, Lt. Barbara Ward, Lt. Jean Phillips, Captain Manuel (Tony) Zuniga, my head nurse; the hard-working surgeon Major Vincent DeAngelis, unhappily drafted out of his New York practice; and Specialists Ralph Broussard, Skip DeLong, and Cass Benavidez, three wonderful corpsmen on Ward 6.

I spent a lot of time taping music from reel-to-reel audio tape recorders. Music was priceless in Vietnam; it brought America up close and personal to us like nothing else could. I spent hours with The Kingston Trio, the Byrds, Bob Dylan, Simon & Garfunkel, Peter, Paul and Mary, Joan Baez, The Beatles, and the like. Music spared me from insanity that year. I didn't mind the protest songs. Maybe they would help end the war.

It wasn't just American soldiers we cared for. For a month at the 36th Evac, I worked on a Vietnamese ward, civilians who had been injured in the crossfires of war. A letter home reminded me: "Today we got a three-day old baby admitted to the ward. Now we have them all the way up to age 84. I'm tired of colostomies, Foley catheters, and old men and women spitting on the floor. But I love the kids; they make working on that ward the worthwhile part. I debrided four burn patients today—takes several hours just to do that." I remember emptying a colostomy bag from a sad old man; it was bulging with live and squirming Ascaris roundworms.

Somewhere along the line, a medic in Vũng Tàu gave me a peace symbol that he'd made out of hammered copper at a helicopter-maintenance shop. It came on a leather shoelace. It was against regulations to wear any sort of jewelry, even earrings, while in uniform. But I tied it around my neck, tucked it inside my fatigues and vowed to wear it until I came home to the farm. I was pro-soldier. But this was my private protest against the war.

Every day, six days a week, twelve to fourteen or more hours a day, I tended to the sick, the disfigured, the wounded, and the near-dead as best I could. The little downtime we had just created boredom; it was easier to be busy.

Most of us learned early on that to survive the accompanying misery and trauma of watching young men suffer and die was to detach ourselves emotionally. It wasn't a conscious decision. And it took time. But I learned to shut down emotions. My skills were honed, and like a robot on an assembly line, I moved to the next patient and the next and the next.

Not that I ever lost compassion, but it was the only way for me to survive—and, really, for them to survive. I wished I'd had had more time to listen and show that I cared more about a patient's psyche than simply hanging his IV or monitoring his ventilator. Each soldier had a story, a home. He was someone's son, someone's brother or husband or boyfriend. But *someone* worth saving. And while careful to not let my emotions impinge the task at hand, I wanted to do all I could to help get that young soldier back to his unit or back to what we had coined "the world." But I couldn't help get that young man get home if I got too emotionally involved, even if at times it seemed impossible not to.

7

Eddie Lee Evenson

November–December 1968

Ann Cunningham had warned me not to get close to any of the soldiers. At Vũng Tàu, I couldn't help it, though it wasn't in a romantic
way. Specialist Four Eddie Lee Evenson was just one of those people
who made the world a better place. He was admitted to my unit with
injuries requiring a DPC (Delayed Primary Closure). I don't remember
where the injuries were or what caused them. I remember *him*. He was
from Thief River Falls, Minnesota, about two hundred miles north of my
home in Buffalo, Minnesota—so we had that in common. When you're
eight thousand miles from home and find someone who lives a three-
hour drive from you in the States, it forges an instant bond. We became
fast friends, not in a romantic way; he was more like a fifth brother to me.

Eddie, at twenty-one, was the same age I was when I arrived in
Vietnam. He was angular and strong, with a ready smile. And because
he was deemed ambulatory, he could move around. But because he wasn't
ready to be released, he was happy to help us out.

No job was too small for Eddie Evenson. He cheerfully emptied bedpans, took blood to the lab, and helped ambulate patients using crutches.

There was no shortage of cynicism and bitterness in Vietnam; Eddie managed to rise above that. He reminded me of my brothers and the folks back in the Minnesota farm country, people who'd return one of Dad's cows that had gotten loose or help him get hay in the barn before a storm rolled in. He was sweet and respectful, the kind of guy who lifted everyone's spirits and diluted the boredom. The corpsmen and nurses loved him. So did I.

"Hey, Lieutenant, let me do that," he'd say with his Minnesota accent.

"What, you wanna do bedpans?" I'd reply with my Minnesota accent. "Well, guess it's better than pulling off those blood-sucking leeches from your buddy's private parts."

He'd laugh; he had a great laugh. Eddie actually *wanted* to do the "dirty work." He looked at it is as some kind of privilege so nurses and medics wouldn't have to do it. He saw us as having a higher calling. He realized we were busy and had little time to spend with each patient.

Eventually, he was ready to return to his unit. As his chopper warmed up beyond, he came to me to say goodbye.

"Promise me one thing," he said.

"Anything."

"Promise me you'll write."

"Of course I'll write," I said. "We're Minnesotans. We keep our promises."

And I did. Often.

My ward was quiet one night, and the supervising nurse on duty asked me to go sit with a patient in the ICU until—well, until he was gone.

He was a young black soldier wrapped nearly head to toe in white. I knew he wasn't likely to make it through the night; his wounds were just too severe.

"Ma'am," he said. "Please stay. I don't want to die. Don't leave me."

"I won't," I said. "I'm here with you."

And I was. At 7:30 p.m., the lights went out for the night. I stayed with him, holding a hand that got colder and colder. He died after midnight. I couldn't let go of his hand. A part of me was going with him and I couldn't let go. I was still breathing, but I was dying with him. I remember pulling the sheet over his face and knew that I would never ever forget him or that night at his side.

Often, a nurse would be the last person a soldier saw, touched, talked to, or smelled before he died. I knew he was dead, and his mother and father didn't. I felt desperate to have those parents there instead of me. I asked God, why? Why allow this carnage? The soldier's loved ones would never know that he wasn't alone when he died. But if hearing truly is the last sense we lose, there's no doubt he heard during that one long night the love of a stranger telling him stories of life on a farm in Minnesota as he fell into peaceful, permanent sleep.

To counter the weight of such sadness, doctors, nurses, and medics often leaned on humor. In Vũng Tàu, I had treated a soldier who'd been bitten by a sea snake, which were common in the South China Sea. Soldiers on R&R in this seaside resort were at risk every time they stepped into the water.

"I'm from the Land of Ten Thousand Lakes," I told the corpsman who'd brought in the soldier. "Never seen a sea snake. What do they look like?"

A few days later he showed up with one in a glass gallon jar and tried to hand it off to me.

"Like this," he said.

Just before Thanksgiving, a storm slammed ashore. Surf rose to twelve feet. The beach was closed. Exciting. My spirits were high, in part because I'd received a certificate of achievement signed by the general himself, and Thanksgiving was done up right. We were treated to quite the feast: shrimp cocktail, roast turkey, cornbread dressing, turkey gravy, hot rolls and butter—the works. We each were given a written message from Gen. Creighton W. Abrams, commander of the U.S. Army. "We should never forget," it read in part, "that in Vietnam our actions are defending free men everywhere. We pray that peace will come to all in the world and that all of us can return to our loved ones in the not too distant future." By the end of 1968, "all of us" meant 540,000 American troops in Vietnam.

I was hoping he was right, though there wasn't much time to ponder the future. "The other evening, I got in twenty-one admissions all at the same time," I wrote home on November 24, 1968. "Was a little hectic. I'm on alone in the evenings except for a corpsman. Besides that, one of the patients came back to the ward loaded on pot (marijuana) and had to have four people carry him in. I had the MPs there. He was soon air-evac'ed out."

The United States' entanglement in the war was unnerving and complicated. For us women in the combat zone, the predatory behavior of some men in uniform could be as well, particularly among those of higher rank.

Every day our unit received visitors: buddies of casualties, platoon sergeants visiting their men, senior officers, generals pinning on Purple Hearts. One day a major with aviation wings on his uniform asked permission to visit a friend. A few days later, back for another visit, he came up to me.

"Would you like to go up in my plane and see the country?"

"Sure, that'd be fun!"

Ever since I'd arrived in Vietnam, I'd loved flying in choppers and planes. Vietnam proved to be spectacularly beautiful and the only way I could see it was from the air. Nurses were forbidden to ride in convoys; travel was limited to specific orders. We were threatened with Article 15 punishment if we broke the rules. But flying meant more than getting a breath of fresh air above the sickly smell of war; the perspective gave context to a geographic world that was otherwise hidden by the sloping walls of our Quonset hut. I loved the rush. Never mind that I'd be breaking the rules.

At any rate, he picked me up at my billet. He was late thirties, early forties, almost old enough to be my father. A major. But apparently a forgetful major.

"Where's your flight suit?" I asked.

"Oh, I thought we'd go to the beach instead—after dinner downtown, of course."

"But I don't have a swimsuit or anything."

"That's OK. You won't need one."

Beginning with that change of plan, I never relaxed the entire evening. Not at dinner. Not on the ride to the beach, where the South China Sea lapped ashore. And certainly not when we got to the beach. He grabbed a bottle of wine and my arm, and—with an increasing sense of control—guided me away from the jeep. There was not a soul on the beach because we had walked past a Do Not Enter sign with concertina wire everywhere.

He sat us down on the sand and pulled out two wine glasses. Dusk was turning to dark.

"I don't want a drink," I said.

"Fine."

He suddenly stood and stripped naked, suggesting I join him. I looked away and knew I was in serious trouble.

"Maybe this'll help," he said, flashing a book in my face with photos of people having sex. "I'll teach you to enjoy it. I'll be gentle."

I started to get up. He shoved me down and gave full attention to my jungle fatigues, which thankfully had lots of buttons. He started madly fumbling with them. When I pulled back, he lunged at me, tearing at my clothes.

"Please," I said, "just take me back."

He slammed me back on the sand and tried to muffle my mouth. I started kicking and twisted my head so I could talk. Officers didn't *do* this kind of stuff!

I thought of my roommate who saw me leave with this guy. I had told her his name. If he killed me and left me there, she'd know who'd done it.

"Stop!" I said, "Or you'll never fly again! I will kill your *career*, your *promotion*, your *family life* back home."

He stopped. But what made him stop wasn't the sudden realization that he was taking something from me that didn't belong to him. No, it was the threat of something being taken away from *him*. Like a madman, he drove me back to my villa and all but tossed me out of the jeep, fuming because I'd rejected him.

I wouldn't tell anyone about the incident for thirty-eight years. But why had I said yes to him in the first place? Because I was still naïve and trusting. I hadn't been in-country long. This was a wake-up call.

Meanwhile, I wasn't going to let one bad night color my views of all military men. "I believe the American GI is the best patient in the world," I wrote in my diary. "They deserve the very best of everything—especially nursing care."

But there were also predators, sometimes unleashed on us by superiors.

I had finished my shift and was leaving the unit at the 36th Evac when the senior nursing supervisor, a lieutenant colonel, called out to me.

"Lieutenant!"

"Yes, ma'am?"

"Lieutenant, I have a good friend coming in today, and I think you'd enjoy having dinner together," she said.

Sounded interesting. I wondered who she was.

"He will pick you up at your villa at seven tonight."

I was incredulous. *He?* And it was all planned? I *would* have dinner with him? Coercion from a superior? Yes. But I could trust her, right? He was her friend. So why, I wondered, wasn't *she* going out with him?

He was a colonel who, after dinner, started driving us toward the beach. The jeep hadn't even gotten warmed up before I had him heading back to drop me off. I learned another lesson that night: the older nurses weren't going to protect us; we had to watch our own backs.

On January 3, 1969, in the Mekong Delta in southern Vietnam, I was on a medevac flight to pick up patients from the 3rd Mobile Army Surgical Hospital. The VC harassed the area frequently with mortar-rocket fire, and we were getting in and out of there fast. As the chopper lowered onto the LZ (landing zone) near the emergency room, I saw sandbags stacked to the limit on all sides of the hospital. We prepared to transport a soldier with an amputation and get off the LZ and out of the way for several incoming ambulances. Suddenly I heard a loud voice calling out to me from the open end of one them, "Diane! Hey, Carlson. Is that you?"

It was a Buffalo, Minnesota, farm boy I knew: Charley Streiff. Wounded. We spoke quickly and went our separate ways. But it had been inexplicably comforting to see a familiar face and a reminder of home.

Speaking of which, I managed a phone call home over Christmas using MARS (Military Auxiliary Radio System), which required users to say "over" after each time they finished talking. I chose a day when I figured Mom would be off work and Dad not working in the barn. They were thrilled to hear my voice and it felt good to make the connection, even if having to say "over" after each comment you made was awkward. It was my one and only call home from Vietnam that year.

I had learned that after spending six months in an assignment we could request a transfer. It was January, and I had just finished a month on the burn unit at the 36th Evac. I wanted to go north, closer to where the fighting was. And went to my chief nurse to say so.

"Ma'am, I'd like to request a transfer," I said.

"To where?"

"Pleiku."

There was a pause, as if she wasn't sure she'd heard me right.

"Are you sure, Lieutenant Carlson? That means going north. Hot fighting up there."

"Yes," I said. "Positive."

She nodded as if to bless my choice.

Though Bob Hope had joked for the troops in Pleiku back in 1964, in the years since the site had become too dangerous for entertainers. It was jungle country, a few kilometers from the Cambodian border in the Central Highlands. I'd heard the 71st Evacuation Hospital was wrapped in concertina wire to keep out the NVA (North Vietnamese Army) and VC (Viet Cong) and that mortar attacks weren't uncommon.

And there was a nearby fire base—an artillery battery set up to give fire support to surrounding units.

None of this deterred me. It was time for a change and a new experience in a different part of Vietnam. And the jungle would be a different world from the beaches and rice paddies I had lived around. I had no ties to the 36th and was ready to go.

My head nurse, Captain Manuel Zuniga, not only wrote me a letter of commendation for the job I'd done—I had no idea he thought I added to the morale of the unit; nobody got accolades when on duty—but presented me with a petition from a bunch of people on staff and the ward full of patients insisting that I stay.

"The hardest part will be leaving all the people here I've made friends with," I wrote home. "Today, after two more weeks of working on my Ward, was my last workday at the 36th Evac. Working with the all Vietnamese ward for a short time was a great experience for me. It brought me much closer to the Vietnamese people and to the realization that they are people with the same needs, wants, fears and feelings.

"Today several of the Vietnamese ladies and kids cried when I told them thru the interpreter that I was leaving. It touched a very sensitive part in me, and I couldn't help but feel rather sad yet so rewarded with the love and appreciation these people show, too. I gave Anthony a book with a message written in Vietnamese to him, 'To my very good friend Anthony. I love you.' I've fallen in love with the kids and it's very hard to leave their beautiful smiles and looks of love."

Before leaving for my new assignment, I packaged up some things to send home. "Please store for me," I wrote. "I marked 'DO NOT OPEN.' Just leave closed and store."

My mother would respect my wishes—until that day in 1983 when she'd suggest it was time to unpack my stuff.

8

Screaming to Death

January–July 1969

In Pleiku, the sound was faint at first, then gradually grew louder: a medevac chopper somewhere in the night sky. For grunts, the sound was a benevolent god with rotor blades; for nurses, an adrenaline-pumping bird that brought us merciless, soul-harrowing work.

In my hootch, I buried my head beneath a pillow and tried to pretend I wasn't hearing it. After working every day for nearly two weeks, I'd peeled off my blood-stained fatigues and fallen face down on the bed, snugly cocooned in thoughts of a day off. Happy, for once, that the mirror shattered in a mortar attack a few weeks earlier couldn't reflect my weary body. I had no mirror now to look into and wonder who was looking back. She wasn't the Minnesota farm girl any longer—or didn't seem to be. She wore no makeup and only needed to pull her hair up on top of her head before her shift.

Above, in the sky, this bird wasn't going away; I knew the sound of a Dustoff—your basic-sized air ambulance—and this wasn't one. The sounds of the blades kept getting louder and the vibrations stronger—like a mosquito that not only was in your tent but dive-bombing your ear.

A giant mosquito. *Thumpa-thumpa-thumpa.* Choppers meant only one thing: more death. More disillusionment. More distrust of everything I'd once believed in.

By the spring of 1969, after eight months in-country, my Vietnam experience had, if possible, turned darker. I'd realized that our government was lying to us. And despite having made a couple of close friends, I'd never felt lonelier. I was so tired I just wanted to go to sleep and wake up anywhere but this war-torn place that I hated as much as I loved.

As the *whomp* of the helicopter blades escalated from the usual to the ominous, I realized this wasn't a Huey dropping off a few casualties. I rolled over and sat up with a start.

"Edie, Barb," I said to the nurses sharing my hootch, "that's a Chinook!"

That meant dozens of wounded instead of a handful.

"Oh, God," said Barbie, "Back to work." Her ER would be pandemonium—until she and the medics brought order and calm.

It was March 7, 1969: a mushrooming nightmare for our medical team. Mass casualties. A "push." In came the wounded and sick. Out went our generator—not an uncommon occurrence but the first time it had happened during a mass-casualty situation, or "mass-cas" like the one we were facing. Ventilators can't pump oxygen into lungs when the generator dies. Pleiku's dust turned the chopper's landing zone into a whirl of crimson fog. Litter-bearers shielded their eyes from the blowing reddish-orange grit as they ferried their wounded buddies into our heavily bunkered emergency room for triage.

Then came the final indignation: the sky began raining enemy fire. Gashes of orange lit up the darkness, turning the already-surreal scene into a new dimension of insanity. In Vietnam, army field hospital wards were uniquely spread apart so that one rocket couldn't destroy the whole complex.

The first mortar round hit close to my ward. *Thud...whump, whump...boom.* A series of incoming rounds landed. Exploding mortar shells sprayed shrapnel and dirt. We grabbed helmets and flak jackets en route to our duty posts, mine a spare ward that we used in such emergencies. I could hear the "outgoing" sound of artillery from our nearby fire base.

Rockets pounded. Officers shouted instructions diffused by the noise. Chaos laughed in the face of whatever sanity was left.

I was ordered to open up the spare ward. What, hours earlier, had been an empty room was suddenly filled with groaning bodies. I felt a sense of dread. A ward master had gotten us our supplies, but it would be just me, my medic, and a single flashlight to get the job done.

"Corpsman!" I yelled. "Need a corpsman with a flashlight in the spare ward—quick!"

A young medic, Specialist McCabe (I can't recall his real name, so have given him one here) was running behind me. "I'm right here, Lieutenant."

I knew the drill, as did all the other doctors, nurses, and corpsmen already in the emergency room or setting up the OR, dealing with their own slices of this apocalypse. Dazed from the load-in, the two of us did a quick assessment.

"Twenty-eight, Lieutenant Carlson," said McCabe after a quick count.

Something more was happening here, and there wasn't anyone from the chopper crew to ask.

"See what I see, McCabe?" I asked my medic. "No boys full of holes. This is really strange."

I did a quick assessment: weak pulses, low blood pressures, exhaustion. The patients were drained of color, struggling with life-threatening dehydration. They were going into shock soon. I couldn't diagnose them, but I knew they needed fluid resuscitation—and fast.

A harried doctor appeared and took a quick look. "Start Ringer's lactate on every one of them. Two liters over the first two hours, then one liter over two hours. I'll be back later."

Thanks to heroic pilots and their choppers ready to lift off at any given moment to save a life, most soldiers arrived at a field or evac hospital within hours of being wounded—some within minutes. But these mud-crusted and disoriented soldiers appeared to have been *days* in getting here, though it was impossible to find out their back story. Nobody was talking. Some were moaning. A few were so hypotensive they were bordering on what we called "expectants," those certain to die. And nobody could help them but the two of us.

This was the night I recognized that whatever came my way, I could measure up. The troops were out there facing kill-or-be-killed scenarios every day, seeing their buddies' heads blown off. They were doing their job. I would do mine.

Compartmentalize, I told myself. Like planting potatoes. Just trust the process. One step at a time. One soldier at a time. One IV at a time.

This is how Mom did it back in Buffalo when, in one ER room, she had a farmer whose tractor had flipped on him and, in another ER room, three victims of a car-truck collision. Do your job, then go home and, in your farm kitchen, whip up a batch of cinnamon rolls to remind everyone of life's goodness. As a nurse, you can't fret about being overwhelmed. You just figure out your first step and start.

I breathed deeply. By now, Vietnam had pretty much blotted out any faith I'd arrived with, but I was desperate.

"Grace," I whispered. "Please, God. Send me some grace."

"What was that, Lieutenant?"

"Uh, *great*," I said. "This is pretty great. Had my first time off in thirteen days—until these guys decided to drop in and spoil everything." Our verbal exchange lightened the gravity of the situation, as was often the case in the war zone.

For me, grace meant *calm*. There is no panic in grace. There is confidence and hope. But thank God for the ward master, a crusty sergeant who'd served in WWII and Korea as a medic, who seemingly always knew exactly what to do and was always one step ahead of me. For the moment, he *was* god. He had set up all the IV poles, tubing, and a bottle of fluid hanging from every one of them. As the last litter-bearer came in I said, "OK McCabe, we're ready. We're going to get fluids in these men before they dry up and blow away."

One by one, we went to work. I soon realized the numbers, the darkness, and the whistling of the mortar shells above us weren't our only concerns. The men were so dehydrated that their veins were collapsed.

I had trouble finding them to insert the needle and get the life-saving liquid going. But by now I had started hundreds of IVs. I was good at this. Slowly and steadily, we worked our way down the first of three rows of men.

I knew what to do. Touch the soldier on his hand as means of connecting with him. "I'm going to start an IV on you," I'd say. "You're going to be OK." Choose the arm with the most probable vein. Wrap a tourniquet around the arm. Scrub the entry point. Insert the needle. Release the tourniquet. Run the fluid. Tape. Repeat. Just like making cinnamon rolls; follow the recipe.

The guys with painful abdominal cramping worried me, but even they settled down as the intravenous fluids took hold. Despite the chaos around us, despite an occasional mortar thud in the distance, a strange peace settled over the ward. I was in a zone I'd never experienced before. Calm amid the chaos.

About a third of our way through the twenty-eight men, we found one who seemed mildly lucid. His eyes widened when he saw the flashlight beam.

"Soldier," I asked, "what happened?"

He stared right through me, eyes fixed.

"Food poisoning?" asked my corpsman. "Water poisoning?"

No response. My corpsman and I exchanged a quick glance of futility regarding the cause of this mass dehydration.

Hours passed. The shelling had stopped. Artillery in the distance rumbled but wasn't threatening. My eyes scanned the bodies beneath blankets for those who may be in distress, those slipping into some degree of unconsciousness; we never would find out what had happened to these guys.

The leather and bronze peace-symbol around my neck, hidden by my fatigues, was soaked in sweat. As the batteries in McCabe's flashlight waned, so did the two of us. My back stiffened from bending over. My fingers had grown numb. My mind faded into sleep-deprived fuzziness.

"You OK, lieutenant?" McCabe asked.

"Fine. You?"

"Couldn't be better. We're done."

"Seriously?"

"Twenty-eight soldiers arrived. Twenty-eight still have measurable pulses."

We mirrored quick smiles. We felt so good you'd have thought we'd saved every passenger aboard the Titanic. I shook my head sideways in wonder and weariness, a far cry from that poster I'd seen on the Army Nurse Corps recruiter's office showing a gorgeous and glowing woman with the caption: "The most beautiful girl in the world, a U.S. Army nurse." And, at the moment, I was nobody's poster girl.

"Good work, McCabe," I said.

He nodded his head slightly in appreciation, not a common gesture in these parts. "Uh, good enough for your usual reward, ma'am?"

I nodded toward the supply room and widened my eyes. "Sure."

I loved my corpsmen and wasn't averse to showing them in ways that not only stretched protocol but would, if we were found out, ruffle the feathers of my superior officer. But this was war, and sometimes rules had to be bent. We slipped into the supply room. Whatever faint light was still left in his flashlight, McCabe shined on a tier of shelves, one of which contained something I'd baked the night before: a batch of cinnamon rolls.

"Two left," I said.

"Perfect."

We slid our backs down the wall, sat on the floor, and right smack in the eye of the storm of war, ate cinnamon rolls. Reveling in every single bite, feeling no guilt at all, though we both knew they'd been baked illegally.

"Oh, my God," he said. "These are heaven."

I had a fleeting image of our hands-on-her-hip nursing supervisor, a woman born sometime before Attila the Hun—and with the same rosy disposition.

"Thanks," I said. "But keep that to yourself."

"Why?"

"The 'lifer' busted me earlier today for this batch. Said I'm toast if she catches me making them again. Something about fraternizing with the 'enlisteds.' Said I'm getting too close to my corpsmen and she doesn't like it."

He shook his head sideways.

"You know," I said, "it's not like I'm stealing ingredients from the mess hall."

His eyes widened. He nodded encouragement.

"I'm just *borrowing* them—well, sort of *permanently* borrowing them."

"Yeah," he said, "and if she does catch you, what's she gonna do?"

"Send me to Vietnam? I mean, really, it can't get any worse!"

He laughed. I laughed. Our shift was over.

"Get some sleep, McCabe. Judging by that bloated Chinook, tomorrow's not going to be much better."

I slept for four hours, but it seemed like four minutes. Back on our post-operative surgical unit by 6:30 a.m., we evac'ed out most of our patients—and checked on a Montagnard child burned by napalm—to make room for the newly wounded. The Montagnard tribal people of the Central Highlands were used to minding their own business but got caught up in the spiderweb of war and coerced by the U.S. government to help us out against the NVA and VC.

As darkness fell, the skies lit up; in Vietnam the night belonged to the enemy. A shell ripped into the earth just outside our ward. The sky flashed brightly again; another blast, almost as close, followed. And another. The NVA was targeting the Pleiku Air Base and the radar placed alongside our hospital buildings.

We needed no coaching—nor did the patients lying in their beds. They hit the floor, yanking out blood lines and IVs. We grabbed their empty mattresses and threw them atop the patients who couldn't move—those connected to chest tubes, tracheotomies, malaria ice blankets, ventilators, and the like. It was a sorry way to protect them from flying shrapnel, but it's all we had.

The quiet gave way to deafening noise. Terrifying thuds. Some IV bottles crashed to the floor. More blasts. More flashes of light in the dark from cracks in the wood-shuttered windows. I grabbed more mattresses, a feeble attempt to save lives in the madness.

While reconnecting tubing and blood lines, I heard it: a child's scream. In the faint glow of the medic's flashlight, I found her. She was perhaps two or three, face wet with tears, hands over her ears. It was the heart-rending little Montagnard girl. I couldn't pick her up; she was burned too badly. God, what had we done? Her parents had been killed in their village. She was terrified, and she was in extreme pain.

Boom...boom...boom.... More shells. More screams from the little girl. I had done all I could do, now I got under her crib and reached up to hold her hand. Just hold her hand. And I prayed to take away her pain, to stop the shelling, and to stop the suffering. Don't let them die, not here, not now.

"It's OK," I whispered. "I've got you."

She heard the comfort of my voice but kept on screaming. Just when you thought you'd seen it all—necklaces made of human ears and all the rest—something like this would remind you that, when it came to war, the potential for man's inhumanity was immeasurable. A few moments later, the little girl screamed herself to death. Literally.

One minute you were enjoying a cinnamon roll with your corpsman, the next realizing that the little girl whose hand you held—the girl you'd promised to protect—had gone as limp as a rag doll.

Moving to the 71st Evacuation Hospital at Pleiku felt like flying directly into a storm, but that's what I needed. I was wiser, smarter, more confident than I'd been when first arriving in Vietnam. Less trusting, yes, but no less intent on looking for the good in people, be they Americans, Vietnamese, or Montagnards. I went from being a 2nd lieutenant to a 1st lieutenant and became the head nurse of a surgical unit.

I quickly formed bonds with a handful of other nurses, foremost among them Edie McCoy. We arrived about the same time, both wanting a change even though the territory looked more hostile. We quickly discovered we were both from Minnesota and traded memories of home. She had a beautiful smile, a quick wit, and an infectious laugh. We were instant friends. She brought a green tomato home from the mess hall and put it on her windowsill.

"What's that for?" I asked.

"I just want to look at something that's alive."

Beyond the combat casualties, even the jungle around us was dead, leveled by liberal sprayings of Agent Orange.

Edie and our other hootchmates—Barbie Chiminello, Maggie LaBarbera, Sara McVicker, and Joan Furey—went to work and came back from work like robots, bumping into each other in the hallway, sharing the one bathroom and shower, but rarely talking about what we did that day. We worked twelve-or-more hour shifts, six or more days a week. Generally speaking, much of my job was taking doctor's orders, spotting and reporting changes in patients' vital signs, starting IVs, hanging blood, tracheostomy and wound care, monitoring ventilators, chest tubes, pain control, and reporting to the nursing supervisor. Morphine and Demerol were my go-to drugs for the wounded.

Barbie had accompanied the body of her brother, 1st Lt. Thomas Chiminello, home after he was killed in his downed helicopter on October 29, 1967. She volunteered for a second tour in Vietnam, in the emergency room. By now, she was an unflappable nurse.

One night, Joan knocked on my door looking like death warmed over. "Read this," she said. "I just needed to get it off my chest."

It was poetry that began with:

Legs ache, head throbs
Every muscle taut. Every nerve on edge
I want to scream but I can't...
I'm sorry, it got to me today
I'm a nurse and maybe it shouldn't
But it does,
And I ask also
Why God? Why?

We worked in wood-framed wards with glass-free windows. Screens and wood shutters were safer. Choppers arrived with regularity, sometimes two or more at a time. Depending on the type of Huey, a Dustoff helicopter could bring up to ten or twelve KIAs or wounded.

In February, the post–Tet Offensive ratcheted our casualties to a new high. I once went thirty-two hours without any sleep. Even when you did catch shut-eye, it wasn't always peaceful.

"We've been rocketed and mortared the last three nights," I wrote home on February 25.

The hospital compound was surrounded by concertina wire and guard towers housing medics or MPs with M16s.

It wasn't just here, of course, that hospitals were taking heat. I got a letter from a nurse friend in Vũng Tàu who said shortly after I left, they'd been hit by a rocket attack and taken mass casualties. Numbers never bled or cried or died, however. It was the individuals you remembered.

A young black-haired girl, maybe twelve or thirteen, arrived, teetering toward death. A pediatric doctor, Captain Dan Rowe, diagnosed her with plague, possibly pneumonic. Quarantine was a joke; all we could do was put up a sheet in the back room separating her from other patients. Dr. Rowe told me to put a sign above her bed, "Do Not Resuscitate." I briefed our corpsman and nurses that under no circumstances should they do mouth-to-mouth resuscitation as plague can be contagious from the saliva. On the next shift, I walked in to find one of our medics, Spec. John Huddleston, performing mouth-to-mouth.

"Huddleston, stop!" I said. "Don't you remember what I told you? No mouth-to-mouth! Stop!"

He wouldn't. I checked the little girl's pulse. She was gone.

"Huddleston, it's too late."

He wept. Unabashedly.

"You know that was dangerous. Why were you doing it?"

He rubbed his hands across his face. "I just wanted to save her life," he said.

I ran out of prayers in Pleiku. I quit writing in my diary—at least temporarily. I did not ever, *ever* want to remember any of this. One night, litter-bearers carried in a teenage Montagnard girl, one of the indigenous people who'd been swept into the war—wrapped in her dark maroon sarong. She grabbed my arm, terrified. I noticed the pupil of one eye was huge and dilated, the other pin-point small, always a bad sign. Of course, she wanted her mother. I was "mom" for those brief moments; I comforted her as best I could, then, on our government-issue desk phone, called Dr. Rowe with my plea for him to take a look, explaining the symptoms.

I could tell I'd awakened him, probably after a fourteen-hour shift.

"Diane," he mumbled, "you know as well as I do, there's nothing we can do for her."

What could I say? I had no response. So I held her in my arms, knowing she would likely die soon. And, then, ten minutes later, there he was, coming through the door: Rowe. Hair mussed. Eyes half-mast. But *there*, ready to help if there was even a glimmer of hope. The girl died anyway. But he had come, a moment I would never forget.

How could that be enough to placate my loss of innocence? Does Dr. Rowe coming through that door override the guy who decapitated the prostitute and then told a buddy "these gooks" can't be trusted?

I'd arrived in Vietnam eight months before, admittedly as a wide-eyed girl fresh off a Minnesota farm and nursing school. The daughter of a nurse who modeled unbridled commitment to her profession and her patients. The girl who never liked to see the school bully pick on the little kids, so she finally kicked him in the shin and yelled, "Stop being *mean*!"

And yet here I was, in a place where war had muddied the waters so violently that all you saw was drab-olive green and browns and the red of blood. Like a kindergartener's water-color tray, every color had merged with the others to create a grayish-black tint of meaninglessness.

Thus far, my indignation had gone only so far. I'd refused to let the crazed soldier with the ear-necklace see his buddy in our ward until he took the adornment off. Now, in a repeat of my playground-bully moment, I wanted to climb to one of the guard towers and shout: *Stop the fighting! This is sick and useless!* I wanted to have Richard Nixon spend a twenty-four-hour shift with me—then tell me to my face that it made sense to escalate this war. I wanted to know that these suffering soldiers and women and children were dying for *something*. A cause. A purpose. A mission worth fighting for. Not just some politician's desire to save face. I wanted to know that men and women, if they had to die, were dying for a reason. And, no, God and country weren't enough.

I was far too exhausted to notice that I'd arrived at some sort of emotional crossroads. Like a leaf on a river, I was feeling less and less like I had a say in where I was going. I was careening unsteadily toward a choice that—whatever it was—might have more control over me than I had over it.

On one hand, you could say I had only myself to blame; after all, it was my decision, after six months in Vũng Tàu, to seek a transfer closer to intense fighting. Guards kept watch from towers night and day. You were always on guard for the unexpected, whether that might be an attack, an infiltration, or the mama san who did your wash stealing medical supplies right out from under you. Or worse: passing secrets to the enemy.

And so, amid the madness, I made a decision rooted in self-preservation, my personal cry to refuse being so warped by war that I could no longer recognize myself if I looked in a mirror. A week after the mortar attack, at just after four in the morning, all was quiet in the compound. Every building was dark. Suddenly, combat boots, their owner purposely walking lightly to avoid detection, padded down a hallway and into the mess hall supply room.

I flicked on my flashlight, startling a mama san asleep on a supply shelf in my path. She ran off. The nursing supervisor be damned; this was war. I found the shelves with the yeast, flour, and other ingredients, and silently started to make another batch of cinnamon rolls.

9

The End of One War

The manila envelope arrived for me in early April, the kind of thing I had never received. Inside was the last letter I'd written Eddie, unopened. I squinted with more concern than conjecture. What was this?

Then I saw it: a note paper-clipped to the letter from his commanding officer.

"I'm sorry to inform you," he wrote, "that Specialist Four Eddie Evenson, A CO, 1st BN, 12th CAVALRY, 1st CAV DIV, USARV, died on March 23 in Japan from injuries incurred by hostile fire in Vietnam on March 6. This letter was found in his possession at the time of his injury."

My body convulsed forward as if I'd been shot. Wait, this was impossible. Eddie Evenson was too good a man to die. We saved him. For what? To go back and die? I saw him in his blue pajamas ambulating patients on Ward 6 in Vũng Tàu. I saw him back in full uniform smiling as he said goodbye.

"See ya later, Lieutenant, maybe back in Minnesota! Don't forget to write!"

No. No. No. I sat alone on the edge of my bed while slowly the reality sunk in: all of these men we were taking care of had nurses, doctors, medics, friends like me who cared deeply about them, loved them. They had combat buddies. Girlfriends. Wives. Fathers. Mothers. Children. Sisters. Brothers. Teachers. Coaches. Pastors. Aunts and uncles. Neighbors. Schools. Clubs. Workplaces. Communities of people who wanted more than anything for that soldier to come home alive.

And Eddie Evenson's death would break all those hearts. In Pleiku that afternoon, I vowed that I would never make this mistake again; I would never get as close to another soldier as I had to Eddie Evenson. I should have listened to Ann Cunningham, my friend from Fort Lee who had accompanied her fiancé's body home from war.

They will die.

I was tired and didn't feel like writing letters home about all this misery. The weather was miserable. The monsoons left our clothes damp with mildew, everything moldy and taking on the reddish-orange hue of Vietnam dirt and mud. The threats of enemy attack were real; we were usually on "alert" mode with the sounds of outgoing and incoming artillery pounding away, the latter sometimes prompting red alerts.

But if the threat of attacks from outside was real, so was the threat of attacks from within. A hootch setup had a handful of units for nurses inside, each with a padlock and a common bathroom/shower. One night I awoke to one of my hootchmates, Maggie, screaming; a huge rat was clawing its way across her. Another night, we were awakened by another rat—a senior officer who'd made a drunken pass at me at the officer's club earlier in the evening. Smashed out of his mind, he was hammering on my door, demanding to be let in. The MPs carted him off. The same MPs who, a few nights later, boasted about the sapper, a "dead gook" they'd found entangled in the compound's concertino wire.

Exhausted as I was, sleep never came easily. Our brains were wired for vigilance—not just for rats, drunks, and insurgents, but keying in the sounds of war triggering us to act. But you learned to leaven the horror with humor or numbness.

Seconds after the scream of a red-alert siren, a shell exploded just outside our wood-shuttered screen. The mirror over my dresser crashed onto the floor, leaving slivers of glass. I crawled over, wincing when my arms hit glass shards. I unlocked my padlock, then banged on Edie's door to let me in. I wasn't going to die alone.

"Come on in, Diane," she said in a lilting voice that belied the seriousness of the attack.

Edie was struggling to get her helmet on over her hair rollers.

"You look ridiculous," I said.

We crawled under her bed and were struggling to get comfortable when I realized she was swathing peanut butter onto crackers.

"How can you eat at a time like this?" I asked.

"If I'm going to die," she said, "I'm going to die happy."

I laughed. She laughed. We couldn't stop. That was Vietnam. I was bleeding from mirror shards embedded in my arms. We'd been seconds removed from an almost direct hit. And we were laughing uncontrollably.

At daylight we found that the hootch near ours was gone. A crater was in its place. By the grace of God, the hootch had been empty. By the time we headed for work the next morning, sweating GIs were stacking sandbags to the top of our hootch.

The makeup of the casualties was diverse. At Pleiku, beyond our own soldiers and Vietnamese, we took care of many Montagnards. With the language barriers, communication was nearly impossible. And they were getting injured, and dying, thanks to the United States' invitation for them to help us out. We stepped up and did our nursing. We cared for them right alongside our soldiers.

"Choppers are flying in with patients night and day," I wrote home. "Yesterday it never stopped. The Air Force is flying extra missions to Japan to get them out of here. This post–Tet Offensive is horrible."

Some soldiers were dead on arrival. Some were about to be. The triage team quickly did its assessments based on the resources, human and otherwise, needed to save them: "expectants" were placed somewhere out of view from the others because they were expected to die no matter what. Someone would stay by their side. "Immediates" were those who needed urgent life-saving attention and surgery. The "walking wounded," guys who were hurt but didn't require extensive attention, were given the lowest priority.

At times you'd see things that made no sense. A young man would survive what would seem to be a fatal injury, his insides ripped to shreds; another young man would die from a "through and through" wound, a single bullet that left both an entry and exit wound. Had it entered the body half-an-inch higher or lower and missed a vital organ, it wouldn't have killed him.

By now, I'd lost any patience with politicians and the press whose body counts were far different from what we were seeing. "Yesterday morning the radio said that American casualties were light and only one was killed the night before," I wrote home. "That night there had been almost a whole battalion of American men killed and those who weren't KIA were brought here, wounded."

It was common knowledge among the medical staff that our score-keepers were padding the figures to assure the folks back home we were winning. Winning, meaning a higher "body count" than the enemy. Unlike other wars, which involved pushing forward to gain territory, villages, and cities to ultimately force surrender, Vietnam offered no such clarity. No such definition. There were no "fronts." No ground permanently won or lost. And so, in the absence of real estate won, what emerged as our measuring stick was simple: corpses. Ours vs. theirs. The U.S. government consistently inflated the number of theirs and deflated the number of ours. That way, it went over better on the six o'clock news.

What's more, the U.S. government tried to hide our atrocities. A year prior to my horrific night in Pleiku, in a place only 150 miles northeast of us, U.S. troops killed somewhere between 350 and 500 unarmed civilians in what would become known as the My Lai Massacre. Later, I learned the official press briefing summed it up like this: "In an action today, American Division forces killed 128 enemy near Quảng Ngãi

City. Helicopter gunships and artillery missions supported the ground elements throughout the day."

If the government was bluffing the press, at the time I wrongly blamed the messenger. Vietnam wasn't the end of the earth; we read an occasional newspaper or magazine, listened to radio. We knew people were demonstrating wildly against the war back home; if they kept it peaceful, I couldn't blame them.

"What makes me so darned mad is the garbage and lies the press tells back home," I wrote to my folks in March 1969. "Either you don't hear the *truth at all*, or the news is exaggerated, and correct figures not given out." Such reports didn't match the lies spewed by the president. I did some sanitizing of my own experiences when writing letters home; I wasn't about to tell my folks about little girls screaming themselves to death or prostitutes being beheaded. But I never lied.

In Vietnam, if there was an alleged "purpose" that drew us all together, I was still looking for it. We each fought our own war. Our own demons. In the spring of 1969, war was killing us in more ways than one. War was robbing our souls, our integrity, our humanity. Our government was lying, God was silent, and integrity was scarcer than American pie.

Not that such integrity was missing altogether. It was in the corpsmen who didn't flinch as we kept two dozen men alive in the dark. The grunts who stood by their injured buddies on our ward, loyal to a fault. The Eddie Evensons who were wounded but determined to go back to their units. And the thousands of brave men and women serving in the U.S. Marine Corps, Air Force, Navy, Coast Guard, Army, and Red Cross, sharing hardships and adversities in a foreign country whose people fought unmercifully to kick us out. Journalists and civilians serving in support of the Armed Forces, were being killed in Vietnam, too; no one was safe.

Under fire, we forged friendships, camaraderie, and bonds that only those of us who serve in war could grasp. It made us tougher, wiser, maybe even better. But beyond the moral and political befuddlement, I found myself getting lost in a personal typhoon. Who had I become? Was I still that farm girl from Minnesota in some way, shape, or form?

I liked to think so. But reports from back home suggested otherwise; if you were in Vietnam, male or female, you were considered a crazed baby killer. Never mind that we saved the lives of hundreds of babies. If you were a woman serving in Vietnam, you were a target of any number of negative assumptions.

What really mattered, I finally decided, was simply what I thought of myself. After transferring to Pleiku, I got a handful of letters from nurses and medics who I'd served with at Vũng Tàu. I was touched by the respect they accorded me and by the realization that amid the chaos, I'd apparently made a difference. I had long carried guilt that I wasn't doing enough. In the cruel barbarity of war, I could only help one person at a time; whatever I gave never seemed to be enough.

I got a letter from Private James Testa, a soldier I'd cared for in Vũng Tàu. He lifted my spirits when saying he couldn't run yet, but he could walk. "And Rome wasn't built in a day." Happiness, he said, was being home. "But happiness in Vietnam was the 36th and you."

I also heard from the mother of Danny Bodin, the neighbor farm boy from Buffalo who'd died in Vietnam in February 1968, six months before I arrived in-country. I'd sent her a note when I heard the sad news. She talked about the weather, about how the flu was going around, but made no mention of her son's death. It must have been too hard to do so, a concept that I couldn't understand now but would soon.

I couldn't forget the kids in the orphanage back in Vũng Tàu. When friends back home asked how they could help, I asked them to send care packages to the kids, and they did.

Rain brought mud. In early March, a storm blew through, ripping off a few ward roofs, taking down power lines, and turning Pleiku's red dust into a muddy mess. "Pillow cases, sheets, treatment carts, medicine carts, you name it, we cleaned it," I wrote home March 6, 1969.

Though the government wasn't saying so, we knew our infantry was inside Cambodia. Knew our soldiers were fighting there. The results were bleeding out on our hospital beds, with amputated limbs and horrific head injuries.

"No patient records will indicate that that wounded man was fighting in Cambodia," our commanding officers told us.

But we knew plenty of our boys were, as they say, "jumping the fence." Not once did I defy a supervisor who told me that—to his or her face. But when I asked a soldier where in Vietnam he'd been wounded and he said, "Cambodia, ma'am," I refused to lie for my government. Instead, on their record I wrote "Cambodia"—every time that was the case. As if to thumb my nose at President Richard Nixon: "Lie if you will, but I won't be your accomplice." The only man I despised more was Lyndon ("we shall win this war at all costs") Johnson, on whose hands was the blood of far too many of my brothers and sisters in Vietnam—and thousands of innocent civilians.

Some of the saddest moments on the ward included seeing officers stop by to visit the wounded and pin them with a Purple Heart. That was the hypocrisy of our leaders: that they could not only keep sending our boys to a war that was clearly not winnable, but that they could pretend a quarter-sized medal was going to compensate for whatever they had taken from these men. Those men just wanted to get back to their units and be with their buddies, win the war, and go home.

The government seemed convinced that you could play this game of chess with human beings and all would be fine as long we took more of the enemy than they took of us. On June 8, when a medic tapped me on the shoulder and told me that an Army nurse, Sharon Lane, had been killed in a mortar shelling at Chu Lai—the first U.S. nurse to die from enemy fire—my first instinct was not: *those dirty VCs. Attacking hospitals.*

Instead, my heart broke as I thought, *her poor parents, her poor family.* And all the life that this twenty-five-year-old woman from Ohio wasn't going to get to experience. But eye-for-an-eye thinking was rampant in this war. I was treating a Viet Cong prisoner who, while I tried to start an IV on him, grabbed at my neck to choke me. Was he scared? Was he thinking I was trying to kill him or hurt him? Perhaps. I didn't know. The two military police armed guards on either side of him carried him out.

He was too dangerous to have on our unit. They probably took him to the POW Hospital in Long Binh…or decided to do something far worse. Rules get broken in war time. I wondered if that POW had committed an atrocity against one of our soldiers. The guards were clearly upset. I thought about one of our American soldiers who had been tortured by the VC, strapped to the ground on his back in the hot sun with a bamboo shoot rammed up his rectum and left to die.

The bodies kept coming faster, as if someone had turned up the speed on a conveyor belt. At times, you worked on young men whose chests were split open or whose faces were scarred beyond recognition or whose plumbing no longer worked, and they'd lost their will to get better.

"Who back home is going to want me like this?" they pleaded with eyes that broke your heart.

Meanwhile, the surgeons working on them were exhausted and disillusioned with the carnage—and who could blame them? They were overworked and underappreciated here in what one of my patients called "the land of flowerless misenchantment." And yet they were doing extraordinary work. The record of the Vietnam War in terms of saving the lives of the wounded was unparalleled in the history of warfare at that time. Fewer than two percent of casualties who were treated in our hospitals within the first hours of arriving died as a result of their wounds.

"I have been caught up too much in things," I wrote in my diary April 14, 1969. "Have not kept track of myself nor my diary. Things have been happening too fast. Post–Tet and all the casualties—the endless casualties coming in."

In April, I took a much-needed week's R&R in Hong Kong, a ninety-minute flight. I loved every minute of the trip: the city was clean, the people friendly, the food great, the shopping fantastic. What's more, I got to phone my folks without having to say "over" after every sentence. At least these are the things I wrote home to my folks about.

I conveniently overlooked telling them that, while delayed getting out of Vietnam, I was being put up at an officer's billet, and while getting ready for bed I heard the loud pop of a gun outside. To this day, I've thought it indicative of a nurse's instincts that instead of running *from* the sound, I ran *toward* it. A soldier with a handgun had tried to take his life—and, judging by the amount of blood spurting out of his chest, had done a pretty good job.

I knelt beside him and touched his face. "Hey, soldier," I said softly. No response.

I put my mouth to his ear. "You're on your way home. Kiss the ground for me when you get there."

Uniformed soldiers yelling the proverbial "what the fuck?" soon came running to help. We all knew it was too late. An MP looked at me and shook his head. The sound of a chopper got lower and lower as it descended to get the soldier.

"Ma'am, you best get back to your billet," said an MP. "Not much more you can do here."

Wearing my blood-soaked nightgown, I stood in the shower for a long time and watched the soldier's blood flow into the drain. Watched his life literally go down the drain. *God, where are you?* I cursed the war and all those in our nation's capital whose fingerprints were on the .45.

But in a testament to how pathetically war can dull the senses, I was so tired I fell right to sleep.

Unlike Vũng Tàu, heat wasn't the challenge here as much as rain and cold. By May the monsoons were slamming us regularly. "It's like a tidal wave every time it rains," I wrote home. And nights could get cold; "had my electric blanket on eight," I wrote.

Pleiku was one of the busiest hospitals in Vietnam in the spring and summer of 1969. By now my disposition was slipping to the dark side. When I got off duty, all I wanted to do was sleep. Forever. "I've taken care of guys over here with diseases I've never heard of before: shigelloses, amebiasis, blackwater fever, and plague," I wrote home on July 4. "This is the crappiest country! It's pretty but is disease infested."

On July 20, while we were patching the wounded, a corpsman announced that two U.S. astronauts had stood on the moon.

"That's great," I said. "Hope they make it home safely."

"Who has time for that?" said Edie. "We have men dying over here. Meanwhile, they send a guy to the moon but can't send us more medics and supplies?"

"Some days we would discharge seventeen and admit just as many," I wrote in my diary. "The beds never cool off."

One day, amid one of our drenching rains, a pilot—a major—came to visit his co-pilot who'd been injured badly while in the cockpit but ejected from their plane before it crashed.

"Sir, there's something you need to know," I said. "Your buddy is blind—and will likely stay that way."

Initially, the major's face froze in defiance, as if not believing me could somehow alter the truth. Then it contorted into part anger, part fear, part horror.

"I am so sorry," I said.

He composed himself and walked down the ward's aisle to see the man. A few minutes later I gathered my things to leave; my shift was over. Outside, the monsoon-powered rain raked the side of the hospital as I grabbed my poncho and headed for my hootch, bent over, hand atop my boonie hat to keep it from flying away. Ahead of me I noticed the blurry figure of a man careening slightly left and right as if drunk or in a stupor. When a cat tried to scurry across the muddy path in front of him, he kicked it with a vengeance.

The yowling scream shivered my spine. Before the dazed cat could reorient itself, the man stomped on it. Again. And again. And again. By now, I wasn't shocked by anything that happened in Vietnam. This was just another surreal moment, one of thousands of heinous acts in a war evolving into one big hallucination. The cat was clearly dead. The man looked back, as if wondering if anyone had seen him. I recoiled; it was the major who'd just seen the co-pilot who couldn't see him back. Was he crazy? Weirdly, I was beginning to understand. The tragedy of war makes good people crazy, even if I still had a glimmer of hope that I could avoid joining that category.

I didn't say a word. The pilot didn't say a word. He turned and hurried away into the storm.

I stood and stared at the pile of fur, bones, and blood, reminded of what had happened to so many of our soldiers, their soldiers, and the poor civilians caught in the crossfire since I'd arrived a year ago: physically or emotionally, they'd become indistinguishable from their once-glorious selves, blurred beyond recognition by war. Would the hate and anger and lies never stop? It was as if the war was killing us in two ways—in the field of battle and in our souls, our integrity, our humanity, or whatever we had left of them.

Enough.

It was time to go home.

PART III: HIDING IN THE LIGHT

My youth and health had mattered so much when the task was that of dragging wounded men back to life; I believed that the vitality which kept me going had helped others who had lost their own to live, and it seemed rather thrown away when it was all exploded upon persuading the grocer to give us a pot of jam.

—Vera Brittain, *Testament of Youth*

10

Goodbye, Vietnam

July 1969

I remember my last patient in Vietnam like I remembered the moment President John F. Kennedy was assassinated. (Speech class, Buffalo High.) At Pleiku, the most critically ill patients were positioned directly across from the nurses' station so we could keep a close eye on them. They watched us as much as we watched them. I think they also knew they were chosen to be there because they were dying.

One of them was a badly wounded GI with a tracheostomy; he was hooked up to a ventilator. He was restless and fearful and couldn't speak. For days, we had communicated with each other by jotting words on a notepad. The back-and-forth messaging eased his anxiety and provided the reassurance he desperately needed to lessen his distress. My DEROS (Date Eligible for Return from Over Seas) orders arrived.

"It's my time to leave Vietnam," I said to the soldier. "I'll miss you, but I have to say goodbye."

A look of panic locked on his face. His eyes darted left and right. He gestured for the notepad.

"Don't leave me," he mouthed in words. He took the notepad and scrawled "Please don't go!!!!"

He couldn't hold back the tears. I never cried in Vietnam, but at that moment I came close.

I hung yet another bottle of intravenous fluid, then touched his ashen face and looked into his sunken eyes. I stroked his soft, cold face. He scribbled something on his notepad.

"Wish I could see my mom again," he wrote.

I nodded, kissed him on the cheek, and left. Though I can't remember his name, I would never forget him. I think he knew he wasn't going to make it—and I don't think he survived, although I've never been sure. But what else could I do? Nothing was neat and clean in Vietnam, good-byes among them, because here's the thing: as much as I wanted to leave and needed to leave, I *didn't* want to leave. If that sounds like a contradiction, it's because Vietnam was one giant contradiction.

I didn't want to leave that soldier. I didn't want to leave my unit, my hootchmates, my patients. I seriously had toyed with re-upping for another year. Another contradiction: Just when we got good—really good—at our jobs, our tour was over, and we turned things over to the new people.

Barbie, my hootchmate, had lost one brother who was a helicopter pilot and had another brother on his way over to Vietnam. And yet she had re-upped for another year. I wasn't trying to "guilt" her, but I couldn't help but ask.

"How can you do that to your parents?" I asked.

In her mind, she had rationalized staying. In my mind, I had rationalized leaving, perhaps because I still remembered my father crying when I left and still remembered all the letters my mother and Nola wrote once I'd gone. They deserved to have me come home. I'd written my folks weeks ago that my ETA in Minneapolis would be about August 9, 1969. Emotionally, this was more about them than about me. But, physically, it was all about me.

I was exhausted. I was sick, having had a low-grade fever for the last week. And I was losing weight. I was 5'5" tall and always thin, rarely over

110 lbs. But now I was flirting with double figures. Copter pilots offered me their hand when we loaded in beneath the rotors.

"Hell, girl, take it or you'll blow away," one said.

I hastily stuffed my clothes and mementoes given to me by patients—poetry, brigade and division patches, a rabbit's foot, a Green Beret, letters, dog tags, a VC flag, a Montagnard bronze bracelet, and more—into my footlocker. I said goodbye to my ward nurses, corpsmen, hootchmates, and docs.

As I approached the helipad, with duffel bag in hand, I encountered more than a dozen desperate and wailing Montagnard women with about as many kids lining up and vying to get on the same chopper. Something terrible must have happened in their village. The pilots and crew hopped out and shooed them away. As the helicopter lifted off, I looked down at the red whirling dust and saw young mothers scatter into oblivion. The apocalypse was behind me.

Or was it?

Leaving railed against every nursing instinct I'd ever had. I had no sense of relief for having survived for 351 days in Vietnam. I had never run away from anything in my life, and this felt a little like I was. More U.S. soldiers died in Vietnam in the two calendar years I was there—1968 and 1969—than at any other time during the war.

I felt no sense of having neatly tied the knot of an adventurous two years of my military life. And I had no picture of what exactly I would be doing with my new life in the states. In a letter home, I'd asked Mom to inquire about my working at the Buffalo hospital. So I must have assumed my future would include being a nurse. But even that image was diffused and uninspiring, like trying to peer out one of the farmhouse's frosty windows and seeing only the faintest of images beyond.

I arrived in Japan, feverish and fatigued. I checked into a Naval Bachelor Officer Quarters in Tokyo, staying ten days while waiting for the fever to break. An elegant, well-coifed woman noticed me sitting alone in the officer's mess. I know she saw me as forlorn; she couldn't have known how unfamiliar it was for me to be sitting at a table covered in white linen with silverware and fresh flowers in a vase.

She introduced herself as the wife of the captain of an aircraft carrier that was arriving soon. It was my first true conversation with someone outside the military in a year. She was lovely, poised, and relaxed—and yet interested in me, where I'd been and where I was going, not that I had much of a clue about either. We talked late into the evening. She insisted on buying my dinner. In my transition home, beyond the two GIs who stood up for me in an airport, she would be the only one who seemed to really care about *me* as a returning Vietnam veteran.

I'd been warned not to wear my uniform home, that such attire would only bait the soldier-haters in the airports. But to *not* seemed like surrendering to the idea that we should be ashamed, that war couldn't be separated from the warrior. For my last leg to San Francisco I threw on the uniform and, for the first time, wore my peace symbol—on the outside.

I thought briefly of home. The farm. Mom. Dad. My brothers. My sister. "Please don't plan anything for me when I get home," I'd written the previous month. "The only thing I want is for everything to be the same as when I left."

As the jet winged its way home, I sensed a numbness, a listlessness, an indifference in me that failed to trigger the usual nurses' response of seeing what's wrong and fixing it. Instead, as the thrum of the engines lulled me to sleep, my last thought was: *If this plane were to crash right here in the middle of the Pacific Ocean, I honestly wouldn't care.*

At Travis Air Force Base near San Francisco, I was initially surprised that when I got off the plane, nobody spit on me, verbally unloaded on me, or gave me a look of disdain. Then I remembered: *You're still in the military bubble.*

It was time for my discharge physical. I understood why I'd been feeling so poorly the last few weeks.

"Ma'am, it appears you have a spot on your lung," said a military doctor after taking x-rays. "We're going to send you to Madigan Army Hospital up in Tacoma, Washington, for another opinion."

At Madigan, I was told to have it looked at every six months. No mention was made of tuberculosis, which I'd later be diagnosed with but not compensated for—even though I'd treated Vietnamese patients with it.

With that I was handed my DD 214 discharge papers. The Army Nurse Corps and I were officially parting ways.

"And where do I pick up my ticket for Minneapolis?" I asked.

"Oh, you're on your own for that," the corporal said.

"Seriously?"

I was not trying to be smarmy but news that the U.S. Army wouldn't get me back home seemed like the ultimate insult.

"Even though I live in Minnesota, you're really not paying for me to get back there?"

"Sorry. Protocol."

Protocol? It was like forking over $3,500 for a new Mustang and finding the dealer was charging you for the bag of popcorn you ate in the showroom. I'd paid a huge price to give to my country and my country couldn't pay a small price to get me back where I'd started this journey?

"You're out of the Army now, ma'am," he said. "Rules are rules." I shook my head and left. As far as last words go, my country could have done better. I'd have preferred "thank you for your service—and here's your pre-paid ticket home." It didn't need to be first-class; I'd been flying in open-door choppers that sounded, and felt, as if you were in giant belt sanders. But, yeah, a "thanks" would have been nice.

That was the first shoe that dropped. The other followed at the Minneapolis-St. Paul International Airport when I arrived at the baggage carousel and was belittled by one of a handful of protestors when getting my duffel bag. I was out of the Army, but I was still wearing the uniform. Two uniformed enlisted men stood by me as we waited for our bags. As I moved to pull my duffel off the belt, one of them said, "I'll get that for you, Lieutenant!"

"Let her carry her own damn bags," a long-haired protestor sneered. "She's in a man's army!"

The GI bloodied the guy's nose with a single punch.

"You know," I said, "we didn't start the war. We're over there defending people like you."

I found it interesting—no, disturbing—that nobody in the crowd said or did anything to support us. Bystanders, they had just stood and watched. It was a metaphor that I would experience often in the years to come.

I would hear of other degrading welcomes for military personnel from Vietnam: civilians spitting, throwing eggs, shouting, swearing, and protesting with in-your-face antics aimed at us. "Go back to Nam, Army pigs!" said some signs. "Baby Killers Not Welcome." One of our 71st Evac nurses, Lynda Van Devanter, tried to hail a cab. "Fuck you, army bitch," the driver said and sped off.

So, you leave as a defender of the free world and return as the enemy. I was stunned at how quickly people could race to conclusions at the simple sight of a uniform—or, in particular, a woman in uniform. That kid who'd hassled me didn't know me. Didn't know our medical team saved the lives of hundreds of South Vietnamese and Montagnard children. Didn't know that I was probably more anti-war than he was—because I'd actually seen the war in living color instead of only on TV, and knew it to be mainly the color of blood. And those of us who wore the uniform basically had pledged to shed ours so protestors like that kid could enjoy the splendors of freedom. All around, our nation was drowning in anti-war violence.

Did many of us in the military like how our leaders were lying to us and putting more soldiers in harm's way, sacrificing thousands of lives so the brass might somehow save face? No way. But I wanted to say to the kid: *Before you paint us all as crazy-eyed baby killers, at least find out who we really are. You might be surprised.*

Mom and Dad were late picking me up, for which I was thankful. They missed the fiasco. It would have crushed Dad; he hated the war, too, but couldn't understand the animosity toward the veterans. He was part of the World War II generation where men and women came home from duty with honor for their service and their victory.

Dad grabbed my duffel and we got in their 1966 Ambassador Rambler to take me home. I can't remember a single thing we said in the car.

11

Picking Up the Pieces

August–September 1969

Soon after arriving at the farm, I saddled up my horse, Camaron, and went riding. It was pure freedom, August heat and all. The earth smelled like fresh rain and clover, our staple crop for the livestock, even with a slight whiff of manure. I rode and rode and rode, never having to look over my shoulder, not worried about land mines or wondering if the sound of a chopper were suddenly going to spoil everything—like the first crack you hear when ice breaks on a skating pond.

But things quickly went downhill from there. My thoughtful mother and sister, Nola, were anxious to invite friends and neighbors for a welcome-home party.

"Thanks for the idea, Mom, but I don't feel like a party," I said.

How could I tell her there was really nothing to celebrate? My response surprised her.

"Diane, so many people have worried about you and wondered about you and prayed for you, too."

"And I appreciate that, Mom. But I don't think I could face all those people right now."

I was now twenty-two years old—I'd be twenty-three in November—and I felt like an old woman. I felt like I had just practiced a lifetime of nursing in one year. By now, Mother had practiced nursing for thirty-two years and still went cheerfully to work. For once, I wasn't sure I could follow in her footsteps.

I walked up the familiar stairs to my room and looked out the window for the view, which hadn't changed. But as I undressed for bed, taking my uniform off for the last time, I realized that all this familiarity was unfamiliar. That this home was no longer my home, could never be home again.

On top of my bedding, I curled up in my old poncho liner from Vietnam and listened to the quiet that could never again be what it once was.

"You were kinda cold when you came home," Nola, my sister, later said. She wanted me to do all the fun things again with her. Nola had grown up; she was seventeen, tall at 5'9", slender, and beautiful with long black hair. I'd adored her from the moment she was born.

She decided what I needed was to reconnect to the traditions of the past. She wanted me to go along with her to the county and state fairs and 4-H exhibits. But crowds and the stimulation of flashing lights in the amusement parks didn't interest me.

"I don't really want to go," I said.

"But you always loved the fairs," Nola said.

"I just don't want to face a bunch of people," I said.

More than the noise and the crowds, I think I was protecting myself from the questions I knew would be asked. At fairs, I always ran in to people I knew, and I didn't want to answer questions like, "Where have you been? How are ya? Vietnam? What was *that* like?"

How could I tell her that I wasn't the same person I was before going to Vietnam? She wouldn't understand. I wasn't sure anyone would understand, unless they'd just experienced what I had.

Ever persistent, Nola changed her tactics. If I had cooled on traditions, she surmised, I had to be interested in dates, right? Before I knew it, she'd set me up with a guy.

"You'll love him," she said. "He's really smart and handsome, and he works at the nuclear power plant in Monticello."

I said yes just to appease her but had little interest in seeing this total stranger who would seemingly have nothing in common with me. To prove it, I stood him up. Just bailed out at the last minute. And had no way of contacting him to tell him so. I felt bad. But I would have felt bad had I gone through with it without any emotion or interest.

I had saved money for a new car, so I talked Dad into accompanying me to Buffalo's lone car dealership. Dad was exceptionally mechanical—a true asset for a farmer to be able to fix his own machinery—but didn't believe in buying new cars. We test-drove a shiny new Mercury Cougar I really liked. Afterward, Dad lifted the hood to check the engine.

"Diane, this is too much car for you" he said. "It's a V-8."

"What's that?" I asked.

Dad and the salesman exchanged eyebrow-raising glances.

"How much?" I asked.

"Twenty-nine hundred."

My father nearly fell over backwards. He'd probably never paid anything more than three digits.

"I'll take it."

"Just like that?" asked Dad.

"It's perfect!"

He shook his head and looked at the salesman. "So, what'll that set her back per month?"

"Oh, I'm not paying for it on time," I said, scribbling on the check and handing the full amount to the salesman.

My father nodded his approval. Like everything else in my short life, Dad never stopped me from making my own decisions. Again, life's lessons had to be learned on our own. He might shake his head or pound his fist on the table in protest, but he never tried to stop me from anything I decided to do, for which I was grateful.

A few days later, Dad asked if I'd like to go along to town to the feed store. I jumped at the chance for one-on-one time with him. We arrived in his truck and approached the cashier.

"Howdy, we're here for the usual," said Dad. "You remember my daughter Diane? We're pretty happy. She's just home from Vietnam."

Given how quickly the woman averted her eyes, you'd have thought Dad had said, "She just busted out of the Minnesota Correctional Facility after doing ten years for armed robbery—and specializes in feed stores."

The woman would not look up. She took Dad's money, gave him his change, said, "Thank you, Newell," then told a fellow employee to get the man his feed. On the way home it was quiet for a few miles.

"Dad," I said, "I know you're proud of me and I appreciate that. But from now on it might be better if you didn't mention me and the Vietnam connection."

He glanced at me and slowly nodded as if he understood—even if I knew he didn't. As a father, how could you understand being humiliated for having a son or daughter who went off to war? And having that son or daughter humiliated in front of you at the same time?

When he'd come of age, serving in the military was a point of pride. Men and women of his generation had served by the tens of thousands in World War II, and their return—not for all, but for many—was similar to Norman Rockwell's "Soldier's Homecoming" painting: all smiles and hoorays from the homefolk. But in a single generation, because of a much different war, those in uniform had gone from being heroes to villains. We were baby killers, crazies, fools, whores, and a host of other names.

Yes, children, thousands of them, died in Vietnam thanks to our government's leadership, or lack of it. But our servicemen in Vietnam included men like John Huddleston and Dr. Dan Rowe. Huddleston was the guy who tried to literally breathe life into a dying child. Rowe was the guy who was happily working as a pediatrician, then drafted and sent to Vietnam—and, in the middle of the night, answered my call to try and save the Montagnard girl. I knew about a world that nobody back home knew about, and my perspective was different because of it. But I couldn't tell anybody that.

If I was at least treading water before, incidents such as the feed-store chill started to pull me under. I'd take long drives in the new car just so I could be alone. I didn't want much to do with anyone, not because I wanted to be stand-offish but because I felt as if I had so little in common with others. It wasn't that I felt superior, though some may have interpreted it as much. It was that I felt different. I'd spent a year doing something that, for all its literal blood and guts, felt important to me. Now I was trying to reconcile with the idea that apparently it not only wasn't important, but it was evil. Bad. Shameful.

At the same time, based on pop culture of the time, I was supposed to believe that four hundred thousand hippies stoned in the mud of a farmer's field was good. Significant. Meaningful. Along with "Gomer Pyle," bell bottoms, and "Chitty Chitty Bang Bang." I had listened to Joni Mitchell in Vietnam and liked her music. But her description, in an interview, that "Woodstock was a spark of beauty where half a million kids saw that they were part of a greater organism" left me wondering what I had missed. Or what she had missed.

Even though I loved most of the music played and the event was held on a *dairy farm*, I couldn't relate to it in the least. I couldn't relate to my own generation. I couldn't relate to my own country. I could only relate to Vietnam veterans—and we were left out in the cold. While our nation had hummed along and the people back home did normal things like party, eat pizza, and drink beer while the six o'clock news played in the background, I'd been watching young men suffer and die.

My family meant well; they were all happy to see me home. But how could they understand the year that had changed me? And, no, I didn't help matters by refusing to talk about it. But Nola arranging a blind date for me seemed an exercise in the trivial. In Vietnam, bullets and shrapnel had left too many men as literal blind dates—guys who couldn't see anymore. I know my views were distorted, but I didn't know how to change them. Much of "back home" seemed trivial.

I went to visit an old high school friend, Judy, who'd gotten married and had two children. We talked for two hours. She never asked about

Vietnam. Maybe it was my fault. Maybe she sensed that it wouldn't be a good idea to raise the subject.

I found it difficult to make commitments to anything or anybody. And easy to let others down. In just a few weeks' time, I'd let Nola down on not going to the fair, stood up a blind date, and was the reason my dad felt humiliated at the feed store.

Thinking I needed to "stick to my own," I decided to pay a visit to the parents of Danny Bodin who'd died in Vietnam the February before I'd left for the war. Danny, two years behind me at BHS, wanted to grow up and be a farmer like his father, who knew my father. He loved his '55 Chev. And he had been caretaker of the Swedesburg Cemetery in which he was now buried. After he died, the family made news when Vice President Hubert Humphrey and his wife, Muriel, who had a summer home nearby, had come to the farm to pay their respects.

Following the service, the Bodin family had pledged to fly the American flag every single day until their own deaths. "What we need is to continue our hope that this country will always be the very best place to live, for our future generations," they told a local newspaper. "We know that in some way, Danny has played a part in that continual process of creating a strong and good nation for all."

I hadn't phoned ahead, deciding just to drop by and pay my respects; Danny had been killed in a war of which I'd been a part. I'd sent Mrs. Bodin a condolence note from Vietnam, and she'd replied with a Christmas card with small-talk inside. Neither one of us seemed to want to talk about it.

I started up the gravel drive, looked at the farmhouse and the flag fluttering in the wind, then eased the brake on. And began backing up. I couldn't do it. Wouldn't my showing up, having survived Vietnam, only remind them that their son had *not*? Wouldn't my presence just rip the scab off a wound that might never heal? What was my purpose? What would I say?

Once again, I'd bailed on something. Though I didn't notice it at the time, I would overthink everything, having lost all confidence in my ability to fit back into a system that, at first, seemed unrecognizable.

I drove home and flopped on my bed in a room that now seemed like a too-small pair of shoes. Nothing seemed to fit anymore. Years hence, after I had started therapy in a Vet Center, my therapist told me to ask my sister what I was like after Vietnam. Nola said, "When Diane came home from war, it was as if she wasn't my sister anymore."

I couldn't disagree. When I came home from the war, I wasn't a lot of things anymore. To others. And to myself. In Vietnam, even if things got crazy, I'd adjusted to the new normal. Now I was having to adjust to another new normal that, in some ways, was harder than the adjustment in Vietnam. There, we were all in the same boat; it may have been rocking like crazy and taking on water, but it was our boat. Here, everyone seemed to be in a different boat—and don't you dare come aboard, people seemed to be saying, if yours isn't just like theirs. I was hard on people. I judged them. I felt guilty about that. I felt guilty about a lot of things.

I found myself worrying and wondering about the patients I'd left. In Vietnam, I felt so *necessary*. Here, no. I also felt that what I did in Vietnam mattered, regardless of my opposition to the war itself. Here, no. I sensed that nobody thought what I did over there mattered.

What only made it worse was that there was nobody I could talk to about such feelings. In 1969 there were no support groups for Vietnam vets. Edie, my closest friend, was still in the Army Nurse Corps, finishing up her commitment. My family tried to connect, but our worlds were now so very different. It was none of the other people's fault; this was their world. It just wasn't *mine*, at least for now. Either they were walking on eggshells or I was. But I was the one to crack, not them.

Nola had always been able to make me laugh. But not after Vietnam. I had not forgotten how to laugh: I simply had come to believe I didn't deserve to.

The bottom line: I'd never been so lonely in my life.

12

Finding a New Life

1969–1974

Trying to find my way in this new world was like trying to find the exit to a farmer's Halloween maze in a cornfield. The routes that others suggested for me seemed like dead ends: welcome-home parties, county fairs, dating. My own choices proved equally inefficient. The new car bought me freedom, but the trip to encourage the mother of a soldier who'd died in Vietnam brought out something that was never a problem for me overseas: my courage, or lack thereof.

I had been with dying men in Vietnam whom I wished their mothers had been with in those last moments. I was that mother. And I could say plenty about their stoicism, about how brave they were, how they were more worried about their buddies than themselves, how proud I was of them, how I comforted them. I'd stayed with them. I'd treated their bodies with dignity.

And now I couldn't face their mothers?

I was always on edge. I'd wake in the morning to the quiet percussion of the farm: cows mooing, dogs barking, and chickens clucking. It was welcoming and comforting and peaceful but worked against a nurse who, in Vietnam, had become an adrenaline junkie, a self-induced chaos drunk. Over there, I was sometimes awakened by the scream of mortars and rockets. I rode in helicopters so loud you couldn't hear yourself talk. I worked in a ward that might have three different languages spoken at once, guys shattered because they'd been told they were losing their eyesight or their manhood. Meanwhile, a monsoon roared outside like a freight train.

Before leaving Vietnam, I'd told Mom in a letter that all I wanted was for everything to be the same when I got back. Now I was realizing that "the same" was too different. Be careful what you wish for.

Back home, I couldn't sleep on top of my bed so would lie on the floor with the same poncho liner I wrapped myself with in Vietnam. I quickly realized this: as much as I had no interest in going back to work in a civilian hospital, I needed to do so soon. I needed to support myself, and I also needed some sort of "rush" that my current life wasn't providing. I thrived on adrenaline, and I was going through a rough withdrawal.

Buffalo Memorial Hospital, where mom worked, wasn't going to do that for me. North Memorial Hospital in Minneapolis might. It had a trauma center and, frankly, that's what I craved. Even though I was assigned general surgery instead of trauma, the reception was promising.

"When can you start?" the woman doing the hiring asked.

"Tomorrow."

To be honest, it was one of the first, and only, bits of affirmation I'd gotten in the two weeks since I'd been back—a sense that someone believed in me.

"Can you do the three-to-eleven shift?"

"Sure, wherever you need me."

"Good. I'm going to make you the charge nurse," she said. "And, oh, we've had some rapes in the parking lot. We'll provide a security escort for you on your way to the car after your shift." Great. I'd had to watch my back in Vietnam, and now here in Minnesota? I took her seriously and had a guard with me without fail.

The bubble burst fast. I knew I was in trouble when my supervisor insisted on hovering over me while I started IVs.

"You must be supervised three times involving this procedure," I was told. Nobody but human resources knew I'd been in Vietnam. I wanted to scream at her, "Hey, I did twenty-eight of these in four hours on dehydrated men in shock with collapsed veins…in the dark…with a flashlight…with only *one* medic…while *mortars* were exploding outside. I *think* I can put in an IV." And not only that, "I've started more in one year than you will start in a lifetime!"

I said none of it. When it came to Vietnam, I'd lost my voice. I hadn't defended my sister and brother veterans. I couldn't even defend myself.

If I showed myself to be more competent than the non-vets around me, people would assume I thought I was some hotshot war nurse. Like, "What are you trying to prove, that you're better than the rest of us just because you've been to Vietnam?" I wasn't trying to prove anything, but my skills honed as an Army Nurse didn't mean anything to those around me.

I had an intern scream at me, "Who do you think you are putting down an NG [naso-gastric] tube? That's our job!" I wanted to scream back that I saw the doctor's order and did as he asked—and that I had inserted a lot of them when it used to be "my" job.

Soon I was doing paperwork and taking care of people who were having gallbladders removed and varicose veins stripped. The fear from a fifteen-year-old having an appendectomy and a sixty-year-old having her veins stripped almost caused me to quit on the spot.

"Miss Carlson, I'd like to talk to you about something," said my supervisor one day. "You must start taking your breaks. Minnesota law says you have to have two fifteen-minute breaks, one before dinner and one after."

"Thanks, but I'm fine," I said, expecting my gentle retort would convince her. "I don't need a break."

"But it's the policy. You need to take a break."

I offered a brief smile. "I don't smoke, and I don't need a break."

She shook her head and walked off, wondering why I was so indignant.

In Vietnam, I'd routinely work a twelve-plus-hour shift without a break.

"Nurse," a patient with varicose veins said to me one late evening as I was writing the report for the night shift before leaving, "I called you thirty minutes ago. I would like a cup of hot chocolate."

Gritting my teeth, I got her one. The next day my supervisor called me in.

"Miss Carlson, last night Mrs. Willoughby said she had to wait thirty minutes for you to answer your call light."

"Yes, Ma'am. I was busy. I assumed it wasn't a cardiac arrest given that she was in for varicose-vein stripping."

"Please, don't get smart with me. This patient is litigious. She has sued other hospitals."

I was incredulous. If this was a sue-able offense, then maybe the tens of thousands of wounded men—and their families and the families of the women who died in Vietnam—could sue our government for a little pain and anguish and inconvenience they had suffered.

I said nothing. Just turned and half-politely walked away. That night I drove home so angry my hands seemed superglued to the steering wheel. *Are you kidding me? In Vietnam, patients weren't worried about any varicose veins in their legs because they may not have had legs, period. And they never complained!*

I was doing paperwork, watching the externs, interns, and docs do much of the work we nurses did in the military. The mother of the appendectomy patient was as persnickety as her son.

"My son is in terrible pain," she huffed.

"Ma'am, I gave him pain meds just two hours ago and—"

"I want you to call the doctor, now!"

"I am following the doctor's ord—"

"Then I will call the doctor directly."

"No, that wouldn't be a good idea."

Next day the doctor wagged an angry finger in my face. "Nurse, don't you *ever* allow a patient or patient's mother to call me directly! Just follow my orders!"

"Yes, sir."

After two weeks of this, I went to human resources and gave notice. The following week I was without a job. In my exit interview, I mentioned that I'd been a nurse in Vietnam and was simply unhappy and planned to work in a military hospital out west. Instead of my supervisor understanding, she cocked her head sideways, as if in a disbelieving sort of way.

"Well," she said, "you certainly don't *look* like you were an army nurse."

I didn't even know what she meant by that, though surmised she must have expected me to be "manly" or a whore, a drill sergeant, or too ugly to find a man so joined the army; pick your stereotype. By now, I knew what I was. I was an outcast facing an intergenerational split on home ground, and the only place I truly belonged was Vietnam.

In the days to come, I worried less about my life in the U.S. and more about the men I'd left in Vietnam. In particular, I wondered what had happened to my last patient, the guy who begged for me to not leave. I had left him like an intimate lover not wanting to leave the bedroom for a last kiss, a last embrace.

After Vietnam, Edie was heading west to finish her two-year commitment at Madigan Army Hospital in Tacoma, Washington. I knew this when I gave notice at North Memorial. I wanted to go to Washington with her and find a job in Tacoma or Seattle.

I was living at home while working at North Memorial and I needed my independence back. My parents and brothers and sister were glad to have me at home. But I was too old and too independent to stay on the farm.

The timing was perfect. I had no trouble landing a job at Madigan as a civilian nurse, so I loaded up my 1969 Mercury Cougar and followed Edie in her hot new 1970 flower-power Plymouth Barracuda. We were off to a new adventure, driving across the country together. We rented an apartment in Tacoma. Once hootchmates in Vietnam, we now roomed together and rarely, if ever, talked about Vietnam. Edie and I understood each other without using words. We were comfortable with each other.

No game playing, no drama, no excuses or need to explain why or why not, or what we were doing—or not doing. And I was working at a hospital whose staff appreciated—yes, actually *appreciated*—the skills I'd learned in Vietnam.

I was offered the position as head nurse on an "officer only" ward. Nobody questioned me. Nobody doubted me. Nobody looked for the worst in me. My skills were immediately recognized and legitimized. I started IVs and inserted NG tubes without criticism.

Working as a civilian at Madigan, I didn't wear the military uniform, of course, but I worked in a surgical unit just as I had in Vietnam. Just as when I worked at the VA hospital in Minneapolis, I also cared for World War I, World War II, and Korean War veterans. Among my patients was a World War I army nurse, crippled with rheumatism and still suffering from injuries incurred while working on a French ambulance train. Oh, how I wished I'd had time to listen to her stories. I loved my job. I loved the people around me. But mostly, I loved my patients, many of them home from Vietnam recovering from war wounds.

In Vietnam, I cared for officers and enlisted men mixed together on the same ward. They all looked the same and were the same when wearing their standard blue pajamas. I found it odd, state side, that they would be separated. In my mind, officers were no more important or better than enlisted men and women. In a hospital, they deserved equal care and equal respect.

Another difference: In Vietnam, I didn't have to deal with families of casualties. Here, I couldn't avoid it. That added another layer of emotion to the whole experience, not one I found easy.

When a captain I'd known in Vietnam invited me to meet him in Hawaii for his R&R, I accepted and went; I missed any sort of adventure. And yet the sexual assault at Vũng Tàu hovered over me like a vulture. So did the words of Ann Cunningham: "Don't get close to anyone over there in Vietnam. They'll only die on you." I was too submerged in feelings of grief and loss to be emotionally available to the man. I was depleted. Drained of desire. No one would hurt me if I pushed them far enough away.

Hawaii was the perfect metaphor for where I was in my life: I wasn't in Vietnam. I wasn't home. I was somewhere in between, lost in the middle of a vast sea that I saw no way to navigate.

When I had time off, I headed for forest trails on weekends to find some sense of peace: Mt. Rainier, Mt. Hood, the Olympic National Forest. My soul knew what my mind did not. Isolation equaled safety. But it didn't make me *feel*. My emotions were cauterized.

Meanwhile, I began to wonder: *Why are you working as a civilian when it's the army life that's working for you?* I had no answer. Within a few months—May 1970—I flew to Chicago and re-enlisted. I was assigned to Brooke Army Medical Center (BAMC), Fort Sam Houston, in San Antonio, Texas.

"Welcome back in the army," Colonel Gann said to me as I arrived at the hospital. I remembered her from the 71st Evac. "By the way, we're promoting you to captain."

I felt relieved that she welcomed me. Returning to the army felt right—and helped me survive my post-war blues. I was truly happy for the first time since leaving Vietnam. I loved the Army Nurse Corps. And they appreciated me.

BAMC was a teaching hospital, which only ramped up the importance of what we did. I was in charge of one of its surgical floors, 13A. It was made up of three units: recovery room, intensive care, and the post-operative surgery ward. Our patients were primarily seriously wounded soldiers from Vietnam; hundreds and hundreds of them flowed through that first year. We also cared for retired veterans and their dependents. I was back where I belonged. I was safe in the military cocoon, safe from the anti-war protestors whom I lauded for their courage to speak out against the war and loathed for their unwillingness to separate those of us who served in the war from the politicians who perpetuated it.

The rebellious anger I'd felt in the civilian sector was replaced by a sense of purpose. I could care again about something greater than myself. But that anger was always just below the surface, like jagged rocks just beneath freshly fallen snow at a ski resort. If the temperature rose just a bit and the snow melted, I could catch the edge of my ski and go sprawling.

Our seventh floor was former President Lyndon B. Johnson's private suite; everyone knew that. One day the chief nurse came to me in the ICU and held some keys in front of me, keys to the seventh floor. I knew what this meant.

"No, I'm sorry, Colonel Cleveland," I said, "but I refuse to take care of that man. I can't." His "more troops" policies had cost thousands of lives in Vietnam. His lies meant soldiers died.

"That man has blood on his hands, the blood from *my* patients. There's just no way—"

"Captain Carlson, the patient is not the former president. It's Mamie Eisenhower. She's being transferred here for care."

"Oh, well, then, 'Yes, ma'am!'"

I was the private-duty nurse for the former president's wife for two weeks. It was an honor to care for her but not particularly challenging.

Soon I was back with the guys critically wounded in Vietnam. We had a patient with relentless complications who endured thirty-six operations. Another patient was a triple-amputee. His beautiful fiancé came to visit him in the ICU.

"I think of her every waking moment," he told me. "She's the only reason I want to keep living." She never came back. Months after his discharge, he killed himself.

I was not immune to tragedy; it was reminiscent of Vietnam. Of course, the atmosphere wasn't as bawdy. No more war humor. Or using slang descriptions. No more "basket cases" or "crispy critters." That was fine. It felt like family. I liked the intensity; it made me feel that what I did mattered. I threw myself into my work, satisfied with the job; my new English Shepherd puppy, Charlie; and a beautiful apartment all to myself for the very first time.

Ann Cunningham, with whom I'd bonded at Fort Lee in Virginia, had finished her second tour in Vietnam and came to visit me. I was a bridesmaid in Edie's wedding in Minnesota, and Barbie Chiminello's in

Massachusetts. I had made good friends. That's all I needed. Until, that is, I met a particular surgical resident from 13A named Mike Evans.

He was from Utah. Just as, years ago, he questioned and left behind his Mormon upbringing, I was questioning my Lutheran upbringing; I simply couldn't imagine a God who could allow the carnage of Vietnam to happen. I'm not sure how much dating Mike had done; I didn't ask. I'd done very little. Everything outside of work seemed frivolous to me. I turned down invitations from all kinds of men: single, married, patients, and former patients. Dating meant questions, and my answers were off limits. Plus, I didn't mind doing things by myself.

Captain Evans was smart, calm, and exhibited both confidence and kindness with our patients. We had a code in the ICU that was our equivalent to a red alert; everyone would come running. Medical staff would be madly rushing around, but Mike always stayed cool. I watched him and our team save many lives.

"So, you were in Vietnam?" he asked.

"I don't talk about it much."

"Where?"

"As I said…."

He cleared his throat. "You know, the best nurses at the hospital are the ones who've returned from war." It was no come-on line; he was just trying to salvage an awkward conversation and I'd already learned he had great respect for vets.

In 1970, when nobody wanted to go to Vietnam, he volunteered. He had finished medical school and thought he should go. He had to rotate through BAMC for his internship and training before going overseas, but by the time his general surgery residency in 1975 was completed, the Vietnam War would be over.

He liked jazz, my cinnamon rolls, and, above all, me. We went on our first date August 30, 1970, and were engaged on my birthday, November 10. The diamond may not have been rough, but I know that I was. I simply was still not interested in men. But he snuck up on me. He was different. He had no expectations of me. He watched me at work and liked what he saw.

He was the first man I'd ever seriously dated. We took drives into the Texas landscape, listened to jazz, and met each other's families. We were married in April 1971. The marital ground rules that mattered to me had nothing to do with trivialities like how to squeeze the toothpaste.

"Vietnam," I said, "is my no-fly zone. Don't even try. Don't ask me about it. Don't tell anyone I was there. Please." He never asked why, he simply honored my request—most of the time. "And I don't want a television in the house." Whenever I was near a TV set, news of Vietnam triggered my worst memories.

When I got pregnant with our first child in 1972, I had to make a choice. Because of a new rule change put in place the previous year, the army would allow me to keep working. Prior to that, pregnant women weren't allowed to serve. But after much thought, I realized that as much as I loved my job, I wasn't going to trust someone else to raise our baby. So, I left the army—for good this time—ironically, only shortly before the last U.S. Army nurse left Vietnam on March 29, 1973.

I soon realized how much I needed to work. Guy, our firstborn, was pure joy; I loved being a mother, but I missed the hospital work. I found a job at a local San Antonio Hospital that had an onsite daycare setup. I could see Guy on my lunch hour and breaks. (Yes, I finally reconciled with taking them.) And because I was working a 3:00 p.m.–11:00 p.m. shift, Mike could pick up Guy on his way home from work and be with him in the evenings.

When I interviewed for the job, I was asked if I knew much about snake bites. The staff was impressed when I told them about my experiences in Vietnam, that I'd cared for all kinds of snake-bit patients and would be happy to do so here.

"We have one of the most renowned physicians in the country for treating snake bite injuries," the woman doing the hiring told me. "And as you know, there are lots of poisonous snakes in Texas. You'll enjoy working there."

"Sounds good. I'll take it."

Who says that? Who welcomes the chance to work in a ward where every patient has been bitten by a poisonous snake? Me. I loved the new challenge. The transition was simple. I felt prepared for this type of work. Though I wasn't seeing much of Mike, we were making this three-part family work.

From time to time, I'd be asked to cover the recovery room, which I had done at BAMC. I'd had plenty of experience with that, too.

Then it happened.

I was in the recovery room awaiting a post-op patient when an operating-room nurse rushed in. "Ms. Evans, we need you in the OR."

"What?"

"It's an emergency, there's a young boy—"

It wasn't a snake bite, but a car accident.

"I'm not an OR nurse. No."

"You don't have a choice! We're down a nurse and you're needed in the OR. Right now!"

Of course, I went. Arriving, I found the surgical team fighting for a little boy's life.

"More sponges!" barked the surgeon. "More!"

He tossed bloodied sponges into the basin. I was told to count them. I had never counted sponges in my life. *Concentrate. You can do this.*

But the smell and sight of fresh red blood jolted me. I was no longer in San Antonio, I was in Vietnam. This wasn't a little boy injured in a car accident, this was a soldier who stepped on a Bouncing Betty. I'd never been squeamish; the sight or smell of blood had never bothered me. But I'd never had a flashback before either. Until now.

"Count them so we don't leave one in the abdomen!" said the circulating nurse.

I froze. She noticed. Her voice raised two notches.

"Count 'em so we don't leave one behind!"

I had slipped into some sort of catatonic state, unable to really think, much less count. Me? Not in control? That had never happened.

It was already too late. The boy didn't make it to the recovery room. The next day I resigned. It wasn't my fault the little boy died; I was just a last-minute replacement for a team that fought hard yet couldn't save him. But deeper things were at work, things I didn't yet understand.

"I'm pregnant, and not feeling well," I told the supervisor. "I need to quit."

"Can you give us two more weeks?"

"I'm so sorry. No. I'm just not up to it."

I walked out. Shattered. Broken. Ashamed. I'd failed. Failed the team. Failed myself. Failed for the first time. Ever.

I couldn't tell Mike that night—and wouldn't for years. I was too embarrassed. Too humiliated.

I slipped into bed, stared into the darkness, and felt as if I were an astronaut floating in space, untethered to anything. Not to Vietnam. Not to America. Not to Mike. Not to myself. Not to God. Nothing.

Though I didn't realize it at the time, post-traumatic stress disorder is like that.

13

Keeping the Secret

1975–1982

When the war in Vietnam ended in 1975, I was a stay-at-home mom in San Antonio, Texas. On April 30, U.S. diplomats, Vietnamese allies, and evacuees desperately clamored up a ladder atop the embassy in Saigon to get on the final helicopter out. Our firstborn, Guy, had recently turned two, and Luke was nearly six months. I was twenty-eight, the wife of an army surgeon. I nursed babies. Changed diapers. Cooked. Ran errands. Did all those domestic chores for children that didn't require me to debride the necrotic tissue from kids burned by Napalm.

As the 1970s deepened, I was being hunted down by something, but I was too busy to notice. Or maybe that's exactly *why* I stayed so busy—because that way I could keep *not* noticing. I could think about the POWs that were finally released or that helicopter lifting off the roof of the U.S. embassy, and just about the time I was ready to melt into a puddle of mush, Guy would say, "Look at me, Mommy," and he'd be literally climbing straight up our living-room entertainment center like Edmund Hillary on Mt. Everest. "Me climber." And, suddenly, I could disconnect from Vietnam and try to make sure my little boy didn't fall and break his leg.

Another time, Guy cried out in the dark hours of night. I was vigilant, it came with war. But after I heard the voice, I wondered whether that was my boy or the soldier boy I left in Vietnam. I couldn't tell the difference. Both wanted their mothers. God gave me sons, hundreds and hundreds of them, before I gave birth to three of my own.

When my own brother died, I didn't cry. "You're a strange woman," Mike told me. "You never cry." He was right on both counts.

I was always running, I just didn't notice until, say, that day when I reached into the kids' closet and smelled a wet diaper that had been overlooked and, baked by heat, smelled just like the children's ward in Vietnam. Or the time we were at a wedding in Missouri and I walked into the house where members of the family were preparing the wedding meal on the butcher block: red meat. Bloody limbs. Huge slices of tenderloin that reminded me of the bleeding legs of the wounded in Vietnam. Suddenly, the smell hit me. I just could not be in that place. I walked out into the woods for fresh air and to calm down, lest anyone suspect that I was crazy.

I never told Mike why I'd quit at the hospital. And, in Missouri, I never told him why I suddenly had the look in my eyes as if someone were chasing me, even if I never quite pin-pointed who that someone that might have been. I was able to make a couple dozen cinnamon rolls and insert twenty-eight IVs into soldiers during a mortar attack—all in the same day. I'd survived Vietnam without shrinking from duty or hardship. I wasn't about to be chased down by something as innocuous as bad war experience.

Not that outsiders ever saw inside me: *Diane? She's fine. Married a surgeon and has kids.* No one but my family saw the startled, distant look in my eyes when a helicopter flew overhead. No one knew how I would drive and drive and drive, all alone, sometimes until I ran out of gas. No one but Mike and our kids knew that I went to the basement and covered my head with a pillow every Fourth of July night, before fireworks exploded loudly into the sky. But outwardly? *Diane? Oh, she's fine.*

Motherhood and moving defined the mid- and late-1970s for me. In 1975 Mike accepted a position as chief of surgery at a military hospital in Heidelberg, Germany. Carrie, our lone daughter, was born there. After two years in Europe, we moved to Grand Rapids, Minnesota, in 1977 only to find the hospital really wasn't in need of another surgeon. Our fourth and final child, Jon-Erik, was born in 1979 in Utah, Mike's home ground. We left soon thereafter because—how else can I say it?—Mormons ruled and we weren't Mormon, Mike having long since parted ways with the faith of his childhood. When one of my sons hid under his bed instead of going to school—the principal was demanding that he pray the Mormon way—I said *enough*. "We move," I told Mike, "or I'll shoot myself." He responded with two words: "We'll move." Then came River Falls, Wisconsin, where Mike was the only surgeon in the county. As such, he was on call twenty-four hours a day, seven days a week.

Otherwise, we loved it. River Falls offered superb schools and a great neighborhood to raise kids and a Golden Retriever. I made wonderful friends and found meaningful volunteer work with resettled Vietnamese refugee families. I chauffeured kids to piano lessons, tennis matches, and took them on road trips to get to know Wisconsin. Mike performed surgeries and played tennis. His family came first in every way, but his priority was his patients and my priority was our kids. I suppose we were, in the eyes of those around us, the All-American family and, in many ways, there was truth to that. But in other ways, it was deceiving.

The backstory: work was forever pulling Mike; Vietnam was forever pulling me. I'd built a towering wall between our marriage and Vietnam, and I'd made it clear to him that if it ever came down, *I* would have to do it—brick by brick. The operative word was *I*. Mike wasn't allowed to try to bring down the wall, nor did he make the attempt—not because he didn't care, but because I wouldn't let him. Nobody was allowed into my secret grief, not even my closest friend. In the meantime, the military experience for Mike was also calling him back. He joined the Minnesota Air National Guard and served one weekend a month and two additional weeks per year as a medical officer. I was proud to see him in uniform again.

We'd go visit my parents just ninety minutes away as often as possible; the kids loved being on their grandparents' farm. Even on weekends that Mike declared himself "off," he was *on*. More than once a police car showed up for him at our house. Accident victim in the ER; they needed him and would escort him quickly to the hospital.

Meanwhile, more than once choppers showed up for me in the middle of the night. Casualties arriving by helicopter; they needed me. I'd wake up in a sweat, check the clock and figure out how many more minutes of sleep I could get before getting the kids to school. My sleep was a tangle of Vietnam casualties calling out for their mothers and my own kids calling out for me. They were both demanding.

Mike was forever the good soldier. Without fail he was up early and gone to work at the hospital before the kids were up. I was up early, too: make the breakfasts and the lunches, sort the appropriate clothes for the weather, make sure the kids knew the dentist and music schedules for the day. *And whatever you do, don't tell anybody about that other life you once had.* Now, more than a decade since I'd walked off the plane from Vietnam, the anti-soldier culture had tainted me as a betrayer of country. I was still ashamed to admit I'd been there. And I was ashamed that I was ashamed.

Until "the night."

In 1982, at a Christmas party in River Falls for the hospital staff, a doctor was aware—apparently through Mike—that I'd been in Vietnam. I was sitting at a table; the doctor was standing nearby.

"So, I heard you were a nurse in Vietnam," he said with a smarmy tone, looking down on me.

Thirteen years of protecting myself automatically kicked in. I didn't respond.

"Well, if you ask me," he said, "all those fucked-up Vietnam vets were fucked up before they ever went to Vietnam."

I stood up and looked him eye to eye.

"The only person who's fucked up in this room is you," I said. I was loud. I was rude. I was shaking and breaking out in a sweat. I sat down next to Mike. The room stilled with an awkward quiet.

"We need to leave," I whispered to him.

The car was silent on the way home. He knew I was a time bomb. And he understood, even if we never talked about it. Mike Evans was my quiet sentry. As an army surgeon, he had enough military understanding to appreciate what I'd been through. As a stateside doctor, however, he didn't know Vietnam like I did. But even though we seldom, if ever, talked about my experiences, he's the one person who seem to implicitly trust me. His unspoken response to moments like these always seemed to be: *I don't know what it was like in Vietnam, and I don't know what it's like for you here in America, but I honor your feelings.*

The party incident wasn't the first time something like this had happened. In Germany, in 1977, at a baby shower luncheon for me, I'd had to excuse myself and calm my nerves in the bathroom when a friend casually, but with pride, mentioned that she'd heard I'd served in Vietnam. In that case, there was no ill intent on her part—her husband was part of the military establishment—but my trip-wire reaction was uncontrollable. Even when I realized she understood—"my brother was in Vietnam, and he never talks about it either"—I still couldn't trust the group at the table, so certain was I that there'd be another shoe to fall.

In such cases, I wasn't trying to host my own pity party. I didn't want people feeling sorry for me because I was another "wounded" Vietnam veteran. I didn't want to talk about it. Beneath whatever veneer I offered in social situations, I was simply sad. And sadness, I realized, was turning to anger. And anger to bitterness. It was as if I had all the pieces—husband, family, security, and—down there somewhere—a good sense of self. But I couldn't seem to fit the pieces together.

Nobody understood. Not the people at the hospital Christmas party and not the people across the nation. In 1981, when the U.S. hostages in Iran were released, nobody thought it weird that the entire country fell over itself honoring these folks. Trees from coast to coast were wrapped in yellow ribbons. Welcome-home songs were written. Reporters prattled on and on about the hostages' amazing resolve. All this for what? For people who were in the wrong place at the wrong time. That defined essentially everyone who ever served in Vietnam. But we didn't get ribbons. We got spit on. Cussed at. Ignored. We didn't get welcome-home songs or yellow-ribbon trees. We had cab doors slammed in our face, feed-store clerks look away from us, and cocky doctors question our integrity without having a clue what we were really like—and, for the most part, what Vietnam was really like. Was I cruel, hardened, insensitive to the Iranian hostages? Where was my compassion and empathy? Who was I? For now, I had no idea.

That day, I picked up all the pieces of the dishes I had thrown against the kitchen wall before the kids came home from school. No one had seen my rage. No one ever would, I silently vowed.

It was as if I was falling down a dark well that had no bottom. Before going to Vietnam, I'd subconsciously learned that if you worked hard and played fair and served others, you were rewarded. You got good grades in school. You won American Legion Citizenship awards in high school. You got top-of-class honors in nursing school. Better yet, you looked in the mirror each night and felt good about yourself. You didn't need any enhancers to affirm your worth—a boyfriend or marijuana or a Twiggy miniskirt. You had something far more powerful: yourself.

You went off to Vietnam and transferred your skills and drive and compassion to the venue of war, a scene unlike anything you'd ever experienced. Amid the madness, there wasn't much time for pats on the back. You played for the team and with the team. You and your colleagues marched to the same tune, working end on end without complaint. And the soldiers expressed their gratitude in big ways and small; some begged you not to leave. Some wrote you letters after you'd gone. Some said they'd never forget you. What's more, you sustained yourself and your patients through that hell without sacrificing the Buffalo, Minnesota, farm girl in the process. You could encounter a guy with a necklace made of enemy ears in the afternoon and not only *not* give in to such cruelty by becoming a who-gives-a-crap cynic yourself, but instead sneak into the 71st's kitchen that night and make cinnamon rolls for your guys.

Then you came home and for the first time in your life there wasn't a hint of validation whatsoever for the years you just sacrificed for your country. Not only no validation, but outright anger, as if you've shamed the entire country. And so you're trying to rekindle some sort of life while feeling like a stranger in a strange land, and you don't even realize that what it's become is a double life. The public life where you smile and take care of children and say all the right things—except, perhaps, at the Christmas party (or, perhaps, *especially* at the Christmas party). And the private life, where you began thinking of how high a bridge it would take to end it all.

As work was being finished up on the building of the Vietnam Wall in the early 1980s, the irony was that this wasn't a memorial decided upon, and paid for, by our government to honor those who served. It was done by what was mainly a group of Vietnam vets. Good for them, I thought. The outcome was welcome: at last, those who died in Vietnam were going to be officially remembered in our nation's capital. No longer would their names, their lives, their service be hidden from the world as if they never existed or were part of one of the greatest tragedies for America. They wouldn't be forgotten.

Meanwhile, despite my lashing out at the Christmas party doctor, I kept my head down about the war. But I did plenty of reading. (We didn't even own a TV at the time, so I didn't see much of that). The suicide rate for Vietnam veterans was higher than that of nonveterans. Some veterans suffered from something just starting to show up in the news: PTSD or post-traumatic stress disorder. It affected one or every compartment of their lives, causing an array of problems, including depression, rage, suicidal tendencies, flashbacks, difficulty maintaining relationships and jobs, pretty much everything you need to find some semblance of contentment. And if that wasn't enough residual, Vietnam veterans were dying by the hundreds from some mysterious deadly ailments. Agent Orange was now on the radar as thousands of veterans sought help at the VA for exposure to the toxic chemical.

Later, I accepted an invitation to serve on Federal Judge Jack B. Weinstein's Agent Orange Class Action Lawsuit advisory board, New York. While I hated what the enemy had done to us, I hadn't aimed my anger at the North Vietnamese. Even though I didn't recognize it at the time, my anger, my wrath, my bitterness was aimed at our own government that knew kids were drowning in the pool but simply looked the other way, whistling their innocence all the time. And at citizens back home—not everybody—who so quickly labeled many of us who served as drug-crazed, glassy-eyed baby killers. No wonder I mostly kept quiet; along with my brother and sister veterans, I had a scarlet letter on my chest: *V* for Vietnam. *Damaged goods. Danger. Stay away.*

With my involvement in the Agent Orange issue, I was putting my toe in the waters of the war I'd been avoiding; it wouldn't be long before I was up to my neck. If that invigorated me, what kept me from killing myself was my children. Guy, Luke, Carrie, and Jon-Erik were my sustenance. I loved being their mother, hated being away from them, and couldn't imagine a permanent separation from them.

So I returned to my "regularly scheduled programing" of keeping my time in Vietnam a secret. The country's misconceptions of what it had really been like to be a nurse in the war were only more skewed by the popular movie and new TV show, *M*A*S*H*. Though it supposedly was about a different war, Korea, and though its humor could be funny and the program widely popular, the overriding messages it left were these: War was just one great one-liner after another. And women, based on "Hot Lips" Houlihan, were sex objects not to be taken seriously.

People back home had no idea what it was like to hold a dying soldier's hand while it went from warm to cold. Or to be awakened by the sound of chopper blades right over your hootch. Or to have a Montagnard child you're holding literally scream herself to death. People didn't understand—not because vets weren't willing to talk about it, but because no one showed any genuine interest. Had they done so, I may have been more forthcoming about my experience. But nobody did. The default format was that vets were to seamlessly fit back into the cultural flow as if what had happened in Vietnam had been no more discombobulating than, say, rearranging the patio furniture.

So, like many others, I carried on in silence, the layers of guilt for doing so building up like Wisconsin snowfalls that freeze and thaw and are replaced by more of the same. Two things threatened me: guilt and emptiness. Guilt for burying my Vietnam experience. And emptiness for doing what I thought was a noble thing for my country and not only getting no semblance of affirmation, but outright hostility.

The guilt cut deeper because I wasn't a homeless vet without any legs fighting the VA for lawful compensation. I was a physically fit wife of a surgeon, the mother of four beautiful children, a person surrounded by friends. I'd had a good upbringing on a beautiful farm. In other words, in many people's eyes I had no excuse for being anything other than a happy-go-lucky mom and wife. And yet I felt as if I'd been sentenced to a life of shame. In retrospect, the realest moment of my life in the twelve years since I'd been back from Vietnam might have been at that Christmas party when I told off that doctor.

Did I even recognize where my unhappiness was coming from? On some levels, yes. On some levels, no. My life was a blur of kids, appointments, and to-do calendars, my busyness fueled by a subconscious desire to not face what really needed facing, even though time would suggest that's exactly what I needed. More than a decade since Vietnam, I'd never sat across from a counselor and spilled my story. I'd never had a therapist help me understand how my time in Vietnam had been the best, and worst, year of my life. I'd never had a friend encourage me to open up about how I was feeling. And I'd never had a meaningful conversation with a fellow veteran.

So, I soldiered on. I had decided that in November 1982 I was going to fly to Washington, D.C., and attend the dedication of the Vietnam Veterans Memorial. Not that it was a given I would actually go. Truth be told, I was also considering heading for the St. Croix Bridge.

One jump and it would be over.

PART IV: FINDING A PURPOSE

It was impossible to remain very long pre-occupied with the effect of the War upon one's own position when the opportunity of changing the position of all women, whether superfluous or otherwise, was there to be seized for the first time in history.

Vera Brittain, *Testament of Youth*

14

A New Journey

1982–1984

Richard Timmerman lived four houses down from us on Wasson Lane in River Falls, Wisconsin. He and his wife, who taught in the elementary school our kids attended, were similar in age to Mike and me—in 1982, I turned thirty-six—and our kids played with theirs. We were casual neighbors until that summer, when, for the first time, I let down my guard.

Rich and I were shooting the breeze on the street after picking up our respective mail when, just for an apparent "conversation continuer," he asked if Mike and I had any special Christmas plans.

"Oh, we'll probably go to the farm as usual, but I'm"—was I really going to reveal this?—"going to Washington before that."

"Why D.C.?" he asked.

"For the dedication of the new Vietnam Veterans Memorial."

He seemed surprised.

"Was Mike in Vietnam?"

For a split-second I was back at the Christmas party; was I suddenly going to learn that Rich, too, thought all Vietnam vets were "fucked up?" But he'd asked.

"No, he wasn't there," I said. "*I* was. As a nurse."

"I didn't know that," he said with obvious interest. "I was there, too. Sixty-nine. Fourth Infantry."

Interesting. My year. And a division whose soldiers frequented Pleiku.

"Ever wounded?"

"Yeah."

"When?"

"March."

"Where were you treated?"

"Pleiku."

Why wasn't I breaking out in a sweat?

"I was a nurse at Pleiku. 71st Evac. And I would have been there in March."

His eyes widened, his mouth opened, his face lit up.

"By any chance, were you a 'Lieutenant Carlson' back then?"

"Diane Carlson, yes," I said, "before marrying Mike Evans."

"Oh, my gosh, you were my nurse! I remember the auburn hair. Yeah, it was you. I don't believe it!"

I shook my head in amazement. It was the first time since Vietnam I'd come across a patient I had treated. It's hard to describe the elation I felt.

I asked about him, he asked about me. Like me, he'd been raised on a farm. He'd considered the idea of becoming a Methodist minister prior to going to Vietnam. Instead, he'd gone to work for the postal service.

"Are you locked in to your airfare for D.C.?" he asked, "because a few other vets with their wives and I were thinking of going together in a van. You're welcome to join us."

I hadn't booked a flight. The idea of spending a long day in a van— four long days, counting the trip back, and that was driving through the nights—with a handful of strangers and their wives wasn't my idea of a good time. On the other hand, these were, in essence, "my people." I hadn't asked Mike to go with me to the dedication; he hadn't been to Vietnam. I was terrified I might break down in front of him, and I couldn't do that.

But these guys and I had Vietnam in common; they knew what I'd been through, and I knew what they'd been through. Not only in Vietnam, but since we'd gotten home. I knew I could trust a van full of vets.

In Vietnam, I'd had many opportunities to pile into helicopters and scan the geography. I loved the sense of adventure. The not knowing exactly where I was headed. The idea that through this experience, in some way or ways, I would be better for having taken the risk. I looked at Rich, feeling as if I were twenty-one again.

"Yeah," I said, nodding my head. "I'll go with you guys. Thanks for the invite."

Mike was cool to the idea. Perhaps he should come with me.

"Honey, I have to go do this," I said. "I just do. I went to Vietnam alone. And I need to do this alone."

Mike nodded as if he understood, but I don't expect he did. Even though he didn't understand the roots of my anxieties, he trusted me to deal with them as I saw fit.

It was now September 1983. The ten months between when I stood at the Wall on November 13, 1982, and when Rodger Brodin handed me the ball of clay and told me to "tell your story" became a catalyst that totally changed my life. What transpired in that year would send me on a trajectory I never could have imagined. And it all seemed to have happened so fast:

The soldier's hug at the Wall—my first-ever "thank you" in person. The touching of Eddie Lee Evenson and Sharon Lane's names in the granite.

The therapy group I first met with, nine guys and a leader who gave me permission, for the first time, to share about how I was feeling when I was on the brink of ending my life.

The first time I opened up to Mike about my experiences in Vietnam.

The rediscovery of my footlocker at the farm.

The news, in 1984, that a statue, the Three Servicemen, was soon going in across from the Wall to honor Vietnam survivors—and to appease the faction that thought the Wall was a "black scar of shame."

The thought that something was missing in this addition: women.

The hospital where I struggled with encephalitis.

The nagging thoughts about leaving this world, about not wanting to leave Mike and the kids and yet lured by the idea that death would wash away the betrayals by our country, the sadness that followed me wherever I went, and the guilt I felt for denying my time in Vietnam.

Then, the fulcrum shift: hearing the still, small voice of the past—not reminding me of the cruel barbarities of war and the betrayal by our nation, but of the courage I'd once had but had hidden away when I got home as if it were the footlocker in the attic with a DO NOT OPEN label on it. Amid my refusing to talk about my past, where was the nurse who had kept twenty-eight soldiers alive with only a flashlight and a corpsman?

The idea that a memorial for women could at least be a start for female vets to get over Vietnam; an affirmation that we'd done something honorable, something worth remembering; a sign that we no longer had to hide our experiences.

And finally, the question to Rodger Brodin: "Have you ever thought of doing a sculpture of a female vet?"

When he handed me the ball of clay and asked me to take it home and mold it into something signifying my experience in Vietnam, he was speaking as much figuratively as literally. He wanted me to come back and tell him of my experiences and the stories of other women who had served in Vietnam; he wanted me to tell him what was in the Pleiku clay. I later learned he thought I'd be so overwhelmed with the challenge that he'd never see me or that ball of clay again. But I came back, carrying that clay, and if I didn't tell him my story with art, I told him with words. He, meanwhile, started imagining what the nurse he was to sculpt might look like. We had a handshake agreement to forge ahead with the project.

Beyond marrying Mike and having four children, it was the best thing that had happened to me since Vietnam. I needed to repurpose the old me, take the same passion I had before and during Vietnam and find a new way to use it for good. I'd spent most of my life dealing with people's physical wounds; now I was going to do something that had the potential to help heal psychological wounds. I would continue my nursing career, helping women heal from the trauma of war. And—who knew?—perhaps helping myself heal in the process.

I might help some of the 265,000 women who'd served around the world during the Vietnam Era, women whose service had largely been ignored. Women such as Lt. Rose Mary Burke, a young nurse from California with a serious no-nonsense disposition who was one of my nurses when I was a head nurse in Pleiku. She worked selflessly and tirelessly under hostile conditions and enemy fire while treating every patient—civilian and military—with dignity and diligence for their safety and well-being. But had anyone thanked her? If not, it was time. Time for her. Time for all women who'd been part of that war.

In the early 1980s, few people even knew women had served in a war that had been over for more than five years; a 1983 book by army nurse Lynda Van Devanter, *Home Before Morning*, was essentially the lone testament to our experience. Because she talked about sex, drugs, and partying, it was met with heated controversy, particularly within the Army Nurse Corps. Some Vietnam veteran nurses related to her story, others didn't. Senior officers in the Army Nurse Corps weren't happy that one of their own had openly talked about her personal life in Vietnam, and in their eyes, she had cast a negative light on the Corps. I defended the book by simply saying that it wasn't my story, but Lynda had a right to tell hers. While it wasn't representative of my experience, I wasn't threatened by her story. Maybe it would inspire other women to write their own.

After returning from the dedication of the Wall, both of us on fire to connect with others like us, Rich Timmerman and I put our heads together to bring Vietnam vets together in a support group. In 1983, after we secured a grant from the VA, a licensed counselor was authorized to participate as the mental health professional; Rich and I were deemed its "facilitators." It would be a vet-to-vet peer group. It was all very "seat-of-

DIANE CARLSON EVANS

our-pants." The whole concept of Vet Centers and peer-to-peer support groups had only started a few years earlier, in 1979.

Rich and I got the word out, identified the veterans, and found a weekly meeting place in the waiting room of my dentist, Dr. Steve Schwalbach, in River Falls. Most of the veterans were from rural Wisconsin—farmers, contractors, local business owners. We led these groups for more than two years. I learned of a new organization: Vietnam Veterans of America.

"Do you take women?" I asked.

"Are you a veteran?"

"I don't know, I suppose. I served in Vietnam. I was a nurse."

"Then you're a veteran. Welcome, Diane."

I became a founding member of Chapter 5, Vietnam Veterans of America, in Eau Claire, Wisconsin.

It felt good to be welcomed anywhere; I wasn't used to that. I drove long distances to go to meetings all over Wisconsin and in Washington, D.C., to participate in the founding of the new organization. I was coming out of my shell slowly but surely. On the advice of a peer counselor, I began to face my experience in Vietnam instead of trying to pretend it hadn't existed. I found new friendships with the Vietnam veterans I had avoided. I realized, for the first time, that nobody was going to advocate for us, so women who were part of the war needed to advocate for ourselves. For the first time in the fourteen years since I went to Vietnam, I was starting to see light at the end of a tunnel that had only seemed to be getting darker.

I typed—on a typewriter, not a computer—a two-page manifesto to "vets, spouses, concerned family and friends of Vietnam veterans," and poured out a heart that I'd been afraid to tap since I arrived back in the U.S. in 1969. It was a rallying cry for each other. To dare to search our souls. To stop doing what we'd all done: "When we returned from Vietnam, we looked at our country filled with turmoil and our country looked at us with suspicion. We had just come from a war zone. Our senses were keen. We felt vulnerable. To protect ourselves from further hurt, sadness, hostility, or rejection we isolated ourselves. We saw suffering and we suffered in Vietnam. We didn't want to suffer in our own country. The easiest way to do this was to become quiet about our experience, not let on we were a vet. We weren't ashamed of it. We just didn't want to be questioned, judged, or ridiculed."

I went on to say, *enough*. It was time to "stop being held hostage to that old war. You're home now. Talk about it, be proud, be instrumental in helping less fortunate vets. We are the only ones who can tell the real story, the truth of the Vietnam War. And we can only do it together, collectively."

I already had an idea of what that was going to mean for me.

When I told Mike and the kids that I wanted to lead an effort to get a memorial erected at the Vietnam Veterans Memorial in Washington, D.C., to honor women who served during the war, all five were on board. Not, of course, that any of them had any idea just what that would entail; at the time, the kids ranged in age from four to ten and were too young to truly understand. And not, of course, that I had much of an idea either. It seemed ambitious, yes, particularly for someone like me who had no experience in organizing groups, in public speaking, in politics, in business, in finance—in pretty much every discipline that would be required to make this happen. But I had a handful of things going for me: the tenacity to succeed, the empathy for my fellow female vets, belief in my brother veterans, and the naivety to guard me from seeing that goal as being impossible to reach.

Mike was more naïve than me. "A memorial for nurses," he said, "that's like motherhood and apple pie. Who's going to be against that?" I was thinking it would take three or four years, Mike even less.

Our ignorance of what this really proved to entail would protect my family and me from the harsher realities that would come. It may have sounded a bit unrealistic to think someone who couldn't even talk about Vietnam could, in two years, be addressing three thousand people in a Dallas convention ballroom, but Mike had an undying belief in me. And I had the idealistic notion that I might be able to re-channel more than a decade of bitterness into something beautiful.

Had I known what it was really going to require, I never would have said yes. *Never*.

Knowing too little to be fearful, I launched the endeavor with an air of optimism. After more than a decade of twisting in the wind, I had focus. Direction. Plans. I had an idea and a sculptor committed to help my idea go from vision to reality. Next, I needed buy-in from individuals and groups who could help me make this happen, deciding first to target women, then veterans' groups, then the government.

By 1983 some people were already entering the relatively new world of computers, but I wasn't among them. I bought a handful of fifty-page, lined spiral notebooks to keep track of what needed to be done; jotted down some names; and picked up the touch-tone phone. My first call was to an army nurse who had served in Vietnam. I'd met her at the Wall dedication. I told her my idea and asked if she'd help.

"Sorry, Diane, no one will give a damn."

I called Ann Cunningham, the back-from-Vietnam nurse who'd lost her fiancé and had warned me to never get close to any guy who was serving there because he'd just die. She was now living in Sacramento, California.

"Are you kidding?" she said. "I don't *do* Vietnam anymore."

"But Ann," I said. "If we don't tell the story, who will?"

"Sorry. Good luck, Diane."

My former hootchmate at Pleiku, Edie McCoy, had come home and married a guy named Bill, a Vietnam vet, and was now Edie Meeks. I'd been in their wedding. She'd want part of this action for sure.

"Sorry, Diane, I don't want to talk about Vietnam," she told me. "I've moved on."

I called a fourth nurse in Orlando who I knew from Pleiku.

"Why would we need a memorial?" she asked. "What good is that going to do?"

I thanked her, said goodbye, and hung up. I bent over and pressed my face into my hands, my newfound enthusiasm already doused. Lying in bed that night, as I mulled the anger and bitterness I'd heard in those voices, I found new and encouraging perspective. This had not been an indictment of me but an indictment of a country that had abandoned these women. In that sense, their negativity only confirmed exactly why I needed to press on: so that women like us wouldn't feel as if we had to deny one of the most profound, if not horrific, experiences of our lives. So that we could feel honor instead of shame. So that we could feel hope instead of despair.

Having researched a bit on how the Vietnam Veterans Memorial had come about, I knew that a handful of men who'd never undertaken anything like this before had pulled it off in less than three years by raising more than $8 million. I didn't think ours would cost nearly as much or take nearly as long.

After running his number down, I called Jan Scruggs, a Vietnam vet who had envisioned the memorial and led the charge to have it built. I admired him deeply. Not only had he served honorably in Vietnam, earning a Purple Heart for his wounds, but had cleared all sorts of obstacles to see that the nearly fifty-eight thousand dead were not forgotten. Surely a wounded Vietnam veteran would support a memorial to nurses and other women who had served their country, who had sacrificed for wounded vets like himself. And I instinctively thought we had to have his organization's support to move forward. Despite my optimism, my nerves nagged me with negativity. *Who are you to be calling someone of Scruggs' status?* But I kept punching numbers.

"We haven't met," I told him, "but I attended the dedication ceremony and want to thank you for what you did for us. I was a nurse in Vietnam."

His "you're welcome" seemed flat and uninspired.

I talked a bit about the "Three Servicemen" sculpture that would soon be placed across from the Wall, a memorial for the men who'd survived the war—a concession then-Secretary of the Interior James Watt insisted on to appease vets who felt Maya Lin's design was too dark and defeatist. His response was perfunctory, as if he were only keeping the conversation going out of obligation.

"Jan," I said, "I want you to know that we're starting an effort to have a similar sculpture installed at the Wall to honor women who served. We'd love your support."

There was a pause on the line.

"You've done *what?*"

"We've started a campaign to erect a statue in honor of women who served as part of the Vietnam War," I said.

No response. I was about to ask if he was still on the line, then came words I'll never forget.

"Well, that will never happen."

And he hung up on me.

I exhaled. Maybe my nervousness had been right; maybe I was out of my league. Maybe this was an idea whose execution would prove impossible. But I could see it. I could see Rodger Brodin's statue across from the Wall and see how it could become a catalyst for healing, for bringing women vets out of the woodwork, for restoring their pride. It would be a gift to the people of our country in honor of those who sacrificed and served that country.

Then I remembered back on the farm when we'd be, say, planting potatoes. You couldn't dwell on the end result, get all giddy about a Sunday dinner with a slab of butter moistening a fist-sized potato. You had to concentrate on the process that would get you to the glory of those mashed potatoes. First, get the seed in the ground.

Perhaps I needed to start smaller. Thinking I'd ultimately need to get the support of the major veteran's organizations, I arranged to speak to American Legion Post 121 in my hometown of River Falls, Wisconsin. It helped that Mike was the only surgeon in town and had operated on a handful of these guys.

"Husband did my hernia!" a guy beamed when I walked in.

But as I stood at the front of the room and scanned the group of a couple dozen men, my anxiety spiked. This was a slice of America, the same America that had so coldly responded to Vietnam vets when we returned—yes, the coldness came even from some fellow veterans of previous wars. And who was I? I was a nurse and a mother who had essentially never given a speech to a group larger than my four children. The fleeting memory of my baggage-counter experience at Minneapolis-St. Paul International Airport weakened my knees. I started shaking. Could I even do this?

For fifteen years now, I'd been stymied by a social syndrome not of my making. I'd been given no opportunity to heal from the wounds of war, the effects of which are why I froze in that operating room in San Antonio when that little boy died. And I'd been afraid to share, even in the living room of friends, about who I really was and where I'd been. But, by now, I'd reasoned the only way we women vets could heal ourselves—and perhaps enlighten the country—was to tell our stories, the symbol of which was to be our statue.

Now, if I didn't have the courage to tell mine, how could I expect buy-in from a single other female vet? As Eleanor Roosevelt once said, "You must do the thing you think you cannot do."

"Good afternoon," I said. "My name is Diane Carlson Evans, and I want to tell you a story about a farm girl from nearby Buffalo, Minnesota, who became a nurse, went to Vietnam, and returned to a country that acted as if my doing that—of trying to keep wounded soldiers alive—was somehow wrong. I want to tell you about more than ten thousand other women who served in Vietnam and thousands more who served around the world. The war is over. The Wall has been built to honor those who perished. And a statue is being erected to honor the male soldiers who survived. Women who sacrificed for the same America we all love should also be honored with a statue at the Vietnam Veterans Memorial."

Nobody booed. Nobody hissed. One man at a front table was nodding his head with enthusiasm; the hernia operation must have been successful. When I was finished, they seem to have been moved. Most clapped enthusiastically. I felt relief that the talk was over, honored that they had appreciated my idea, and inspired to move forward with the project. Only later did I stop to realize why I'd found the response so meaningful: since I'd arrived home from Vietnam, other than the guy who hugged me at the

Wall and my Vietnam veteran support group, this marked the first time I'd felt affirmed in a room where I'd admitted I was a Vietnam veteran. It didn't melt fifteen years of rejection, but it started the thaw.

But these were veterans with whom I had common ground that compensated for my female gender. My second coming-out speech as a veteran at the River Falls Lions Club came in a room filled with men who mostly were not veterans. This was dangerous. I told a similar story. When I finished, I looked down to gather up my notes. One person started clapping. One.

However, as I started to walk away from the podium the entire room erupted into loud claps and cheering, which morphed into a standing ovation. I looked up. I was overwhelmed. No longer would I keep my head down.

By February 1984, Rodger Brodin had finished a thirty-six-inch bronze statue replica. As a Marine, he was passionate about this. He was one of those rare individuals with genuine empathy for others. "Keep your eyes open to see the beauty all around you," he once closed a letter to me. "Take time to count your blessings. The light can soften some of the shadows of the past."

A handful of people, I learned on those early phone calls, were interested in partnering with me on the project. I organized the first meeting to discuss the vision and purpose for a Vietnam Women's Memorial. Besides me and Brodin, we were joined by his two brothers Neil and John; Steve Markley, a Marine Corps veteran and the Vietnam Veterans Leadership Program Director in whose office we met in Minneapolis; Gerald C. Bender (Jerry), a Marine Corps wounded veteran and attorney who I'd met at the Minnesota Welcome Home Parade; and Donna-Marie Boulay, a Minneapolis attorney and former Army nurse whom Markley knew and, with my permission, had invited in. All vets. All volunteers. All people who'd wanted to help. That day in February 1984, we named the effort "Vietnam Nurses Memorial Project."

At the time, I knew of no other women who had served in Vietnam other than nurses. I was nominated president and Donna-Marie vice president. We both had been army nurses in Vietnam. For now, we were part of this fledgling group with one massive goal: place a statue in Washington, D.C., to honor women who'd been part of the Vietnam War.

Rodger's statue, patterned after a female police officer in Minneapolis, portrayed a single nurse in fatigues holding an empty helmet and with a stethoscope wrapped around her neck. He had designed it to harmonize with the Three Servicemen, giving the nurse a weary expression to capture what he called "that moment of exhaustion and emotional pain and searching of understanding."

We laid the groundwork, developed a mission statement that included objectives, wrote bylaws, filed articles of corporations, applied for Internal Revenue Service nonprofit tax status, and wrote a policy-and-procedure manual filled with guidelines for our roles and the objectives. The attorneys in our group were of immense help.

Within six months, we made an important course correction. Even if we wanted Brodin's statue to remain our memorial, we realized we'd been shortsighted in only honoring nurses. Though nurses were the most visible women serving in Vietnam, we learned that women had served in an array of other capacities around the world related to the war: intelligence officers, WACs who counted caskets as they arrived home to San Francisco, medics who unloaded endless casualties—soldiers too sick to come home—at Camp Zama near Tokyo, Red Cross volunteers, burial officers in Washington, D.C., and more. There were female doctors, air-traffic controllers, clerks, journalists, USO entertainers, all sorts of ways women stood up for their country. In fact, some 265,000 women had some part in the war, with approximately 7,500 nurses in Vietnam and several hundred more civilian women.

We changed our name to Vietnam *Women's* Memorial Project (VWMP) to embrace not only nurses but all military and civilian women who had served in support of the Armed Forces during the Vietnam era. And we settled upon a motto: "A Legacy of Healing and Hope."

Our mission, we decided, would embody four ideals: to place the monument on the grounds of the Vietnam Veterans Memorial in Washington, D.C.; to educate the American public about how women Vietnam-era vets, with compassion, care, and dignity, sacrificed and labored in their roles; to locate women who served during the war and create a first-ever "Sister Search" database with the goal of promoting connection with each other for the process of healing; and to facilitate research about them.

On August 12, 1984, we held a special event in St. Paul, Minnesota, to unveil Rodger Brodin's statue, which we called *The Nurse*. We invited a Gold Star Mother to lift the veil. We didn't know whether three dozen or three hundred people would show up. More than a thousand did, including the press and dozens of women vets. There was no turning back now. We had publicly announced our intentions and triggered no backlash whatsoever.

To gain awareness and raise money, we organized a seventeen-state tour. Rodger created four thirty-six-inch bronze replica statues to travel all over the United States as a tangible symbol of our mission. An advertising agency created a flyer for us: "A small donation makes a monumental difference."

We set a goal of $1.3 million to accomplish our mission. None of us were to be paid and none of our money could come from the government; all had to be raised from private individuals, civic, and veterans' organizations and businesses. Despite the initial hesitation from the handful of female vets I'd called, two climbed on board as word spread about the project. With newspapers running articles about the proposed statue, nurses and other women and male veterans alike came out of the woodwork. We started recruiting volunteers. My kids spent hours stuffing envelopes and sticking on stamps. We started getting mail.

From an anonymous letter that included a check for fifty dollars: "…For the nurse on the air evac flight who helped me get home. I still love her."

From a woman in Michigan: "We are sisters of the same generation, but I was part of the Silent Majority. I didn't stand up and stand behind you when you needed me most. Thanks for a second chance."

From a veteran in New Jersey, the following comprised his entire letter: "Thank God for you."

From an Air Force flight nurse: "Tet was the hardest challenge I ever faced. I went for thirty-two hours straight without a rest. I had the enormous burden of helping to decide who should get immediate attention and who should be placed aside to die. The stench of death constantly reminded me of the need to move faster and faster. The taste and smell still come back today."

From an ex-GI from Illinois who'd been critically wounded in Vietnam: "I experienced hearing the two clerks standing in the doorway of the x-ray room betting on how long I would live; my fondest memory is of her, the nurse whom I will never know but who will always hold a special place in my heart. Because of my wounds, I could not see her approach the gurney where several people were working on me, including the priest administering Last Rites. She cradled my left hand in hers, and in a soft and caring voice said, 'You'll be all right, you'll be all right.'"

But the response that went to the deepest part of my heart was from a small girl. She wrote: "This is all I have, but I want you to have it because if it wasn't for you, my Daddy wouldn't be here."

Enclosed were two one-dollar bills.

15

Resistance

1985–1987

Early on in the memorial journey, I arrived home in River Falls after the hour-long drive from the Minneapolis-St. Paul International Airport; Mom was watching the kids and Mike, of course, was still at work. I punched the button to hear our phone messages, three-quarters of which, as of late, related to the campaign.

"This message is for Diane Evans," a man's voice growled, "the fucking woman who thinks women deserve a statue. You'd better watch out or—"

I hit "stop" and called the police—again. This was the second one of those.

Another day, I answered the phone and the caller said he was Tom Carhart. Trouble. I knew the name. Vietnam veteran, West Point graduate, hater of the Wall and leader of the fight to add the Three Servicemen statue. I had read about him in the newspapers.

"Who do you think you are?" he huffed. "Forget about adding a statue to women. One statue there is enough!"

Click.

At a copy shop that I frequented regularly, one of the regular clerks looked suspiciously at the material I was having printed, then at me.

"You one of them feminazis?" he asked.

Not everybody was behind us. In fact, as the campaign deepened, we would learn that a lot of people—including some extremely powerful people in Washington, D.C.—were dead-set against us. At times, I was described as a radical feminist out to further my own cause—and climbing on the backs of dead soldiers to reach my moment in the sun. My vision triggered hate mail, angry phone calls, and threats. Women hadn't been in combat, hadn't suffered, and hadn't comprised anywhere near the numbers that men had, the thinking went; why did they deserve a statue all for themselves?

Once a magazine editor asked me how many patients I'd cared for in Vietnam. I'd never thought about it. But when you combined the soldiers, the Vietnamese, the Montagnards—it was easily into the thousands. But nobody in America knew that or seemed to care.

If the first part of our campaign had been like a pleasant raft trip down a lazy river, the flow soon picked up new and dangerous speeds, the rapids grew higher, and somewhere in the distance, I could hear a couple of waterfalls pounding. But we pushed ahead. I booked more speaking opportunities. We set up a national infrastructure of volunteer coordinators who would help publicize our mission to, and solicit funds from, their specific regions. The American Nurses Association donated a small space in its Washington, D.C., office for our national volunteer coordinator to use.

I tried to lead our team like I'd led my team in Pleiku when I'd been head nurse. It was all about teamwork. Everyone was important. Everyone needed to be moving toward the same goal. And nobody could be consumed about getting the credit.

Early on, we diffused our leadership. On Donna-Marie Boulay's urging, the two of us became co-chairs with a third co-chair, Steve Young. Boulay would focus on shaking the legislative tree in Washington, D.C., and I would be the veterans' liaison with a focus on getting national vets' organizations on board. At the time, shared leadership seemed like a good idea. Only later would I be reminded of the prophetic words of a colleague well-versed in leadership who warned me, "Diane, co-chair is no chair."

I was busy making decision after decision, among the more trivial a choice to no longer use a particular copy shop and the more profound to attend a February 1985 meeting in Washington, D.C., whose topic was recognizing contributions of military women in service to our country. Headed up by the associate director of the Office of Public Liaison, it drew dozens of women from the Pentagon and the Veterans Administration. In addition, there were representatives of all the military services, overseas civilian organizations such as the Red Cross, the woman who'd served as campaign director for the building of the Vietnam Veterans Memorial, and, of course, me, the newcomer whom a D.C. commission staffer had called "that woman coming in out of the cornfields."

It was an important meeting that created a handful of critical connections for us with people who could help. And out of it came legislation, passed the following month, to build a memorial to all military women who had served since the time of the American Revolution. It would be called Women in Military Service for America (WIMSA) and would be built at the entrance to Arlington National Cemetery headed by a respected Vietnam veteran, B.G. Wilma Vaught, USAF (Ret.).

This was a wonderful idea but was far different from our project. We supported WIMSA but it had a broader, more educational focus than ours. Our memorial was specific to a recent war that had ripped the fabric of America, was not to include any sort of museum, and was to be located near the Wall, where the names of the nearly fifty-eight thousand who died in the war were memorialized in granite. Ours was meant to complete an *existing* memorial. It was to be a figurative portrayal of women serving in Vietnam as honoring such women—an end unto itself—and, as a means to an end, a catalyst for women to share their stories with America, to connect with one another, and to heal from the chilly reception many received.

The WIMSA project would not prove to be either of the waterfalls I'd heard coming, but it would be a reminder that not all military women row in the same direction.

As four thirty-six-inch bronze replica statues, Brodin's *The Nurse* made its way around the country to raise both awareness and money for our project, the outpouring of interest from people wanting to volunteer was remarkable. Our office was flooded with comments, questions, donations, and offers to help. After the four "sorry, Diane's" I got from my first calls, well over one hundred military and civilian women veterans had now decided to jump headfirst into our uncharted waters. And two of them were among those four who originally opposed the idea with vigor.

After World War I, major veterans' groups sprang up to give soldiers—mostly men—a place to gather, talk, heal, and, of course, drink. But after Vietnam, women who served went their separate ways, tried to get on with their lives, and seldom connected with each other. There were few veterans' organizations specifically for women and fewer therapy groups. Beyond a handful of nurses I'd served with, who I saw rarely, I didn't connect with female veterans for thirteen years—until the Wall dedication. But now that was no longer the case. And the strong "count-me-in" response far outweighed the naysayers, like the person who scribbled an anonymous note to us reminiscent of a statement I heard from the first female vet I'd called: "Do you think anyone will give a damn?"

Yes, I honestly did. And to that end I met with Judge Dan Foley, a World War II veteran and an appellate judge in St. Paul, Minnesota. I'd been told by my River Falls American Legion Post—I joined after giving my speech—that Foley was a key contact if I wanted to get anything done with the American Legion. I called him with great nervousness; he was a judge, an influential leader in the American Legion, and allegedly "knew it all." I knew little. But he put me at ease, invited me to lunch, talked of our common small-town Minnesota roots, and gave me more information in an hour than I ever could have hoped for.

But his key advice left me feeling as if I'd been sentenced to what sounded like a really long term. "First, take your proposal to your local post and ask them to consider and pass it, then go on to district, then to the state convention, and they will take it on to the national convention. Get that done this year."

Several hundred miles of road trips and a flight to New Orleans later, I did. At the 67th National American Legion convention, Resolution 16 was ratified, calling on the Department of Interior, Commission of Fine Arts, National Capitol Planning Commission, and all others to dedicate an area near the Vietnam Veterans Memorial "to erect a statue honoring the women who have served during the Vietnam War." The Legion had nearly three million members with five thousand delegates at the convention, so that was a huge win for us.

I repeated this process with the Veterans of Foreign Wars (VFW) beginning in Wisconsin. After my success with the Legion, I thought Veterans of Foreign Wars would be an easy sell; after all, VFW members have served on foreign soil and many of them in combat. And our memorial was about honoring nurses and other women who had supported the men in Vietnam, an overseas combat zone. How could they be against us?

After getting enthusiastic support and buy-in among VFW members in Wisconsin, I ventured to Dallas in August 1985 for the organization's 86th National Convention to share our resolution for the memorial with their three thousand delegates. These were people who ostensibly would have an appreciation for, say, the nurses who patched up many of the 304,000 wounded soldiers in Vietnam and were often the last people thousands of soldiers had seen before dying.

The VFW National Commander, Billy Ray Cameron, the first Vietnam veteran to assume the organization's top position, assured me our resolution would find smooth sailing among representatives from all fifty states. Confidently, I stepped to the microphone for people in favor of Resolution 739: "Recognize the Women Who Served in the Vietnam War."

"We are educating our nation that women have witnessed, firsthand, the horrors of conflict and made the ultimate sacrifice to their country,"

I said to thousands of delegates. "The monument is intended to complement and complete the Vietnam Veterans Memorial in Washington, D.C. The Three Servicemen representing all men who suffered or served in Vietnam stand to the left of the Wall. We want our statue to stand to the right where she will be watching over the names of the men and women who died and the Three Servicemen.

"I fought in Vietnam—not with a weapon, but I fought in combat zones for young men's lives in the surgical and burn unit. There was someone's son who died in my arms. It left a scar that has taken years to heal. When women veterans are given respect and recognition for their contributions, their strength will come through in the healing process that dictates that wounds heal when wounds get the attention they deserve."

Finally: "We are not a 'special-interest' group. We are veterans, comrades. By honoring these women of the Vietnam era, we as an organization are honoring ourselves. I encourage you to adopt this resolution."

After I spoke from the "pro" microphone, only a handful of others lined up behind me to voice support for the idea. Meanwhile, more than a dozen lined up at the "con" microphone to speak against the idea.

"If we honor the nurses at the Vietnam Wall," said one man, "then helicopter pilots will want a statue, and bomber pilots, and pretty soon we'll have a tank at the Wall."

"We are not tanks," I said, "we are women!"

"My post cannot support a memorial that does not include all the women in the VFW instead of just the women who served in Vietnam," countered another vet.

Later, the voice vote was loud, angry, and lopsided. The answer to my idea for a women's memorial was a resounding "no."

I was shell-shocked. I all but stumbled into the lobby outside the ballroom, stunned by the vitriolic response. Suddenly, a sharp finger from behind jabbed at me under my shoulder blades. I turned around. "You Vietnam vets are all alike," said a World War II-era veteran, his face in my face. "All you do is think about yourself. You already have your memorial. What about all those women who served in World War II and Korea?"

My father the farmer once gave me some sound advice: never get in a pissing match with a skunk. I held my tongue and dodged the sputum. But the red-faced man wasn't finished.

"What's more, you *lost* your war. You shamed America!"

"Look who's talking," said a man who appeared out of nowhere. A Vietnam vet had stepped between me and the WWII vet. "You've had *forty years* to honor your women. Where's your memorial for *them*?"

The Vietnam vet nodded toward me. "At least she's taking action to honor the women who served in Vietnam, which is more than you've done." The finger-pointer gulped, turned, and walked away. I was still in shock, left with a sense of "what just happened?"

If this was our memorial team's first national-level rejection, it wouldn't be our last. And the common denominator would often, but not always, be this: men unhappy about women daring to step onto what they clearly saw as *their* playing field. Now, nearly two years into the campaign, what had kept us going was the same thing that kept us going in Vietnam: for every soldier we couldn't save, one would pull through. And at the darkest hour, there'd be a lone candle of hope in that life saved. A reminder that, as much as possible, we had our wounded men's backs—just like that Vietnam vet who confronted my detractor had mine.

I didn't have time to enjoy the small victory. A Dallas TV reporter suddenly had a microphone in my face. "Ms. Carlson Evans, we understand you lost today in your attempt to—"

"What makes you think you deserve a memorial all to yourself?" interrupted a woman of WWII age wearing her VFW hat, a reminder that not all our opponents were male. "You already have the Wall, with the names of eight women on it. Those of us who served in World War II don't have *anything*."

I calmed myself by clearing my throat.

"Ma'am, I'm sorry you don't have a memorial," I said. "You certainly deserve one. It's not that we're trying to exclude you and women like you. But if you want a memorial, *work* for one. Nobody's doing this for us. *We're* doing this for us—without pay. All volunteer. And ours is for the space at the Vietnam Veterans Memorial, a place you wouldn't want your memorial."

The woman walked off in a huff. The reporter shook her head.

"I don't know how you could be so civil to her," she said with the camera off.

I had expected pushback from those who had never served in the military; by now, I was used to the chip-on-the-shoulder person like the doctor at the Christmas party for whom I became the lightning rod for his anger about Vietnam. I hadn't expected pushback from fellow vets of other generations, particularly served up with such venom. And particularly from women. But I was still naïve. Before this war on the home front was over, I'd find enemies who not only were fellow vets and were women, but who would be sharing the same foxhole with me.

Billy Ray Cameron nodded me over to a corner. "I'm so sorry, Diane, I can't believe what happened in there today. I honestly thought this was a slam dunk."

I just dropped my head and rubbed my forehead.

"Look," he said, "we're not dead yet. I talked to the parliamentarian. There's a recourse, whereby a turned-down proposal can get placed back on the agenda the next day. A motion has to be made and seconded and would need a majority vote to 'reconsider.'"

"I'm all for it. But how do we convince state delegates to buy into this by tomorrow morning?"

"You just come with me tonight and talk, and we'll change some minds."

Cameron, head of emergency services in North Carolina, was a popular VFW commander with whom people loved to align themselves. That evening I was treated to a style of backroom politics I didn't know existed. Basically, it consisted of Cameron identifying several states with which he had particularly good relationships, then, throughout the evening, entering their hospitality suites. Timing was everything. We waited until later in the evening, when, shall we say, the delegates were in particularly good moods. He introduced me. I said a few things. He said a few things. We smiled, shook hands with the delegates, and moved on. Soon, two states—Pennsylvania and Wisconsin—were on board and contributed immensely to changing some minds.

It worked. In the morning, Cameron phoned to say we had several states' delegates who agreed to make the necessary motions and speak to it favorably. We had lived to fight another day. And what happened on that day was less about anything I did than what Cameron did.

When he announced the parliamentary procedure that was allowing the VFW to re-visit the Vietnam Women's Memorial proposal, boos rumbled across the massive ballroom like high-mountain thunder. But Cameron hushed the crowd with a gentle push-down of his extended hands.

The room grew still as he took off his National Commander's hat and placed it on the podium. What was that about? He walked down off the stage onto the convention floor, behind the "pro" microphone, looked the delegates directly in their eyes.

"I am speaking to you as a veteran of a foreign war. If it wasn't for Vietnam, I would not be here on this stage; that's the war that qualified me to be part of this outstanding organization."

He paused. "I was seriously wounded in that war. And, frankly, I wouldn't be here if it hadn't been for those nurses. They saved my life. And they deserve our support, as do all the non-nurses who were part of the Vietnam effort and who will be represented by the statue."

A trickle of polite applause rippled through the audience, then got louder. When it was my turn, I discarded my prepared remarks and apologized for not being clear the previous day about who the memorial was for; not just for nurses, but for all women who played a part in the Vietnam War. I also clarified that I wasn't suggesting that women who served in the Vietnam era were better than women who served in any other war.

"The Frederick Hart statue [the Three Servicemen] honors all men in Vietnam as our statue will honor all women," I said. "I urge you to reconsider this resolution which will put the VFW on record as supporting a memorial which honors all the women who served during the Vietnam War."

A burst of clapping broke out. By now, with hundreds of speeches under my belt, I could tell whether my audience was with me or glancing at their watches to make a 2:00 p.m. tee time. This audience was totally different from the previous day's, even though it was the same people.

But then came resistance. A female delegate from New Jersey said she was going to vote for it, but "after [the previous day's] meeting, there was a certain gentleman from the hotel in the elevator, and I asked him of his opinion, and he said, 'Don't vote for that baloney. They are using that resolution to make money.' I disapprove of the resolution."

Make money? And changing her vote because a guy in an elevator opposed us?

Then the tide turned. Said a male New Jersey delegate: "We certainly can't stand and say that we deny our support for the memorial because of the sex of the statue."

A woman who had served during World War II said, "This is an inspiration...let's honor the Vietnam women, and I will salute them. I love them."

My heart jumped.

"I personally don't feel this is a money-making project," said a male Pennsylvania delegate. "This is a thing of the heart, dedicated to women of all services of the United States."

When the testimony came to an end, Cameron stepped back up to the podium and put his National Commander's hat back on.

"All in favor of the proposal to endorse the Vietnam Women's Memorial?" Cameron asked.

The "aye" response was vibrant.

"Opposed?"

Not so vibrant. I exhaled. We'd won. But I braced myself when I reached the lobby, expecting the detractors to come at me like heat-seeking missiles as they had in this place the day before. I was ready to fight back.

Instead, men with glistening eyes took my hand in their two hands and shook it. One hugged me with fervor.

"Yesterday," he said, fighting back tears, "I voted for the memorial and today I did, too. I can only hope that you were the nurse who was with my son"—he paused to gather himself—"when he died. That you were the last person on this earth he saw before passing."

I loved my mother and she was as wise as the day is long. But when she'd told me long before the war, "Don't ever expect gratitude, it will never come," she was wrong. Bit by bit, I was starting to feel that gratitude, and it felt good. It was the sustenance that kept me—that kept all of us—going. Women veterans would learn that, *yes*, people did give a damn.

My spiral notebooks were filling with to-do items. One notebook alone had 567 such reminders, among them: "Call Jane about labels… write Francis Kohn…make plane reservations…write goals and objectives for conference…complete the requests for telegrams from the VFW… check out Bush's campaign PR person…get big spread in the *Post*…set agenda for Monday…mail the expense analysis…return message from Dottie Beatty…talk to Karen about shipping out the posters…."

When I decided to lead this fight, the commitment was a little like the one I'd made to the U.S. Army Nurse Corps before going to Vietnam: in retrospect, I had no idea what I was getting into. For the memorial quest, I had no idea that I'd be flying or driving on an average of sixty trips a year. No idea that I would become so distraught about missing my daughter Carrie's piano recital or my sons' tennis matches or the in-fighting and vying for power on the board of directors that I'd wear down the appliance my dentist had given me to keep me from grinding my teeth while sleeping. No idea that I would run up $650-a-month phone bills and twice have to use police surveillance at our house because I'd gotten death threats. No idea that newspaper columns would make my blood boil.

"It's a political statement, a nod toward the women's movement," wrote columnist Bill McClellan of the *St. Louis Post-Dispatch*, "and a political statement of any sort has no business at that memorial."

But progress was being made. By 1986, the American Legion, Veterans of Foreign Wars, Disabled American Veterans, Vietnam Veterans of America, Paralyzed Veterans of America, AMVETS, VietNow, Military Order of the Purple Heart, and Jewish War Veterans were all officially behind us. They represented well over seven million people—and with their auxiliaries, several million more.

I had spoken at every one of these organizations' conferences and became a member of most of them, believing it was important for the VWMP to establish a reputation of trust and credibility. We inspired women active in their organizations to promote our efforts. We targeted civic and humanitarian groups of both genders. And, in a first, a huge pharmaceutical company whose surgical hand scrubs had been used in Vietnam approached us—Stuart Pharmaceuticals, later becoming Zeneca—with the offer of a $500,000 partnership.

In September 1986, we put on our first high-visibility fundraiser, outside near the Lincoln Memorial. Thanks to Linda Schwartz, one of our newer board members and a leader in Vietnam Veterans of America, we landed two influential co-sponsors: U.S. Senators Edward Kennedy (D-Massachusetts) and John Kerry (D-Massachusetts). About three hundred people gathered beneath a sprawling tent. Senator Kennedy took to the podium, commending those "gallant and courageous women who served our country in Vietnam" and stressing the need to "recognize those women who served under the colors of our flags…."

Said Kerry, a Vietnam vet himself: "Any of the names on the Wall could be any of us here. Our mission is to remember, and no one can remember in the way we ought to remember until there's a statue that reflects the service of women in Vietnam."

Momentum was building. General William Westmoreland agreed to serve on our Honorary Council, as did General George Price, a vocal proponent of the Vietnam Veterans Memorial. Newspapers, TV stations, and radio stations were calling for interviews—even *Penthouse* magazine! For the first time, they seemed genuinely interested in our story, the most common comment being: "I didn't know there were women who served in Vietnam."

More than $750,000 had been raised from corporate gifts and more than $100,000 worth of in-kind services had been offered, among them Northwest Airlines agreeing to fly the *Nurse* statues around the country for free. We had bolstered our board, which, besides Schwartz, now included P. Evangeline Jamison (Jamie), a retired Army Nurse Corps lieutenant colonel who had served during World War II and the Korean and Vietnam wars. Jamie had donated a considerable amount of money to the project and everybody loved her warmth, generosity, and humor.

Not everything was perfect. In Wisconsin, working out of my house and commuting an hour to our tiny Minneapolis office for meetings, I was starting to sense I was getting left out of some important decisions. At one point, a board member authorized an expenditure to a public relations firm far exceeding the project's by-laws authorization amount— with no approval from the board.

Ever since I'd been introduced to the idea of team nursing at St. Barnabas Hospital back in the 1960s, I'd embraced the concept of people trusting each other so implicitly that the patient was the ultimate beneficiary. For the first time since the VWMP had formed, I doubted that we were all in this together. And that hurt because, of course, I blamed myself. Perhaps I shouldn't have been so egalitarian with the leadership.

Despite these ripples on the water, we were feeling good, particularly when the Vietnam Veterans Memorial Foundation co-founders—Jan Scruggs and Jack Wheeler, who had led the fight to build the Wall and placed the Three Servicemen statue across from it—offered us their official blessing to place a monument honoring women on that site. This was a necessary endorsement before we could proceed—given their Memorandum of Conveyance document authorizing the Vietnam Veteran's Memorial Fund's authority to weigh in on potential additions. And Scruggs, of course, was the prickly guy who'd blown me off when I'd first sought support two years before. I appreciated his about-face, though his backing of us would prove to be tepid at best. The third co-founder, Robert Doubek, couldn't bring himself to support us—a precursor to even more intense resistance.

Everything was lining up for federal approval, though our task of getting that okay got more difficult when, amid our furious campaign, Congress passed a new law in 1986 called the Commemorative Works Acts (CWA). It was a complex piece of legislation hurried into law after the Three Servicemen addition to the Wall rankled the Commission of Fine Arts, which has a say in what memorials are allowed, and not allowed, on federal properties. In short, the CWA had made it nearly impossible to add any sort of memorial on the Mall, much less one that trumpeted women.

In an attempt to quell the uproar from veterans who found the Wall "dark and defeatist," Interior Director James Watt had strong-armed the addition of the statue of men to honor those who had survived. That irked the arts commission, which was of the mind that the increasingly rare swaths of federal land in D.C. were threatened to be filled with what they called "kitschy memorials that had little artistic value."

Meanwhile, CWA became a quandary for us. On one hand, it was the addition of the all-male statue of soldiers that had inspired me to fight for a memorial for women in the first place; on the other hand, beneath its noble veneer, the CWA seemed destined to scatter so many obstacles in the way of proponents of would-be memorials that organizers would quit in frustration. Many wondered if that wasn't its entire purpose.

But we weren't quitting.

Never mind that because the CWA went into effect *after* the Wall was in, Scruggs, Doubek, Wheeler, and their team didn't have to deal with it. Never mind that beyond the CWA, we also needed approval from the Secretary of the Interior, the Commission of Fine Arts, the National Capital Memorial Commission, and the National Capital Planning Commission. We brought in attorneys and landscape architects, gathered information, huddled in countless meetings, and prepared testimony, all of which simply got us to the starting line for these final approvals.

From what we'd learned, these latter two commissions were unlikely to dispute our proposal if the Secretary of the Interior and the Commission of Fine Arts were on board. Thus, we requested a hearing with the Commission of Fine Arts, which was set for October 22, 1987.

Meanwhile, board member Donna-Marie Boulay, along with Senator David Durenberger (R-Minnesota), met with Secretary of the Interior Don Hodel on September 10 in an attempt to win his support.

They were successful. Before the hearing, Hodel released a letter saying that the proposed statue fit within the provision of the 1980 Public Law 96-297, which authorized the establishment of the Vietnam Veterans Memorial. The proposal, he pointed out, was endorsed by the National Park Service. And he favored it, too.

It appeared our long wait might finally be over.

16

Showdown

October 1987

In my Washington, D.C., hotel room, I returned the phone to its cradle after once again saying goodnight to Mike and the kids back in Wisconsin via long distance. (I dreaded our monthly bill.) By now, more than four years into my quest to have a memorial placed in Washington, D.C., to honor 265,000 women who had served in the military between 1963 and 1975, such distant "goodnights" had become standard operating procedure for the Evans family. And yet as I stared out the window at the traffic below on this Autumn night in 1987, I sensed, for the first time, an end to the journey. I sensed closure. I sensed victory.

At 10:00 a.m. the next day, the Commission of Fine Arts would hold a hearing on placing the Brodin design portrayal of a military woman near the Wall of names. Those of us on the Vietnam Women's Memorial Project board were cautiously optimistic that the result would be approved, overcoming the last major obstacle in turning our dream into reality.

It couldn't come soon enough. Frankly, I was weary. If my year in Vietnam had taken a physical and an emotional toll on me, this battle, too, had worn me down. I'd been a busy stay-at-home mom in 1983 when sculptor Rodger Brodin had handed me the ball of clay and told me to tell my story. He'd used my experience in Vietnam, my boots, and my telling of my sister veterans' stories to create the bronze statue that we'd now proposed to be placed near the Vietnam Veterans Memorial.

By now my fifty-nine cent, wide-ruled notebooks in which I kept my daily list of what needed to be done were filling up fast: people to call, letters to write, money to raise, interviews to do, speeches to give, luncheons to attend, information to find, senators to engage, *thank-yous* to offer, brochures to create, plane reservations to make, favors to ask, events to coordinate, requests to make, agendas to set, packages to mail, copies to pick up, messages to return, events to attend—so much on the "to do" list. Later, an associate perused the files and determined I'd already completed more than fifteen thousand tasks—and that doesn't include the myriad accomplishments of others involved.

But you can't obsess about the illustrious final outcome you seek. That will come with the diligence of the day-to-day grind: *one phone call at a time, one letter at a time, one speech at a time, one organization's endorsement at a time....*

And you can't forget why you're doing this: for women who deserved recognition, respect, and a better chance to heal. For women who, more than a decade after the war ended, desperately needed to find a sense of home that they'd left but never found upon their return.

Sometimes I'd be overwhelmed by the whole process. I'd try to remember a simple image to steel into myself the "why" of that process, what the end game was: to shine light on women who toiled honorably in the shadows. I know that I paid a price for my service in Vietnam but considered it the greatest privilege of my life. We all paid a price. Now, it was time to acknowledge that such moments *happened*. To acknowledge *we were there*. To acknowledge *we, too, served*.

As I readied myself for bed the night before the commission meeting, I couldn't help but wonder if the next day's entry in my notebook might read: "The coup de grace! We did it!"

We were confident for a handful of reasons. We had buy-in from every major veterans' group and over forty civic and professional organizations. The Vietnam Veterans Memorial Fund, after initial resistance, approved. And earlier in the day, when we'd all but given up hope, Secretary Hodel had sent his written endorsement.

How could the commission say no? We'd jumped through every hoop, dotted every legal *I*, crossed every bureaucratic *T*. And it was simply time for change; of 110 memorials in Washington, only three honored women. Certainly, the commission could see the imbalance here and realize that art was an appropriate expression of remembrance for the women who served during the Vietnam War.

With nothing left to do, I crawled into bed, turned off the light, and stared into the darkness. Beyond the whir of traffic and the occasional honk of a horn, all was quiet. No choppers in the sky. No worries that a mortar attack would suddenly shatter the peace. No ill-defined war with an enemy hiding in civilian clothes and a purpose you never understood.

Unlike Vietnam, the memorial fight had an enemy you *could* see, even if I sometimes felt wounded by friendly fire, by people who I never considered to be my enemy but who seemingly considered me theirs. It was a microcosm of a pattern that we'd seen from the get-go: push-back, push-back, push-back, then a group or individual would ride to our rescue. Or we'd ride to our own rescue.

Our "Sister Search" effort had reached out to, and found, thousands of women vets, many of whom hadn't connected with a fellow female vet since the war. And, in virtually every state, our volunteers had plastered the walls of businesses, libraries, and city halls with a poster we had done of Rodger Brodin's nurse statue.

Now, virtually all that was left was approval from the commission the next day. I exhaled, like a climber about to make a final ascent of a rarely reached peak, cautious but expectant. I rolled onto my side, and soon was asleep.

The next morning, I joined three women vets, all of whom had served in Vietnam, all of whom were serving on our VWMP board of directors, for coffee in the hotel restaurant. Lt. Col. Evangeline Jamison, U.S. Army Nurse Corps—Jamie to us—was across from me; Col. Jane (Amelia) Carson, another Army Nurse and on active duty at the Pentagon, to my left; and former Women's Army Corps Capt. Karen Johnson to my right.

Casually, I scanned the October 22, 1987, *Washington Post*. The big news was still fallout from the "Black Monday" stock-market plunge three days before. But, suddenly, a headline hit me like a semi-truck. It was in relation to a story on our proposed women's memorial. "Honor Without Integrity," it said.

What? It couldn't be. Not this. Not *us*. Not today.

My eyes scanned. My heart raced.

"Oh, my God," I said.

"What?" asked Jamie.

"Story says the memorial 'is not a very good idea. To be precise, it's a bad one.'"

"How can they say that?" asked Karen.

"It 'would create a serious symbolic imbalance in one of the national's preeminent commemorative places.'"

"That's ludicrous," said Jamie.

Each paragraph seemed more venomous than the previous one.

"Arts critic named Benjamin Forgey says the memorial is 'complete as is,'" I said.

"Sure, now that they've added the three-man statue opposite the Wall. But what about us?" said Jane. "Was the war in Vietnam complete without us?"

Exactly. Forgey defined "complete" as the Wall complemented by the Three Servicemen. In his mind, the addition of a women's memorial would throw that fine-tuned balance into utter chaos. The Three Servicemen, wrote Forgey, "are intended to stand for all who served."

Were onlookers just to *assume* that a male always represents a female—and be satisfied with that? Or was it possible—just *possible*—

that, with the male-heavy governmental bodies making such decisions, females had not been given their due?

Forgey was quick to point out that the Three Servicemen obviously represented women, too; fine; but would he have been equally quick to accept a statue of three women representing men? I mean, wouldn't it have been *obvious*?

A hotel waitress tried to freshen my coffee, but I pushed the cup away. I was angry. Blind-sided. The timing was suspicious, right before the hearing. At the very least, the reporter might have listened to testimony regarding our proposed statue before proclaiming us spoilers of the Vietnam Veterans Memorial. Or at least heard our side before sharing his opinion. And the choice of words he used to describe our proposal ran the gamut of cruel and mean-spirited. In its acidity and depth, the venom was the same vitriol of the vet in Dallas who'd poked his finger at me, only this was a well-camouflaged poke at every American woman from San Diego to Boston. My optimism wilted.

"I feel like the die has already been cast for the hearing today," I said.

"Don't panic, Diane," said Jane. "The *Post* isn't the commission."

I slowly shook my head sideways. I wanted to believe that she was right, that the commission would look at this with a broader perspective, that they would listen—truly listen—to our testimony and realize the memorial would enhance, not detract from, the honoring of those who served in Vietnam. But I wasn't holding my breath.

The Commission of Fine Arts is located just off Pennsylvania Avenue, a stone's throw to the northwest of the White House. Its six-person board was accustomed to hearings that drew scant audiences in a large board room that provided dozens of chairs for onlookers. They existed to ensure the "integrity" of any "architectural development" in Washington, D.C. Its decisions rarely drew crowds or malicious controversy. But from the looks of our crowd, this wasn't one of those ho-hum issues.

Thanks to calls we'd made to female vets at the Pentagon, and to a smattering of newspaper stories (including, perhaps, the one in this morning's *Post*), the hall was packed with a standing-room-only crowd comprised mainly of women in uniform: Air Force, Navy, Army, and Marine Corps. And Red Cross. I glanced back. Off to our side, Robert Doubek, part of the trio that had led the fight for the Vietnam Veterans Memorial and a staunch opponent of our memorial, seemed to be hyperventilating at the overwhelming female presence.

"Quick," whispered a uniformed woman wearing the nursing caduceus symbol, "someone get him a paper bag."

The operators of television cameras, including those from the three big networks—ABC, CBS, and NBC—adjusted their lenses. Reporters flipped out notebooks and glanced at their watches, already worrying about early-run deadlines.

The six commissioners, a few rosy-cheeked after walking back from a quick tour of the project site, took their seats. None was a veteran. Two were women, Diane Wolf and Carolyn Deaver. And one was clearly the man in charge: The Honorable J. Carter Brown.

Even if he had but one vote like the others, the clear political clout belonged to Brown, a man who'd been chairman of the committee since 1971. At fifty-three, he was the aristocratic darling of the national arts and intellectual scene. *U.S. News & World Report* called him America's "unofficial minister of culture."

A blue-blood graduate of Harvard (summa cum laude), he had a pedigree (Brown University was named for his family, which made the initial endowment for the school). He had a portfolio (the U.S. National Gallery of Art, under his directorship, had made such an accelerated rise that it was now rivaling New York's Metropolitan Museum of Art for exhibitions and donations). And he had a touch of pomposity, once daring to call the U.S. Marine Corps' Iwo Jima Memorial "kitsch." (Tell that to the families of the 6,800 U.S. servicemen who died on that island—to protect, among other freedoms, his right to express his opinion on artistic expression.)

As growing numbers of people settled into their seats, you could make the claim that Brown and I were each captains of our own ships—and, yes, try as I might, I *did* sense that he and his board were the enemy, particularly after reading the *Washington Post* article. I'm not a conspiracy theorist by nature, but I couldn't help but wonder if some sort of fix was in place. I couldn't help but wonder if the board members' minds weren't already made up, and that our testimony today was simply a dog-and-pony show for the press—and a way for Brown to feel he'd "heard from all sides."

I looked at Brown; he looked beyond me and others on our board. He had curly hair, blue eyes, and a suit that fit his lean build well. I wore a black blazer—it was the eighties and women who wanted to appear successful often dressed to look like men—but, in a nod to the woman I was, I completed the ensemble with a knee-length tweed skirt.

Beyond our genders, the two of us were night and day. My father was a farmer; his father was once dubbed by newspapers in 1900 as "the world's richest baby" after the child's father and uncle died within three weeks of each other, legally giving the $10 million family fortune to the kid before he was out of diapers. I'd attended a country school with two in my eighth-grade graduating class; Brown attended boarding schools in England. I'd spent a year in Vietnam, trying to figure out how to save the lives of dying soldiers and innocent civilians. Brown lived so aristocratically that, when a colleague once bought him a Big Mac, he struggled with how to open its wrapper. "Carter was mystified by the packaging," the colleague told the *Washington Post*. "It was like we'd just landed on a space station."

And yet nobody could deny the respect and power he wielded in the arts world. Meanwhile, who was I? Not a Washington, D.C., insider. Not a legislator. Not a professional fundraiser. Not anyone with notable experience in trying to get buy-in from the likes of The Honorable J. Carter Brown and his commission. But here I was, playing David to Brown's Goliath.

Promptly at 10:00 a.m., Brown called the meeting to order. A tenseness settled over the crowd. After some ancillary business, board member Frederick Hart recused himself from voting because he'd been the artist who had created the Three Servicemen statue opposite the Wall.; however, he said, he was happy to offer his testimony if "that was the pleasure of other commission members."

I couldn't imagine how it possibly should be. If Hart had a conflict of interest, which he clearly did, why would the commission allow testimony that clearly could influence their decision as a board? Isn't that the point of declining to be involved, to avoid prejudicing the others by your bias? But, as my eyes widened, Brown and the others quickly agreed that his testimony was more than welcome. You could hear the whispers among our rank and file. It was as if a judge had sustained an attorney's objection of a witness's testimony—but allowed the jury to consider that testimony nonetheless. Bad start.

To begin hearing people's views, Chairman Brown called for the reading of some written testimony in favor of the project. The letter was read from Hodel, the Secretary of the Interior, ending with: "I, therefore, am recommending that this commemorative statue, representing all women who served in Vietnam, be added to the Vietnam Veterans Memorial."

At that last line, the pride among the women at the hearing was almost palatable. But when I looked for similar signs of encouragement from the commissioners, I saw none. Their expressions were less animated than the faces on Mt. Rushmore. Brown's eyes seemed to scan the rim of the ceiling, not us. To him, I was some woman fresh from the cornfields, the female version of Jimmy Stewart in the movie *Mr. Smith Goes to Washington*. In short, I didn't belong in his rarefied circles.

He gave the floor to one of our founding board members, Donna-Marie Boulay; an attorney, it was her persuasiveness that had convinced Senator Dave Durenberger (R-Minnesota) to back our effort. After introductory remarks, she alluded to the Three Servicemen statue.

"What we see, as do our families and our friends, is a missing element. We yearn to see a statue with which we can identify, which will speak our history, our contributions, while eloquently depicting who we are, what we did, which will symbolize our spirit, our roles as listener, nurturer, healer, patron, will tell future generations that women served."

Donna-Marie had nailed it. My confidence level rose. One by one, those favoring the memorial offered their support. Among them,

Durenberger; our executive director, Suzanne Mills-Rittman; sculptor Rodger Brodin, whose statue prototype we planned to use; and our landscape architect, Elliot Rhodeside, who pointed out that our design effort had been "to integrate the statue into its context with dignity in a simple, compatible way."

Then I was up. I was more primed than nervous. In some ways, I'd been waiting four years to say this. I introduced myself as co-chair of the project and a Vietnam veteran who was "privileged to have served my country." I focused my argument on how women's contributions to U.S. military efforts had been virtually ignored for centuries. "After viewing the memorials in Washington, D.C., one might conclude that women played little or no part in building our nation," I said. "That was wrong."

"I am reminded of President Lincoln's Gettysburg Address in which he spoke of the nation's need to honor both the living and the dead." And, at Civil War's end, of "the need to bind up the nation's wounds, with 'malice toward none and with charity for all.' That need to bind a nation's wounds will never be fulfilled until America officially honors all of the veterans of the Vietnam era—the living and the dead; the man and the woman."

By the time I took my seat, the commission's secretary had begun reading the names of members of Congress who wanted their support for the project noted: Senators Nancy Kassebaum, Robert Dole, Barbara Mikulski, Rudy Boschwitz, and Alan Cranston; and Congressmen Steve Gunderson, Bruce Vento, Lane Evans, and Vin Weber. The stack of support buoyed my spirits.

But when chairman J. Carter Brown regained the floor, he did so with an air of perfunctory relief, as if now that they'd gotten us out of the way they could get on to what really mattered. The six people on the board had accorded none of us even a token smile. And Brown continued to lift his eyes to the ceiling as he talked, as if he were literally above us. At times, his voice would drop and his eyes close, as if so enthralled with his own thoughts that nothing else mattered. When he later weighed in on the issue, one of his *sentences* rambled on for 202 words, its specific point lost in translation but its general thrust crystal clear: he opposed our statue.

This wasn't only my perception, but that of others in attendance. "His tone," remembered Col. Jane Carson, "was sarcastic, belittling, like: *Why are you wasting my time on such an insignificant matter?*"

Hart was first up. I was incredulous that he was being allowed to speak and have his testimony considered. I settled back with a sense of resignation. Sure enough, he wasted little time in stating he was strongly opposed to the memorial, that it would disrupt—specifically, "demolish"—the "fragile balance" of the Wall and the Three Servicemen statue he, of course, had created.

Wait. Did he say "demolish?" The hypocrisy of his argument was as obvious as the Washington Monument. The sky would fall if a women's memorial were added but the sculpture of three men he created wondrously complemented the Wall.

Then came Robert Doubek, co-founder of the Vietnam Veterans Memorial Fund. As tended to be his style, he immediately reminded the audience of his great importance. He and the other two men responsible for the Wall had been "nominated for a congressional gold medal in April of eighty-five. In further recognition, I, along with Mr. Scruggs and Mr. Wheeler, was pictured in the cover story in the *National Geographic* in May of 1985."

And exactly what did this have to do with our memorial, our topic today?

He went on to exalt the power of the Wall, something of which nobody in the room, myself included, needed convincing; it was a magnificent monument. Perfect, in fact.

Once he reluctantly left the subject of himself, Doubek got to his point. "If something ain't broke," he said, "you don't fix it." To allow the women's memorial, he said, was to open a "Pandora's box" of requests for figurative sculpture from other groups such as "Native Americans, aliens, Orientals, Slavs, and Arabs."

Seriously?

"The main argument for adding a sculpture of an Army nurse appears to be the majority who served in that occupation were women," Doubek said. "Granted that gender is probably the most basic human distinction and that our society is very sensitive, and rightly so, to gender bias, but can anyone really argue in good faith that the Memorial misrepresents truth or history because there is no sculpture of a woman? Can that woman identify with the flag, can that woman identify with the uniform? Cannot women see themselves reflected in that wall of names, and, indeed, the inscription at the top of the Wall that says, on the top line, 'In honor of the Men and Women of the Armed Forces?'"

We had no qualms with that whatsoever; on its own, the Wall, which included the names of eight women who'd died serving in Vietnam, was just as he said it was: dedicated to both men and women. But, like Hart, what Doubek conveniently ignored was the addition of the Three Servicemen statue. All men. Instead, he argued that our memorial would be illegal—never mind that the Secretary of the Interior, in his statement read only moments before, had clearly stated it was perfectly legal—and would, if approved, set a dangerous precedent. Better that the women confine their monuments to the "all-women memorial" that the Women in Military Service for America was planning to place in front of Arlington National Cemetery someday, he suggested.

For Doubek, as for so many others, when the political smoke cleared, here's the truth: this was a turf war, plain and simple. We were intruding on their masculine spot. This was, I had been told, the most prestigious ground in America, so I could just take my "big idea" elsewhere.

Architect Kent Cooper testified that the women's memorial would "open the floodgates…to the proliferation of statuary." He wondered if a plaque might be more appropriate. A letter in opposition to our memorial was read from the Vietnam Veterans Memorial designer Maya Lin. No surprise there; she'd long opposed any addition to the memorial she had designed, including the Three Servicemen statue. "I cannot see where it will all end," she wrote.

Finally, came a sharply worded letter from Secretary of the Navy Jim Webb, himself a decorated Vietnam veteran, which only compounded my disappointment in his stance. "There will never be an addition of another statue at the Vietnam Veterans Memorial," he wrote. "All these special-interest groups want statues, including the K-9 Corps."

Ouch. Women being compared to dogs? And why, exactly, were women a "special-interest" group, but men weren't?

By now, my optimism was ebbing. After four years of dusk-to-dawn work, it was painful to watch people write us off as not only unworthy of honor, but of being guilty of threatening to ruin the memorial already there.

Still, I reminded myself, the commission itself hadn't weighed in—and, they, not anybody else, had the final say. Hart's decision to recuse himself from voting meant five people would decide our fate. Two were women. If Carolyn Deaver and Diane Wolf sided with us, we could still get approval provided at least one of the three men backed us. Brown, obviously, wasn't going to be *that* vote; from the get-go, his body language and words were tinged with a going-through-the-motions hue that bordered on disrespectful.

Before taking the vote, Brown asked his fellow commissioners for their views. Neil Porterfield said he feared that the proposed women's memorial—three hundred feet from the Wall and tucked in a grove of trees—would destroy the dynamics of the Wall and not accomplish what we'd hoped for. *Our memorial would barely be seen from the Wall.* The memorial, he said, was unnecessary as a means of "healing" the wounds from Vietnam. *And he, of course, knew what we needed better than those of us who were actually there in Vietnam and there when our country shunned us upon our return.*

Carolyn Deaver said she initially disagreed with adding Hart's statue but had since come to believe that it enhanced the memorial. But now "it should be left as is." *And why, exactly, did the men's statue enhance while ours would detract?*

When Diane Wolf announced her opposition, it hit me: We were doomed. It was over. And our salt-in-the-wound penalty was having to listen to Chairman Brown prattle on, knowing he already had enough votes to ensure the outcome he wanted. Only moments after agreeing with another architect, Joe Brown, that a simple plaque would be best, he dared to say our proposed memorial had the feel of an "afterthought, sort of a put-down, almost a ghettoization" of women. *And a plaque wouldn't?* Never mind that those of us pushing for the memorial found it evocative, noble, and honorable—Brown apparently knew better than us what was good for us and what was not.

Then, with no apparent sense of how condescending it was, Brown hammered home Webb's point about statue proliferation—using yet another dog reference. Everybody wants a memorial, he suggested; "the Park Service has even heard from the Scout Dog Associations."

I was tempted to stand and shout "enough," my inner child wanting to let the school-girl me kick the bully in the shins. Instead, I bent forward and buried my face in my hands. Brown's subjectivity was particularly telling when, after finishing with his long-winded testimony, he realized he'd forgotten about the final commission member, Roy Goodman.

"Roy, I am sorry," he said, "I forgot to ask whether you had any comments."

The irony is that Goodman, left for last, actually *did* have comments—and he was on our side. He was the son of a World War II vet who'd been chief of surgery at Mobile Operational Naval Air Bases and had grown up with a deep appreciation for the contributions women had made in war. "I have been profoundly moved by the presentation that has been made by the group in favor of this project," he said. "Since ours is a business of making difficult decisions, I would...vote in favor of inclusion of what I regard as a deeply moving and, in the total balance, highly appropriate memorial in recognition of the real role of women in the Vietnam War."

If he'd apparently absolved himself of guilt for forgetting about Goodman, Brown seemed unimpressed by his colleague's stance. Porterfield, perhaps sensing that Goodman's gutsy testimony might inspire others to reconsider and flop, hurriedly made a motion.

"I move that we disapprove this proposal for the Vietnam Veterans Memorial."

"Second," said Deaver without hesitation.

The vote was taken. It was four-to-one. Just like that, the hearing was over. We'd lost.

When the meeting adjourned, I was too numb to notice much around me. Only later would Jane Carson tell me that she'd worked her way through the tangle of people to find me leaning against a wall, head down. Probably so. I don't remember. What I do remember is walking down the steps of the Commission of Fine Arts building and onto the sidewalk, feeling somehow betrayed by my country—again. Women had spent a year in the blood and mud of Vietnam, and this was their thank you from a board almost devoid of the empathy to see a memorial through anybody's eyes but their own?

"Excuse me," came a male voice from behind me. "Ms. Evans, can I get a word with you?"

I turned around to see a TV news reporter I immediately recognized. It was Sam Donaldson, ABC's White House correspondent. He had a microphone in hand and a cameraman at his side.

"Mrs. Evans, given the rejection by the Commission of Fine Arts, what's it going to take now to get a statue of women at the Vietnam Memorial?"

I paused momentarily. "Well, one of two things," I said. "Either an Act of Congress or an Act of God."

And I would be right.

PART V: REFUSING TO DIE

Perhaps, after all, the best that we who were left could do was to refuse to forget, and to teach our successors that we remembered in the hope that they, when their own day came, would have more power to change the state of the world than this bankrupt, shattered generation. If only, somehow, the nobility which in us had been turned towards destruction could be used in them for creation, if the courage which we had dedicated to war could be employed by them, on behalf of peace, then the future might indeed see the redemption of man instead of his further descent into chaos.

—Vera Brittain, *Testament of Youth*

17

Second Storm

For the first time since the project began, I cried. Cried a lot. Huge buckets of tears while sitting in my hotel room with board member Evangeline Jamison, who did the same. We had come so far, and our triumph had seemed so close. Now this. The commission ruled against our statue proposal and denied us the site as well.

"I'm dumbfounded," she said. "They didn't listen to a word we said."

"Nope. Their minds had been made up long ago. That wasn't a hearing; it was a 'get-back-to-where-you-belong-women' response."

I exhaled. "It wasn't their job to decide if we were worthy of the site," I said. "The site was already ours, based on the legislation for the Vietnam Veterans Memorial. It clearly states the ground is for the men and women who served in the Armed Forces of the Vietnam War. That's us. We were good enough to serve in Vietnam, but not good enough to be represented like the men. In fact, the implication was that we would harm what was already there."

"I know. They warned that we would—what was the word Hart used?—*demolish* the fragile balance of the Wall and the soldiers."

"And, correct me if I'm wrong, but did they not compare us to *dogs*?"

"Twice."

"We paid the price for the Wall controversy," I said.

"How so?"

"Don't you see? For the beating the commission took over the Wall and the addition of the Three Servicemen statue, which they ardently opposed. Watt overruled their no-statue decision. Crammed it down their throats. No way were they going through that humiliation again. And so, I think to protect themselves, to protect their pride, they threw us under the bus."

Outside, horns honked. The incessant whir and whoosh of cars continued. The heater in our room hummed. Inside, all I could suddenly hear were chopper blades and that last soldier pleading not to leave and the voice of that cocky kid in the airport telling "soldier girl" to "carry her own damn bag."

"Jamie, it doesn't matter how far away from Vietnam I get, I can never outrun it. Or the way things were when we got back. Ever since I stepped foot in D.C., I've felt scorned. I'm either stepping on land mines or trying to avoid them. Second-class. A whiner grabbing for something that isn't mine. And guess what? It *isn't* mine. It's *ours*. It's every woman who helped the cause in Vietnam and not only never got thanked but sometimes has been denigrated."

For many female vets, the four-year journey had been like this huge hope of rescue after finding ourselves thrashing about in turbulent post-war waters not of our choosing. We were drowning and suddenly saw, in the distance, this little life raft: our memorial. We started swimming frantically for it—or at least those who already hadn't gone under. Closer. Closer. Closer. We were almost there. Almost there. We reached for the gunnel and—whap—someone from inside took an oar and rapped our hands. We fell back into the water and sunk into the liquid abyss, hurt, disoriented, not even sure which direction we needed to go to find the surface.

Slowly, in the weeks and months to come, we got re-oriented. But we were once again alone, out in the middle of the ocean, treading water. And now the raft was only a tiny spot on the horizon.

The *Washington Post*, naturally, lauded the commission's decision. An editorial branded the project's proposal a "bad precedent that would bring agitators out of the woodwork" and "promote similar efforts by ethnic groups, from individual services, and others representing specialties or units within the service."

Under the headline "Feminists used Vietnam dead, nurses for own ends," a *St. Louis Post-Dispatch* columnist, Bill McClellan, wrote: "The statue of a nurse has more to do with a cause—the feminist movement—than it does with nursing." In fact, he said, it has "almost nothing to do with Vietnam." *Time* magazine headlined its opposition to our memorial: *A memorial too many.* Its writer referred to our proposed statue as the "intruding nurse."

Others were outraged. Women veterans were astounded that an "art" commission had taken it upon itself to arrogantly decide that women's healing process had been completed by the addition of the Wall. And that J. Carter Brown had decreed that the three male figures were already "symbolic of humankind and everyone who served." A letter-writer to the *New York Times* termed the proliferation-of-memorial argument as "specious," "specifically sexist," and "an insult to the women of all the services. Women are not an 'ethnic' or 'specialty' group."

The *Boston Globe* backed the memorial: "It is on its own merits that the Vietnam Women's Memorial Project deserves support. As the project's staff notes, to this day 'many women have never told their friends, colleagues, or even loved ones about their tour of duty in Vietnam.' They were young, most in their early 20s, and if the nation did not understand—or fully accept—the experiences of the young men who served in Vietnam, even less did it understand the experiences of the young women who served with them, in a war that had no front lines and in which were no safety, and no shelter from its horrors."

The VWMP circulated an open letter through veterans' publications, chiding the Commission for ignoring the wishes of thousands of American citizens and their elected representatives; for having not a single vet on its commission; and for violating the legislative mandate to review the *artistic* merits of monuments because "they didn't question the artist and made little reference whatsoever to the artwork." They focused on the location and that women didn't belong at the Vietnam Veterans Memorial any more than the eight names on the Wall. We had to be dead to get there.

We knew, of course, that the commission in general, and Brown in particular, disapproved of Rodger Brodin's *Nurse*. "The poor nurse looks like she's about to up-chuck in her helmet," he told a reporter.

Another statement by him wouldn't come out in the *Los Angeles Times* for another two years, but Brown's sentiments were already clear by October 1987: "The poor sculptor got assured (by the women) that whatever he did would automatically be plunked down there. He came and testified and seemed a reasonable type. I don't know that they are stuck having the same artist. We try to focus attention on these memorials, not just a group in Minnesota."

Clearly, Brown saw us as a bunch of hicks from "Minne-no place" who had no business *foisting* what we thought was art on *their* lawns. All he saw that day at the hearing was a bunch of presumptuous women daring to think we knew what art was. He didn't see what this was all about: The sacrifices in Vietnam. The pain of coming home to a country that turned its back on us. The small sliver of honor that would help us unite and heal.

The four no-vote commissions, seemingly devoid of empathy, never saw the deeper meaning of the memorial. "The monument," explained American social philosopher and architecture critic Lewis Mumford about such symbols in general, "is a declaration of love and admiration to the higher purposes men hold in common."

We believed in Rodger's piece of art. And we believed in Rodger, who was a gentle giant, benevolent, a man of integrity without whom we never would've gotten this far. But as we collected ourselves and talked about where to go from here, we began to doubt whether his *Nurse* would ever be approved by the Commission of Fine Arts. And we would have to go through the commission again. On the other hand, I'd come to believe something else: the commission's job wasn't to rule on any particular site for our memorial, just whether whatever memorial we chose was appropriate for that site. True, the Commission of Fine Arts would still have a voice in this matter. But how strong would that voice be if we attained a congressional mandate granting the site?

"I think we need to go for a site by going to Congress," I told the board, "and worry about the actual memorial later." There was only one site where we belonged: on the grounds of the 2.2-acre Vietnam Veterans Memorial. The names on that wall, the men represented by that statue—those were our brothers and sisters, in war and in peace.

Some board members disagreed. "We've been given nothing," said one. "Let's take what we can get."

"And what's that?" I asked. "A nice little plaque? Let's not take what we can get, let's take what we *deserve*."

One of the hardest lessons I'd learned since I'd joined this fight was that to get what you want, you have to play politics; it's what got us that second-day hearing at the Veterans of Foreign Wars convention in Dallas. It's what got us lots of our gains, even if we'd strived to take the high road, to be ethical, in doing so.

The media seemed weighted slightly against us. While we had gotten some support, *The New York Times* and *Boston Globe* foremost among it, editorial headline after editorial headline barked, "Leave the memorial alone." Among the more pompous responses came from *The Indianapolis News*, which editorialized that adding the women's memorial was like "painting the Statue of Liberty in Day-Glo pink" or "adding Elvis Presley's visage to Mount Rushmore." Another huffed that we must resist "trinkets, tacky lawn ornaments" at the Wall. If I'd already felt disenfranchised, as if women were the snubbed daughters of the Vietnam War, this response wasn't helping. Congress was still our last, best hope.

I knew we were in for a long, tough fight and, while not starting over, had to redirect our efforts in a handful of ways, some involving personnel, some involving publicity, and some involving leverage. To the latter end—and in relation to the God-or-Congress comment I'd made to ABC's Sam Donaldson after our defeat with the Commission of Fine Arts—it was time to start lobbying legislators at the national level. Congress seemed like the more practical choice for our immediate needs.

Less than a month after our commission defeat, we'd convinced Senator Dave Durenberger (R-Minnesota), who'd worked with us to get the Secretary of Interior's support to introduce a bill in the Senate. Meanwhile, Representative Sam Gejdenson (D-Connecticut) agreed to introduce a bill in the House authorizing the building of a Vietnam Women's Memorial at the Vietnam Veterans Memorial. Senator Alan Cranston (D-California) and others quickly followed suit. On May 7, 1988, the board decided to move our office to where our future work would be centered.

We moved our headquarters from Minnesota to Washington, D.C., and set up an office, thanks to the help of Vietnam Veterans of America. We went through two executive directors in five months before hiring Diana Hellinger, a former National Organization of Women Legal Defense Fund staffer, to take the helm as executive director. She had the right skills at the right time and was in her element—an efficient multitasker who understood Washington, D.C., had good intuition, and the political savvy—and personality—to influence decisions. I loved working with her. We found insiders, many of them within the veteran's service organizations, who could coach us on how to maximize our lobbying efforts, and we went to work on a legislative push to reach our goal. In short, we went back to work with renewed resolve, but with slightly different approaches.

On the public relations front, we broadened our efforts to gain support from a wider swath of the public. Thus far, we had a strong infrastructure of dependable, reliable, and enthusiastic volunteers working untold hours who'd helped us get endorsements from forty national organizations. But, in our earlier efforts to appeal to nurses and women in particular, we'd limited our reach. New strategies to target the broader public were needed.

To that end we established a new national advertising campaign featuring dog tags, each imprinted with a woman's name: "Not all women," it said, "wore love beads in the '60s"—with Brodin's statue, small, at the bottom of the ad. It was unanimous among our board to place on the tags the name of our board member Evangeline Jamison, who'd served in three wars as an Army Nurse. On the reverse side was space for seventy-five signatures that could be sent to Congress. The effort was astonishingly successful, posters being sent to D.C. from shopping malls, veterans' clubs, nurses' organizations, and others. In D.C., Congress's postal people finally said: "Enough. You've made your point."

On the home front, I committed virtually any time not working on the memorial to my children and, occasionally, to Mike—with one exception. I started running. I had to do something for myself—I'd already given up quilting and sewing—that I could do alone and at five in the morning before getting the kids off to school. I could get exercise, fresh air, and think all at the same time.

Meanwhile, life was a memorial/child balancing act—sometimes the juxtaposition painfully difficult, sometimes laugh-out-loud funny. Once, I was on the phone to Charlie Atherton, the Secretary of the Commission on Fine Arts, when Jon-Erik, just off the school bus, rushed into my office from the across-the-hall laundry room.

"Mom, mom!" he said, "There's a chipmunk clunking around and around in the dryer and it really stinks!"

I placed my hand over the receiver.

"Jon-Erik, *shhhush*, I'm on an important call."

I went on talking to Charlie as smoothly as if nothing had happened. Getting off the phone and working with Jon-Erik to remove the poor little critter brought me back to reality and kept me humble. My most important work was not in D.C. It was right there at that moment with my youngest son.

In early 1988, I redoubled my efforts on the speaking circuit, flying out of, and into, the Minneapolis-St. Paul International Airport so often I was on a first-name basis with the folks at the gate. In the two years prior, I'd either spoken at, or been part of, 113 events in Wisconsin, Colorado,

Texas, Louisiana, Minnesota, Indiana, Montana, Iowa, Michigan, California, New York, Ohio, Illinois, Kentucky, Mississippi, Maryland, New Jersey, and Washington, D.C. Mike and the kids, who should have mutinied by this point, kept encouraging me.

"Don't give up," he said.

His encouragement and the same from many of the wonderful board members kept me going. There's an adage that if you don't care who gets the credit, you can get a lot done. But I also learned that if you don't take the credit you deserve and also give credit to those other deserving people, someone else will gladly take it. Give credit where it is earned and deserved, or deceit and betrayal may replace it.

By now, my mother was with us often, watching the kids, and I was on my third or fourth mouth guard. I was losing weight—Mike was worried—and gaining a worrisome sense that, despite our redirection, maybe not everyone on the board was in step with the others. But I couldn't worry about that; there were planes to catch and piano recitals to watch when I came home and planes to catch and tennis matches to watch when I came home and planes to catch and planes to catch and planes to catch....

For four years, we'd been fending off resistance from the outside—the Commission of Fine Arts, the press, the haters who phoned with death threats, a founder of the Vietnam Veterans Memorial, and the like. Now, just as we were mustering a reorganization, an attack came from an unlikely place: within our board.

Over the years a board member had quietly launched a power grab that backfired when she authorized a six-digit payment without board approval, a clear policy violation. For this reason and many others, volunteers threatened a mutiny unless she was removed. Rodger threatened to quit if she wasn't removed. The board asked for her resignation; when she refused, she was let go. She fired back with a multi-page letter telling me—as she would later tell members of Congress—that under my leadership, we would fail to get the memorial approved.

This was not what we needed. The press picked up the story with zeal—infighting among women!—and I feared it could hurt us all on sorts of fronts: the general public, the Senate and House that would soon be deciding on our bills, and the leadership of our team.

Two lawsuits sprung up—one by her, one by me—and were quickly dropped. I got a rap on the knuckle from the House Subcommittee on Libraries and Memorials, which was concerned that—given that six-figure authorization without board approval—we weren't watching our dollars carefully enough. And when I reached out to Durenberger, the Minnesota senator who'd worked closely with the woman we'd let go, he wasn't happy. We'd done what we knew to be right to restore trust on our board. But that didn't mean others—people who didn't know all that we knew and to whom we couldn't, for legal reasons, be totally forthcoming—would necessarily see it the same way.

All we could do was let the proof be in the pudding—to show people that, despite this aggravating twist, we'd operated with integrity, spent donors' money wisely, and kept our eye on the prize: a memorial for women who'd served in Vietnam. No volunteer or board member was making a cent on this venture. We simply wanted women to get the long-overdue honor they deserved.

Not everyone was convinced. At home, I got late-night phone calls from people who had no idea what was going on but in the absence of information, assumed the worst—particularly of me.

"You," said one such caller, "are nothing but whale shit."

I felt like I'd been kicked by a horse. She was a dedicated volunteer whom I respected. I was open to criticism if it was constructive. But how would this help our efforts? A friend had turned foe. She wasn't the only one. Our family was driving in our blue minivan as I read a letter from one of our board volunteers who resigned. It was vicious. I burst into tears. I don't think my children had ever seen me in tears. Guy, my oldest, looked at the letter.

"Mom," he said, "she's full of crap."

I smiled, then started laughing. I tried to hold to the edict suggesting you should listen intently to those you respect at a deep level—I had been doing so—and ignore the rest. This was more difficult. I'd never been closer to simply waving the white flag and saying: *Enough. You win.* I was human, and despite the armor I had put up, I could be easily hurt. Discovering that some board members had allowed their personal egos to blur their focus on our goal threw me off kilter. I hadn't expected it.

One night, agitated after another such call, I lay next to Mike, unable to sleep.

"What's wrong?" he asked.

"That's it," I said. "I'm done."

"You can't quit now. What about all those women vets who are waiting for that memorial? Diane, you're so close."

I hated him for saying that. And loved him all the more.

If he had said, "The kids and *I* need you more, give it up," I would have.

18

Resurgence

June 1988–April 1990

One year. Two major crises. One external—defeat at the hands of the Commission of Fine Arts. One internal—betrayal at the hands of a board member. We needed to revamp our leadership team with an emphasis on trust, review our financial controls, and restore our sense of mission. By the end of July 1988, I was the sole remaining original person left from the VWMP's founding board of directors in 1984. New directors had come on board who were strong allies, and together we forged ahead.

"Nurses Face Monumental Frustration" was the headline in a 1989 *Los Angeles Times* story on us. "More Trouble for Vietnam Women's Memorial" was one in the *Army Times*.

In some ways, it was like starting all over again. But that was only from the standpoint of getting approval. We'd built a solid base of grassroots support and, perhaps most importantly, learned some critical lessons through the school of hard knocks.

If you read books on leadership or start-up businesses, you know such scenarios are far more often the rule than the exception—the common denominator, of course, being people. Surprise: we're fallible. Two people can start out with the same goals but wind up with vastly different opinions about where the organization has been, where it currently is, and where it needs to go. But as the leaves turned yellow, orange, and red in the fall of 1988, I sensed a new resolve to finish what we had begun.

We expanded our board, which upped our energy levels, broadened our skill sets, and sharpened our perspectives. We redoubled our fundraising efforts and were relieved to find that people still believed in us. By the end of the year, donations would reach $500,000. We made the transformation to a new computer technology—my mother volunteered to buy our first computer—which made it easier for us to do our newsletters and brochures. And, with the ship once again steadied, we resumed our lobbying efforts for the final push by testifying time and again at congressional hearings. For the first time we had boots on the ground in Congress.

The resistance continued in the congressional hearings. As I attended behind-the-scenes staff meetings and testified at hearing after hearing—I would ultimately do so at more than thirty—I realized I'd come a long way from my first talks at the River Falls American Legion Post and Lion's Club meeting at a hometown restaurant. Now I was speaking in the hallowed chamber of the United States Senate and House of Representatives.

"Who decides who America will remember?" I asked the Senate in 1988.

These hearings could be contentious, which was challenging enough, but we were also dealing with fallout from our internal turmoil. Mary Stout, President of Vietnam Veterans of America, had gotten behind the effort early on, the first veterans' organization to vote in full support of the memorial. When I learned that, due to the retaliation from a member of our staff, I'd been scratched from a speakers list, she gave up her seat for me at a hearing.

Back in February 1988, we had testified on our bill before the Senate Subcommittee on Public Lands, National Parks, and Forests. The committee's reaction was supportive—Senator Dale Bumpers (D-Arkansas) argued that it's critical for children to view the women's statue at the "healing place"—and they had sent our bill, now changed to SJ 2042, to the full Senate. When the Senate, in June, passed the bill ninety-six to one—only Daniel J. Evans (R-Washington) voted against it—we were encouraged, even if some cynics suggested it was an election year and nobody would dare oppose a monument honoring women.

Encouraged, but not ecstatic. That's because the bill was as significant for what it *did not* say as for what it did: it did not say that the memorial had to be a *statue* or had to be *at the Vietnam Veterans Memorial.* After considerable bickering between the Senate and the House about whose bill would take precedent and what, exactly, it would say, we unhappily settled for a watered-down version in November 1988. Public Law 100-660 would authorize "the Vietnam Women's Memorial Project to establish a memorial on federal land in the District of Columbia or its environs to honor women of the Armed Forces of the United States who served in the Republic of Vietnam during the Vietnam era."

Behind the scenes, members of Congress would not commit themselves to a statue per se, nor would they specify the Mall site, which is where the Wall was situated. Already weary of the fight, some of the new board members were pushing for us to take PL 100-660—President Reagan signed it on November 15, 1988—and call it good.

"It's a bird in a hand," I was told. "It's ours. Done. Signed."

"It's better than nothing," added someone else.

I wrote a statement to the board about why we shouldn't give up on the mission: a statue. Two board members resigned immediately. Their bitter and lengthy letters accused me of being "rigid" and thinking I knew more than the commissioners knew and that I was deceiving the public by fighting for an unattainable goal. They lost faith in me because they said they weren't wed to a statue and, thanks to me, we would wind up with nothing.

Part of me understood. We were all tired. We could rationalize that we'd won and go take a vacation. Learn our children's names again. Go to a parent-teacher conference without looking at our watches. But deep in my soul, I disagreed with the something's-better-than-nothing choice. We had come too far, battled too hard, and—most significantly—would be settling for too little. For me, this was a fall-on-our-sword issue. In my thinking, we'd only accepted the watered-down version as a placeholder to buy us time to get what we'd worked for all along: a statue near the Wall of names.

I guess I was "rigid," but all of the resolutions and national endorsements by more than forty organizations supporting the VWMP mission still read "statue." We had not changed course and asked those invested in a statue for a memorial design if they would accept something else.

I wasn't interested in a plaque in Foggy Bottom or—however honorable—at WIMSA's Arlington location, which worked against our desire to stand visibly with our Vietnam brethren; I wanted women to take their rightful place among the nearly fifty-eight thousand service men and women remembered on the Wall, and near the Three Servicemen honoring the men who had survived. And I had envisioned a *portrayal of women*, not some plaque or rose garden or bench. Nearly a decade after the war had ended and five years since we had started our campaign, was that too much to ask for? Not a tickertape parade. Not roses. Not praise. Simply a sliver of American soil upon which would stand a memorial to every woman who'd served in this dreadful war, a rallying point, a healing place. One little spot that said: *remember these women*.

By now, trust and mistrust had emerged as major themes in this battle; we'd seen that within our own camp and with the Commission of Fine Arts. If the language in the bill allowed for wiggle room, I didn't trust for a moment that when our proposal reached the Commission of Fine Arts again, J. Carter Brown and his board would grant us what we wanted. Instead, they'd try to throw us a bone with hopes we'd simply go away. They'd try to give us *what they think we needed*, which is exactly what we heard from them in Round One.

Brown was already on record as saying we'd be better off finding a spot at WIMSA in front of Arlington National Cemetery and had mentioned at the hearing that a plaque might be more appropriate. No, the bill had to stipulate "statue" *on the grounds of the Vietnam Veterans Memorial*. We had to figure out a new route to find a memorial that would appease the arts commission. First, however, we needed to find a location.

Maybe it was latent optimism from my growing up on a farm—the faith that if you plant a seed, it will ultimately bear fruit. Maybe it was my latent optimism that the most badly wounded soldier was going to pull through. But deep inside, I was holding out for some eleventh-hour miracle that might galvanize the nation to our cause and influence Congress to give us the final push we needed.

Somewhere amid flurries of meetings, phone calls, and lobbying, I heard the quiet voice of my mother: *Nothing comes easy.* As I dug in on this, the remaining board members decided they would, too. We'd go for the original plan: a statue on the grounds of the Vietnam Veterans Memorial. And our key to making that happen wasn't about strong-arming this senator or that congressman to vote our way, we decided. The key was getting our story told; if we could do that, the public would get behind us, put pressure on Congress, and we'd get the votes we needed. That was the hope.

On the publicity front, we got some attention when the fledgling TV series, *China Beach*, contacted me in 1989 and said they were looking for real women veterans of the Vietnam War to participate in the program. The idea was to do interviews with women who had actually been in Vietnam and interweave their true stories with a fictional episode of the show.

Frankly, I hadn't been a fan of the ABC series, even though people kept telling me I looked like Dana Delany, the actress who played nurse Lt. McMurphy. My father loved the show. I tried, but I couldn't watch it exploit our service with so much emphasis on sex, booze, and drugs. It was Hollywood, not real life, and didn't capture the Vietnam experience as I'd known it. I was reluctant to participate and asked our board members what they thought. They urged me to go for it and shed some light on how important the actual stories are.

The producers did use many of the stories from the interviews for future programing and some of us appeared on the program to share our stories.

"Only recently have I realized that the American women who served in Vietnam had similar shared traumas on returning to the U.S.," Delany said in introducing the short piece on real-life nurses. "They have had to bear their feelings alone for too long."

I met, and spoke with, Delany at length. She became one of our ardent supporters, traveling to Washington, D.C., several times to help us with fundraising events.

Though we were finally making news, too often the press missed the real story—women who'd sacrificed boldly for their country—and trumpeted the trivial. After our ninety-six-to-one victory in the Senate in June 1988, an Associated Press story in the *Milwaukee Journal* was headlined "Trouble hits statue plan for memorial." Huh? Underneath was a ten-inch story pitting *M*A*S*H* actress Loretta Swit, a.k.a. "Hot Lips Houlihan," as a defender of the statue, against Wall designer Maya Lin, who argued against it, saying it was "a misdirected attempt at tit-for-tat equality for women."

The fog of politics and Hollywood were obscuring deeper things. So, we hired a talented Washington, D.C., publicist, Mary Beth Newkumet, giving her explicit instructions to reach out to the thousands of women across America who had served during the Vietnam Era and have them tell us their stories. The response was phenomenal. Letters and telegrams began pouring in, many with checks attached. Veterans reached out to find nurses who'd helped keep them alive. Children thanked nurses for keeping their daddies alive. Within a few months, the tide of negative press started to slowly shift. Finally, the Red Cross and other civilian women's deeply hidden stories began surfacing and shedding light.

"Diane, it's happening," said Jamie, who'd stuck by my side since joining the board, as we sifted through baskets of heartfelt letters—and an occasional "Go to hell, whiners. You didn't carry a rifle."

"Yes, it is," I said. "The question is: Is it happening fast enough, and broadly enough, to influence Congress?"

"Still looking for that miracle?"

I nodded. A week later, we got it.

The phone call was from a woman with CBS's *60 Minutes*, a news show with one of the highest ratings in television, watched each Sunday night by millions of people across America.

"I'm calling on behalf of Morley Safer, one of our reporters. Is this Diane Evans?

"It is."

"Oh, good. We're exploring the possibility of doing a segment on nurses and their fight to get a memorial—"

"A statue."

"Uh, yes, a *statue* placed in Washington, D.C."

"At the Wall, specifically."

"Er, right, at the Wall. Anyway, we know about the Commission of Fine Arts turning down your request back in 1987. But is it true that the chairman of that commission, J. Carter Brown, compared female nurses to scout dogs?"

"Yes, that would be accurate," I said. "I believe his quote was something to the effect that if females got a statue then everyone would want one, because they'd already heard from the Scout Dogs Association. And another man who opposed the statue compared us to the K-9 Corps."

"Interesting. And can I ask how that made you feel?"

"In a word, *appalled*. I know scout dogs are important, but still—for a woman to be compared to one?"

"Sure, I understand. So, if we go ahead with this segment, would you be willing to be interviewed, and would it be possible for you to help us find a handful of other nurses to interview?"

"Yes, I'll be interviewed, and I'll get you the others."

After saying our goodbyes, I hung up the phone, clenched both fists, and thrust them in the air—even though I was alone at the time. But it was telling that to find four other nurses who would speak, I needed to contact more than twenty. Part of it was many women were not used to speaking in public and, like me, might be plain nervous. Part of it was women who found it simply too painful to talk about Vietnam. And part of it was women who'd been conditioned so long to stay silent that, in a sense, they'd lost their voices.

The episode ran in February 1989. It was called "The Forgotten Veterans" and was reported by Safer, a fifty-seven-year-old journalist who'd been a war correspondent in Vietnam and seen nurses in action. It began with graphic film of just that—nurses, medics, and doctors in Nam working feverishly over fresh, bloody, and shattered bodies. In another scene, Dustoff medevac choppers touched down in dangerous landing zones to pick up the wounded.

Safer talked about how well-documented the war in Vietnam had been and yet few knew about the thousands of nurses and other women who had served, many of whom had had just as difficult a time readjusting when they got home as the male soldiers.

The report then cut to me, a woman who didn't even talk to her own military husband about Vietnam and was suddenly going to be talking to millions of people around the world. I was shaking as I told Safer about the day I was just home from Vietnam and went to the feed store, where the clerk shunned me. And how I told my father not to mention to anyone that I'd served in the war. "But," I said, "I still think about Vietnam every day."

Safer talked about our hope to place a statue at the Wall, how we'd been working for nearly six years and hadn't been able to get governmental approval. Then he referred to the Commission of Fine Arts turning us down and J. Carter Brown saying if women were given a statue, what was to keep the Scout Dogs Association from seeking one, too?

He interviewed four other nurses besides me: Linda Schwartz, one of our board members, who was an Air Force nurse whose sister was at Kent State in 1970 when four unarmed college student war protesters were shot and killed by the National Guard; a nurse who was in Vietnam stationed with her infantry husband when a chaplain broke the news that he'd been killed in battle, specifically "his head had been blown off;" and another nurse who talked about the mass casualties, how "we wanted to save them all."

Maggie Arriola, a nurse from Minnesota, told perhaps the most riveting story about a young soldier who'd come from a chopper missing both arms and both legs. A single eye dangled from its socket.

"He said to me, 'I know I don't have any arms or legs, but please tell my mother I love her.' I couldn't stop crying. And then they whisked him off for surgery. I felt guilty all these years because I never even knew his name, so I could never tell his mom."

At one point, Safer showed Brodin's statue and said it seems fitting that women be honored with a memorial because "they saw the war every single day."

When the segment was over, I sat with Mike and the kids stunned. As the program shifted to time zones to the west, hour by hour, it marked the first time in history that the entire country was seeing and listening to female military nurses as they were in Vietnam—and in the aftermath. You can talk until you're blue in the face, but an image of a soldier in a field hospital with an American nurse coolly cutting away his bloody uniform exposing what's left of a leg, wrapping a dressing over a head injury, or holding the hand of a dying patient—that speaks louder.

I ached for the those who'd lost loved ones in Vietnam; the footage and interviews couldn't have been easy for them to see. But I exalted in that, finally, our story was being told. By now, we figured we were going to need an additional $2 million just for the memorial, preparation of the site, and the dedication. After the *60 Minutes* piece, our phone lines lit up with praise, encouragement, and donations. Our mailman complained about his bags having to double in size.

"You know what this means, Jamie?" I asked. "We're going to have to hire more staff."

"That's the best problem we've had in a long time."

"You know what else this means?"

"What?"

"I bet most members of Congress saw that episode—and between their seeing it and letters and phone calls they're going to get from people who saw it, they won't be able to say no to our memorial…at the Wall."

Meanwhile, for months, we heard stories of connection and inspiration because of the episode: other nurses emboldened to speak up because those of us had done so on the show; family members thankful for taking care of their sons; wounded men who recognized a nurse who had been there for them. I heard from one myself—a guy named Bob McDonough who remembered, correctly I might add, how he'd asked for a beer, something not allowed for patients. But I'd hidden one in a pile of sandbags for him, just outside the ward.

"That was me," he said. "Vũng Tàu, 36th Evacuation Hospital, 1968." McDonough now lived in the Bronx. "Thanks. I never forgot that act of kindness."

Not all the stories were uplifting. While suicides among male Vietnam Vets were written about often back in the 1980s and '90s, I never saw a single story about nurses who took their lives, though I had learned of some. But the *60 Minutes* piece triggered letters from families whose loved ones had been women serving in Vietnam—including those who had ultimately committed suicide. Why hadn't we heard about these tragedies? Because obituaries often didn't mention that the deceased woman had served as part of the Vietnam War. Because after coming home from Vietnam, too many veterans blew away in the wind without our nation appropriately drawing attention to, and grieving over, their losses.

That had to change. And we were convinced the statue could be a catalyst for that. In the same way the "Sister Search" was already building bonds between female veterans, so could the statue, and our organization, be connection points for female vets who needed to realize they weren't alone in their grief.

Of all the responses to the *60 Minutes* piece, I found two most memorable.

One was from a man in his forties from Brooklyn who had been listening to the segment because he was blind. Suddenly he was screaming to his wife, "Get in here, get in here! They're talking about me on TV!" His wife raced from the kitchen to the living room, where her husband sat in his wheelchair—because he had no arms and legs.

"I gotta talk to her, I gotta meet her and thank her," he said.

"Who?"

"The nurse in Vietnam who took care of me after I got hit. I heard her talk about me on TV."

Amazing. The man Maggie Arriola had taken care of had lived!

The other memorable response was from J. Carter Brown, who wrote *60 Minutes* and assured them he "never would equate women with canines."

On Halloween Day 1989, the Senate convened to, among other things, consider whether to agree to our stipulation that the statue be located at the Vietnam Veterans Memorial, where the two other monuments were. It was do-or-die time. If we didn't win here, we wouldn't win, period.

Nothing in Washington, D.C., seems permanent. Eight months after the *60 Minutes* piece aired, the Senate, saying it could not dictate design, replaced the word "statue" with the far-broader "memorial," with which none of us was thrilled. We'd have preferred the specific designation; the wording didn't mean the memorial couldn't be a statue, just stipulated that it didn't *have to be* a statue. But having already determined that we couldn't win this fight with Brodin's *Nurse*, we resolved to stay focused and find another memorial design worthy of the women who served—in the spot we preferred, three hundred feet behind the apex of the Wall.

On November 17, 1989, the House followed suit with backing for a "memorial." A week later President George H.W. Bush signed legislation authorizing the placement of a "memorial" to "honor women of the Armed Forces of the United States who served in the Republic of Vietnam during the Vietnam era." In Area I of the Mall. Next, we would have to convince the review agencies that the site be on the grounds of the Vietnam Veterans Memorial since Area I covered acreage outside the 2.2 acres of the Wall site.

Over the next five months we worked with landscape architects and engineers preparing a site selection study and design drawings. We applied for final approvals from the reviewing agencies. In April 1990, with our legislation in hand, the National Capital Memorial Commission and Commission of Fine Arts approved specific sites in Area I for the Vietnam Women's Memorial. There was only one hoop left to jump through: the National Capital Planning Commission, whose hearing was set for the next month.

Finally, when it came time for me to give my testimony at the National Capital Planning Commission, I took a deep breath and, as always, reminded myself this wasn't about me or my speech. It was about them: the women who so deserved this. In my hands, I clutched a ten-page document that I had been up until three in the morning writing and re-writing. When I got up to go to the lectern, I set it down and didn't look at it. After all these years, I knew in my heart what I needed to say, and it was short. I explained our reasoning for the location and our vision for a memorial. I talked of how long we'd fought for this. And I ended with a question that I hoped would seep deep into the soul of every commissioner in the room.

"Is it not of pre-eminent historical and lasting significance to the Nation that women of the Vietnam War saved thousands of lives?" I had practically memorized the Commemorative Works Act. Those words—*"pre-eminent historical and lasting significance to the nation"*—were in the Act. "Our wall of names," I continued, "would be much higher and much wider without the contribution of these very brave women. They deserve to stand on the grounds of the Vietnam Veterans Memorial in near proximity to the Wall."

Finished, I sat down. The room was quiet. The vote was unanimous. Our battle for the site was officially over.

Finally, seven years after I'd taken that ball of clay home, we had won, even if we still had a few hoops to jump through.

"We're celebrating!" said Jamie. She took us to Ruth's Chris Steakhouse and treated us that evening. We were only too happy to share the news with folks sitting near us as Jamie jokingly bragged, "These are all my girls; they all have different fathers." We reveled in a victory that had been a long time coming but now seemed every bit worth the wait.

Now all we needed was a memorial.

In the two years it took from the turndown by the Commission of Fine Arts to approval by Congress, an uncomfortable truth had confronted our board: though we still wanted the memorial to be a statue and though we wished it could be Rodger Brodin's *Nurse*, we had come to believe that could never happen.

We could decry J. Carter Brown's arrogance, we could shake a fist at his condescending attitude, but the reality was that if we wanted our memorial, Brown and his board would never give the greenlight if it was Brodin's work.

"It could be a work of art done by Michelangelo, which it isn't, and it would still detract from the enormous power of the memorial," he said. But that was just a smokescreen. Over time, we'd developed trust with the commission's secretary, Charlie Atherton, who treated us with great respect and was always forthcoming and honest with us.

"Diane," he told me, "I can't say this any more clearly: there's no way the commission is going to approve that piece of art." Behind-the-scenes staff meetings confirmed it.

Though we had launched with every intention of placing Brodin's statue design at the Vietnam Veterans Memorial, there was no *guarantee* it would happen. He understood that. But back in Minnesota, a Minneapolis *Star Tribune* columnist, Doug Grow, came to Rodger's defense, ending his column with a staccato, "He was robbed."

I responded with a letter pointing out that "Rodger Brodin is one of the finest people I know. A Marine Corps Vietnam-era veteran, he cares deeply about vets and it shows in every work of military sculpture he had done. But, given the regulatory hostility, his statue could not be placed."

The Vietnam Women's Memorial Project had backed Brodin's statue 100 percent, I pointed out. But the Commission on Fine Arts couldn't be convinced. "The VWMP was no more able to place a public statue in Washington than it could have put an addition on the White House." I ended my letter with a staccato, "*We* were robbed."

When we first proposed Rodger's statue in 1984, we had no guide-book nor any way of anticipating the tedious regulatory review process for proposed national memorials. Indeed, Congress only enacted the rigorous Commemorative Works Act two years later. Rodger was at our side when we presented our case for his statue in 1987 to the Commission on Fine Arts. And while he testified that he would modify his statue, the Commission rejected our site and design proposal. With regret and deep appreciation for Rodger's talent and dedication, the board decided to sponsor a national design competition.

It seemed like a good idea at the time—and ultimately was. But like seemingly everything else we'd achieved, nothing seemed to come easy.

19

Finding Our Memorial

May 1990–October 1991

As spring became summer in 1991, the quest to find the perfect memorial began. For nearly six months our six-person board, with the counsel of our attorney, Paul Mahon, met with Michael J. Pittas, a professional design competition advisor, and others—artists, veterans, federal agency officials, landscape architects—to establish and fine-tune the criteria for the contest. For starters, we deliberated over what parameters the piece of art could and could not be. For example, the memorial had to be designed to be open and accessible in all seasons and at all hours. It couldn't have a roof or domed structure. It could not visually compete with the Wall; there were size limitations. And "the visitor must know in an instant that these women served during the Vietnam era."

The final "Vietnam Women's Memorial National One-Stage Open Design Competition Program, Design Standards, Rule and Procedures" were approved by all three review agencies: the Commission of Fine Arts, the National Capital Planning Commission, and the National Capital Memorial Commission.

In August 1990, we announced the rules and procedures to govern our competition. The board wanted to be egalitarian in our approach—and arts-savvy in our final selection—so we decided that five of our nine jurists would come from the arts and architecture community. They were Lita Albuquerque, artist, Los Angeles; James Freed, architect, New York City; Craig Hodgetts, architect, Santa Monica; Raquel Ramati, urban designer, New York City; and Martha Schwartz, environmental artist, landscape design, San Francisco. The four Vietnam veterans were me; Rear Adm. Frances Shea Buckley, USN, Ret.; Adm. William J. Crowe Jr., USN, Ret. (11th Chairman, Joint Chiefs of Staff); and Brig. Gen. George B. Price, USA, Ret.

It would be a "blind" competition—jurists would not know the identities of the artists who had designed particular works—and the panel would choose a first-place winner ($20,000), a second-place winner ($10,000), and as many as five honorable mention winners ($1,000 each).

While artists were free to use "any art form" as their memorial, the design needed to "honor women from all branches of the Armed Forces of the United States who served in the Vietnam War."

The rules stipulated that while the Vietnam Women's Memorial Project board was confident this process would provide the desired design, *it was not bound to choose the winner* as the memorial to be placed at the site. The jurists' recommendation was strictly advisory. In essence, we, the board, had the final say.

"The VWMP," the rules read, "...shall make the final decision and shall not be required to, and is under no obligation to, adopt the winning design as the proposed Vietnam Women's Memorial."

For two days, inside the National Building Museum in Washington, D.C., judges perused thirty-inch by forty-inch sketches from 317 entrants. I was as amazed at the diversity of ideas as I was sometimes stunned. I furrowed my brow and tilted my head sideways trying to understand what an eight-foot ball of string had to do with women serving in Vietnam—our many "strands of stories," apparently.

I fell in love with Number 181, named "Vietnam Women's Memorial," a wonderful illustration of a statue of a nurse, a male wounded soldier, a woman holding a lone helmet in her hand gazing up into the sky, and a woman cradling a baby in her arms, amid piles of sand bags. When I studied the drawing, it seemed to me that the artist had either been a nurse in Vietnam or had extra-sensory perception to understand what it had been like for us. It seemed to have been designed to view "in the round"—and every angle offered a different nuance. It had strength, hope, pain, despair, everything we experienced. I could already see it in the grove across from the Wall.

Beyond it and a handful of other statues—one looking like an all-too-familiar rendition of Brodin's "Nurse"—the offerings were modernistic pieces of art that showed little or no correlation to women and war.

At the end of the first day, when the jurists started talking about what they saw as strong possibilities, I was blindsided. The non-veteran jurors were rallying around an entry that said nothing to me about women and war. It was a flat fountain piece that sprayed mist into the air. Aesthetically appealing, yes, but generic, as if it might belong at some civic center, not at the Vietnam Women's Memorial, illuminating the experience of women who had served in Vietnam. I wanted to see courage, honor, respect…not balls of string and sprays of mist.

My fellow vets on the jury agreed. But from what I could tell, only one of the five non-vet jurists weren't particularly taken by "Old Faithful" and its predictable spray of water: Raquel Ramati, the urban designer from New York. During a break I approached her. Like me, she was leaning toward more figurative pieces that, just as the Three Servicemen depicted men at war, showed women at war.

"Raquel," I said, "why are you the only non-vet who *gets* it?"

She smiled. "You don't know this because it wasn't on my resume, but I'm Israeli and served in the Israeli army."

"Oh, my gosh."

"Yeah, you know how it is. I've seen dead bodies in ditches. You and I—we've seen death. It's not that these artists are trying to exclude war, but you don't *get it* unless you were there."

"Why do women have to look like 'mist?'" I asked. "Why can't we be real like the men? Did you see the statue that has three women and a wounded soldier—maybe one of them looking up for a helicopter? She's real. You can see her pain. You can just see the veins in her arm."

"I hear you."

It didn't help matters that in the "three women" design that I, and many other vets, liked, one woman appeared to be holding an injured Vietnamese baby in her arms. Some people could construe that as a political image, something congressional representatives and the Commission of Fine Arts had warned us was off limits. And after our selection, we still had to get approval from that commission, the same group that had thwarted us three years ago.

On the second day, as the discussion continued, someone defended "Mist" by pointing out the artist's suggestion that the light spray depicted "the virtue" of nurses. I could only shake my head in disbelief.

"For me, the mist suggests that women are invisible," said Rear Adm. Frances Shea Buckley, a retired Navy Nurse who had served on the *USS Repose* off the shores of Vietnam. "And doesn't that contradict the whole point of this memorial coming after all these years of women vets being treated as if they'd never existed? As if they weren't there in Vietnam? Didn't serve?"

"How would women begin to relate to that memorial?" asked Adm. William J. Crowe. "I don't see how."

"I agree," I said. "The memorial is about healing. But how is a vet going to feel any sense of that if they have no idea what the memorial is trying to convey? Where's the connection to those whom this memorial honors?"

The design competition criteria also stipulated that "the visitor must know in an instant that these women served during the Vietnam era."

But the jurists seemed unmoved.

"What does this say about who we are and what we did?" I asked.

The other three vets got it. But the non-veterans couldn't be persuaded. "Mist," some jurists decided, was the first-place winner and, to add salt to the wound, the statue of a single woman—one looking strangely similar to Brodin's "Nurse"—was second. In the end, the jury decided to combine them as both first place-winners to appease us veterans with a statue and the non-veterans with abstract art. The illustration portraying three women and a soldier over sandbags only won honorable mention.

My heart sank, my hopes wilted. Why did everything have to be so damn hard? How many times had I felt so close only to be blindsided? How much more could I endure? I went back to my hotel room, devastated, disbelieving, and discouraged. It was as if our desire to be inclusive of non-veterans on the panel had boomeranged, as if we'd created this "fair play" Frankenstein that had turned on us.

My anger wasn't that the rules were being circumvented, that we'd been hoodwinked, that the jurists had been deceitful. No, they'd done their jobs and played by the rules. As a board, we simply hadn't foreseen how differently a civilian might see the memorial compared to a veteran. The artist behind "Mist" had played by the rules of the law, but not the spirit of the law. The spirit that said women and war and service should be the focus of this piece of art, that the piece should "honor women from all branches of the Armed Forces of the United States who served in the Vietnam War." I'm not a literalist—I get nuance, subtly, and metaphor in art—but, as a nurse who'd been there, and in response to the Three Servicemen statue, this offered absolutely no emotional connection whatsoever to my experience. "Mist" seemed comforting but obscure. And wasn't obscurity the opposite of what we were seeking?

But I reminded myself that just as there was a second day at the VFW convention, there was still hope for us here. When our VWMP board convened, we voted unanimously to commit our time and consideration to the artists who had won first place on the competition. We invited them to develop their designs as required by the National Capital Planning Commission (NCPC) and other review agencies. It took several months working together with good faith on both sides.

Since the winning design included a water feature, we were advised to work first with the NCPC to learn if this was feasible, mechanically and otherwise, on the grounds of the Vietnam Veterans Memorial.

Meanwhile, our volunteers from around the country were weighing in about the two choices: neither inspired our people in the least. Most liked the three-women-and-a-wounded man-with-sandbags design, which had won only honorable mention.

"The rules are explicit," I told the board. "The monetary awards must go to the winners chosen by the jury." A few heads nodded. "Now let's wait for the final review from the NCPC. We need to know what they have to say. Then, since it's been made very clear that the jury's choice is only advisory, we will move forward from there."

After its engineering analysis and soil laboratory testing, the NCPC soon ruled that a water feature on the proposed site for the Vietnam Women's Memorial did not meet the fundamental requirements for that location on the Mall. It would require sump pumps, would freeze, and would be inoperable several months of the year. The co-winner's design plan included the single figure of a female statue which did not meet the criteria stipulated in the design competition nor the approval of the VWMF board of directors. Both memorials were out.

It was time to decide where to go from here. The board reviewed the five honorable mentions and by unanimous vote decided to explore the design by Glenna Goodacre, a fifty-one-year-old internationally known sculptor from Santa Fe, New Mexico. The more we studied her sketch, the more we believed it met the design competition criteria.

I called Glenna and told her we were unable to move forward with the co-winners' designs; now we were considering the honorable mentions.

"We're very interested in your illustration and vision for the sculpture. We're wondering, however, if you would be willing to work with us and modify it for our consideration."

"What do you mean?"

"We've been told that the memorial must not make a 'political statement.'"

"What are you referring to?"

"One of the standing women is cradling a baby. Of course, in Vietnam that would mean a Vietnamese baby."

"Right. The Vietnam veteran women I interviewed to get insight and inspiration told me they cared for the wounded and sick children."

"And I would have been one of those women, Glenna. I worked on a burn unit and there were hundreds of them. But GIs had been labeled 'baby killers,' remember? Would you be willing to remove the baby?"

She mulled the question and said yes.

"Could you sculpt a small model, a maquette, and bring it to Washington, D.C., for us to see it three-dimensionally—as a sculpture not a drawing?"

"Of course, and when do you need this by?"

"Two weeks."

"Two *weeks?*"

She was incredulous at what I was asking, but not too incredulous to say yes. "You're fortunate that I work fast, but what will that standing woman do now? I'll have to put some serious thought into changing the design as a whole."

After we said goodbye, I felt buoyed; she sounded thoughtful and optimistic. I felt that maybe—just maybe—we had our sculptor. During the next two weeks Glenna and I spoke frequently.

"I put a clipboard in that woman's hands, and it didn't work," said Goodacre. "I tried having her hold a duffel bag—awful. I gave her head-phones like an air traffic controller might use. All terrible. Then I realized she didn't need to stand or hold anything—except an empty helmet. She would kneel between the standing woman looking up, and the wounded soldier. She would hold his helmet. She would portray the futility and anguish of war."

Her connection to our service experience in Vietnam was uncanny. Hopeful and excited about the real possibility of a design that would meet our criteria, I could hardly wait to meet her. She said she would bring the maquette in clay.

By the end of two weeks, Glenna sent photographs of her render-ing in clay—a twenty-four-inch maquette that provided a much clearer interpretation than her illustration for the competition.

"But can she sculpt?" asked a board member.

"Have you ever been to Santa Fe or to New Mexico?" a board member replied. "Her sculptures are everywhere—in galleries, on street corners, and internationally. And you probably can't afford one."

We set a date for Glenna to fly to Washington, D.C., to display her vision to the board, to veterans, and to key stakeholders, particularly representatives from the veterans' service organizations. We reserved a hotel conference room and invited these people to meet Glenna and see her clay maquette.

On a warm day in June 1991, I greeted our guests: more than thirty women and men representing such organizations as Vietnam Veterans of America, the American Legion, Veterans of Foreign Wars, and Disabled American Veterans, major individual contributors, and others who believed in, and were helping with, our efforts.

I tried to stay calm, but how could I? For us, this was do-or-die time. If this group gave the statue a thumbs down, it'd be as if we'd once again almost reached the mountain top, only to slide helplessly down. As if we were all but starting over—again. After nearly a decade of work, how many more "close-but-not-quite" endings could we endure? But we'd come this far; I wasn't about to lose hope.

"Thank you for being here today," I said in welcoming our guests. "We've invited you because we're interested in how you, as people who have supported our efforts, feel about the design we are seriously considering. We don't want to go through another hearing at the Commission of Fine Arts without knowing how the people the memorial would honor actually feel about it."

When people were seated, Glenna walked in, as we'd planned, pushing a room-service cart upon which her statue perched. Talk in the room softened to whispers, whispers to silence. All eyes were on Glenna and her proposed memorial design. This was our moment.

Suddenly, *thunk*. On the maquette, the head of the seated woman on the sandbags fell off and rolled to a stop on the conference-room carpet. A collective gasp rippled around the circle. A woman covered her mouth with her hand. I instinctively buried my anguish with a nervous smile. *What were the chances?* But Glenna Goodacre didn't miss a beat.

"Well, don't that beat all," she said with a touch of her Lubbock, Texas, twang, breaking into an infectious smile.

People responded with smiles of their own joined by a few titters of laughter. Glenna's relaxed response had instantly disarmed the initial "oh-my-God" reactions. Like a magician, she pulled out a couple of toothpicks from her pocket and replaced the head with the wisps of wood as fortification.

"There we go," she said. "Happens all the time in this kind of heat."

People's dread turned to relaxed laughter, like at a funeral when the first light touch of a eulogy is read. You could tell everyone had instantly fallen in love with her—and not just because, as it turned out, her daughter was a model, and married to jazz musician Harry Connick Jr. Everyone loved her laid-back genuineness. She was prepared, brilliant, and talented. And, like us, she, too, felt the addition of the Three Servicemen statue had left something missing at the Wall, the latter of which she called a "brilliant design."

"Art is interpreted differently by everyone," she said, looking at her statue. "In the figure standing, some will see a woman looking into the sky, waiting for a helicopter. Others will see that helicopter as God. That's OK. But whatever diverse responses people might have, I hope they see these women's compassion, their anxiety, their fatigue and, above all, their dedication."

After she talked a bit about her design, including the inspiration for the wounded man as a focal point, Glenna left the room and I addressed the guests again.

"Our purpose here today is not to force anyone to like our recommendation for the memorial," I said. "Our purpose is to simply give you a chance to see it and tell us how you feel. Not: *Can we live with this?* But: *Is this what we want to honor women who served in Vietnam for months, years, and decades to come?* It meets all the criteria put forth by the VWMP. The question is: What do you think?"

The pivotal moment had come. I scanned the room, looking to see which way the wind was blowing on Glenna's design. A few people nodded their heads as if on board. But was it simply people being polite or a ringing endorsement?

"I like it," said a woman. "I like it a lot."

"It's beautiful," said someone else.

"Thank you so much for including us in this decision," said a third person. "I absolutely love what Glenna has done."

"I'd be proud to have that represent me and the other women who served," said a fourth contributor.

I felt cautiously optimistic, but we needed more than a cluster of people behind this. "OK," I said. "Let's have a show of hands. If you think Glenna's statue is what you'd like to see as the Vietnam Women's Memorial, please raise your hand."

Without hesitation, every hand reached upward. Every hand. An unexpected wave of relief washed over me. I exhaled and led a lusty round of applause. I couldn't wait to tell Glenna.

In the autumn of 1991, it was on to the Commission of Fine Arts—once again—for what we needed for our final approval. They had approved the site for the memorial and the design competition criteria that the applicants had to follow in our quest to find what we wanted. The question was: Would they approve of Glenna's design itself? When facing the commission four years before, I'd been confident—only to see the commission dash our dreams, at least temporarily. Could they possibly do it again?

After all, it's not as if we'd swayed the entire country with our "tell-our-stories" campaign and the *60 Minutes* piece. *Newsweek* columnist George Will, whose elitism mirrored that of the commission, called us an "irritable faction" intent on "politicizing the commemoration process" and contributing to what he called "monumentitis." Not, of course, that he'd written a similar column with the Three Servicemen statue's approval.

At any rate, as I walked into that same room where, in October 1987, the commission had voted four to one against us, I couldn't help but feel a chill of uncertainty. My hopes had been so high that day, only to have been crushed by—what?—arrogance, shortsightedness, or, perhaps, fear. By now, I'd learned to take nothing for granted when human beings were involved.

Glenna stood before J. Carter Brown and the commissioners, confident, poised, and articulate as she explained her design. A commissioner said the outstretched left hand of the standing figure would be a potential hazard. *Oh, please, they weren't going to turn us down because our statue was a hazard, were they? Weren't two figures on the Three Servicemen carrying weapons, protrusions that would seem to be more dangerous than an outstretched hand?* They offered other refinements to the statue. Glenna did an admirable job being patient, but her artistic freedom and the commission's…I'll just euphemistically call it "attention to detail" were stressing us both.

In the end, however, they voted unanimously to approve the *design concept* for the Vietnam Women's Memorial. The National Capital Memorial Commission and National Capital Planning Commission followed suit. All the hearings were behind us, though the Commission of Fine Arts still had to sign off on Goodacre's final work.

20

The Statue Comes to Washington

March 1992–September 1993

In the spring of 1992, the board immersed itself in working with George Dickie, landscape architect on the landscape plan and sculpture setting for the monument, and on how we were going to get a one-ton statue from New Mexico to Washington, D.C., and show it off in the process.

Meanwhile, Glenna Goodacre began creating it. She had connected with our vision on a level so deeply that it was as if she were one of us. As if she had been predestined to do this.

From the beginning her mantra for the design was "hope and healing." No detail was left unconsidered. She said her first concern in designing the sculpture was to arrange the four figures in a composition that would be interesting from all angles: a true sculpture in the round. She had perused lots of photos from Vietnam and she'd picked up on how often sandbags were used as protection from mortar attacks, so used that image as something of a foundation. A nurse is sitting atop the sandbags, holding a wounded soldier. A bandage covers half of his face, creating

what Glenna calls "an anonymous figure with which veterans can identify. Even though he is wounded, he will live. I want this to be a monument for the living."

Behind the nurse, a woman in an army cap looks upward, as Glenna
says, "in search of a medevac helicopter or, perhaps, in search of help from
God." And next to her a woman kneels, staring at a lone helmet. "Her
posture," Goodacre said, "[reflects] her despair, frustrations, and all the
horrors of war." At 6'8" high, the statue would be literally larger than life.
Glenna purposely did not reveal insignia, branch of service, or rank. She
wanted it to be a tribute to every woman.

Glenna spared no expense on this project—the statue's granite base,
for example, was coming from Cold Spring, Minnesota—and we knew
we couldn't, either. She was an internationally-known sculptor; people
paid hundreds of thousands of dollars for her artwork. With our attorney,
Mahon, leading the way, we worked out a deal for $350,000 and a copy-
right, which she turned over to us.

That, of course, was a huge chunk of money, but, then, this was a
huge project. A project on the National Mall. Our construction permit
alone ran $400,000. Frederick Hart had been paid $320,000 to create the
Three Servicemen.

In Santa Fe, Glenna ordered one thousand pounds of oil-based clay
from California, asked women veterans to donate period uniforms, hats,
and boots, and had her studio set up with the steel armature and urethane
core necessary for designing and sculpting a national monument.

On March 11, 1993, Charles Atherton, the Secretary of the
Commission of Fine Arts, came to Goodacre's studio to see if what she'd
done met the commission's approval. Some members of the VWMP
board were on hand, along with Glenna, of course, and White House
photographer Dirck Halstead, who shot an array of what, for us, would
become historic photos of Glenna putting on the final touches.

This was it. The studio bustled with anticipation. Finally, the room
quieted. Atherton gently nodded his head. "The statue," he said, "meets
our criteria."

The last hurdle had been cleared. For what had been, at times, a very public battle, we'd won the war in the obscurity of Glenna's studio with Atherton's five-word proclamation to a handful of people. But that was good enough for me. I quietly reveled in our long-awaited victory, my body tingling with joy, my mind already imagining the good-news phone call to Mike and the kids.

"Let's celebrate!" said Glenna.

Nobody needed convincing. We headed to one of her favorite restaurants, the Pink Adobe, and clinked our glasses of champagne in triumph. I looked to my left and recognized actor Gene Hackman seated at the next table; this was his regular hangout, I learned. I looked to my right and saw a beaming Glenna and relieved, happy members of our board. There was no turning back. We had our memorial.

A team of artisans came to the Goodacre Studio from Loveland, Colorado, to make the sections of rubber and plaster mold and take them to Art Castings of Colorado. The bronze sections were welded together; the foundry finished the bronze on August 20. The sculpture was sand-blasted, then the patina applied by Patrick Kipper, a master craftsman patineur. Using a five-thousand-year-old method called "lost wax casting," the soft clay original sculpture was cast into a durable metal one. The piece came to Santa Fe for the send-off to Washington, D.C.

"I put a lot of myself into that piece," Glenna later told *Southwest Art* magazine. "I still remember the butterflies in my stomach the day I signed it. I'll probably never do a piece that means so much."

As the statue was finalized, we brainstormed the logistics for getting it to Washington, D.C., from New Mexico in time for its dedication on what we hoped would be Veterans Day and made plans for our groundbreaking ceremony. On a scorching hot sunny day, July 29, 1993, a dozen of us sliced our shovels into the soil to commemorate the construction of the memorial. Chairman of the Joint Chiefs of Staff, Gen. Colin Powell, a Vietnam veteran, then offered one of the most beautiful tributes I've ever heard.

"You went. You served. You suffered. The names of eight of your sisters are etched on the 'Wall' for having made the supreme sacrifice. And yet your service and your sacrifice have been mostly invisible for all these intervening years. When you finished what you had to do, you came quietly home. You stepped back into the background from which you had modestly come. You melted away into a society which, for too long now, has ignored the vital and endless work that falls to women and is not appreciated as it should be.

"I knew you were there in Vietnam. I knew you as clerks. I knew you as map makers. I knew you as intelligence specialists. I knew you as photographers and air traffic controllers and Red Cross and USO and other kinds of volunteers. And above all I knew you as nurses when you cared for those who were wounded and when you cared also, as one of them, for me.

"And yet now, almost twenty-five years after my return, I've begun to realize that I didn't really, really know you well enough. I didn't know what you have been going through all these many years. I didn't know in my heart truly what memories and nightmares you brought home with you."

He talked of how, in preparing for his talk, he'd begun skimming a book called *Visions of War, Dreams of Peace*, a collection of poetry by women veterans edited by Vietnam veterans Lynda Van Devanter and Joan Furey. How his skimming became reading. And how by day's end, he'd read nearly every poem in the book.

"I realized for the first time that for male soldiers, the war came in intermittent flashes of terror, occasional death, moments of pain; but for the women who were there, for the women who helped before the battle, for the nurses in particular, the terror, the death, and the pain were unrelenting, a constant terrible weight that had to be stoically carried.

"It was a pain that had to be stowed again in a corner of your mind and put in an isolated place of your heart, or you wouldn't be able to continue your work. The nurses saw the bleakest, most terrifying face of war: the mangled men, the endless sobs of wounded kids—not just now and then, but day after day, night after hellish night."

He went on to talk about how the memorial would be a "circle of healing" that was long overdue. "The monument will ensure that all of America will never forget that all of you were there, that you served, and that even in the depths of horror and cruelty there will always beat the heart of human love—and therefore our hope for humanity. My fellow veterans, you and your sacrifices will never be forgotten. God bless you all and thank you very much."

In 1992, I had contacted Jan Scruggs about dedicating the memorial more than a year later, on Veterans Day 1993. Scruggs had helped spearhead the creation of the Vietnam Veterans Memorial that opened in 1982 and had been in charge of the Veteran's Day and Memorial Day programs ever since. Not incidentally, he was also the man who, when I first sought his backing for our memorial, had hung up on me, saying "that will never happen."

Now, he was singing the same song. "You can't have Veterans Day or Memorial Day," he said to me about the dedication planning. "Those are my days to plan."

"Jan, our statue will start its journey to D.C. in August and will be ready to be placed in the fall. Veterans Day is the logical choice to dedicate it. It's appropriate."

"I don't care. You can have any day you want. You can have Mother's Day. But not Veterans Day."

"These women we're honoring are all veterans, so Veterans Day makes perfect sense. Memorial Day is for the dead and Mother's Day is for mothers. We're not honoring these women for being mothers. Some aren't. We're honoring them for their service to America—as *veterans*."

"Look," he said, "I'm the Pope of the Vietnam Veterans Memorial, and you're not getting Veteran's Day."

"Jan, that's not how it works, and you know it. The National Park Service will have something to say about this, and they are the authority, not you," I said.

The next thing I heard was a click. The line went dead. Again.

Amid the two-steps-forward-one-step-backward advance of our team, what continually amazed me was how often just when we needed someone to have our backs, someone did. A Vietnam vet had done that at the Veterans of Foreign War conference in Dallas in 1985 when I'd been accosted by a World War II vet after making my pitch. Now, among those guardians was Charles T. (Chuck) Hagel, director of the USO. Chuck had served on our board of directors in the early 1980s as treasurer, was a true advocate for women veterans, and was a friend of Scruggs.

"I'll handle Scruggs," he said. "Start planning for Veterans Day." He did and we did. Scruggs had acquiesced. Without hesitation, the National Park Service granted us the necessary permits and authorization to conduct ceremonies at the Vietnam Women's Memorial.

Another such "guardian" was David O. Chung, who'd served in the Air Force in Vietnam. He saw to it that our bronze monument got safely from New Mexico to Washington, D.C., a logistical nightmare that was far more complicated than many would assume. With our vision in full blossom, it would become a whistle-stop tour that involved twenty-one cities, eight thousand miles, and enough tears and hugs to create an appropriate prelude to our November 11, 1993, dedication. We didn't want to simply get our statue from Point A to Point B. We wanted to show it off, create interest, inspire people—and, yes, raise money; we still owed more than $300,000.

David had first heard of our memorial in 1986 at a "welcome home" parade in Chicago for Vietnam vets. Forty-three, David had been wounded in Vietnam during an ambush and had a deep appreciation for what nurses had done over there. I had met him at a Vietnam Veterans of America convention in 1991 when he'd heard me speak about the plans for the memorial's dedication, and how we needed a driver and a truck to carry the memorial to Washington, D.C. David came up to me after I left the podium.

"I work for Federal Express," said Chung, who was involved in the company's training programs in Memphis, Tennessee. "I can't promise you anything, but I do know Fred Smith, the company founder and president, personally."

It was another one of those miracle moments where the right person appeared at the right time. But FedEx's involvement didn't come easily. Some higher-ups—non-vets—thought linking the company to the Vietnam War, even if it involved honor for those who'd never received any, would lead to bad press, not good press. Ultimately, though, Chung connected with a high-ranking manager who believed in the idea and helped convince Smith, himself a Vietnam veteran, that FedEx would find it an honorable investment. Another huge backer of our efforts were Melvin Simon & Associates, owners of the Mall of America in Minneapolis, and Chrysler, each of which had kicked in $100,000.

The logistics were not simple: get a one-ton statue safely over a wide, twisting route, and show it off to America—without taking it out of the truck. There were all sorts of considerations that I hadn't anticipated: axle weight, traffic, taxes, tolls, you name it. For every question, however, Chung found an answer. He connected with a manufacturer in Wisconsin who helped FedEx modify a twenty-two-foot truck to have moveable curtains on both sides, so the statue could be seen from both angles. He had the truck retrofitted so it could hold, and secure, the statue. And so intent was he on doing this right that he chose the only people he trusted to drive the truck—himself and a man who served with him in Vietnam (also a FedEx employee), Chuck Raphael.

Those were simply the physical challenges. Events had to be set up in all of those cities, police escorts organized, vets' groups coordinated. For all this, we hired an event planner, whose director didn't always see eye-to-eye with David. To honor our female vets, a group of Native Americans—all Vietnam vets, mostly Navajo—pledged to walk all the way from Arizona and New Mexico, where the statue would begin its journey, to D.C. The Rolling Thunder motorcycle group, among them many Vietnam vets, joined the convoy, too, to provide unofficial security.

The journey east began in Santa Fe, New Mexico, on August 28. Hundreds gathered for the sendoff, including artist Glenna Goodacre, myself, VWMP board members, and the Native Americans who were part of "Walk for the Women." They blessed the statue, placing an eagle feather on it for safe travels.

It was a three-ring, moveable circus that had enough headaches to begin with. But Chung encountered further resistance when, as the driver, people mistook him to be "the enemy." Chung, Asian-American, looked Vietnamese to some people—some of whom got in his face about it. David is primarily of Chinese ancestry, with also Polynesian, Middle Eastern, and Native American heritage. But, above all, he is an American—an American who served his country proudly. The confrontations he encountered by small-minded people only underscored how slowly the wounds were healing from a war that had been over for nearly twenty years.

"I had my ghosts from Vietnam," he said. "On top of that, I didn't need people calling me 'Gook.' I call myself something else. I call myself a survivor."

Despite such incidents—and threats of anti-war protests that never materialized—the healing aspect that we'd hoped for the statue began manifesting itself soon after the trip began. Servicemen who'd fought in Vietnam and nurses who'd patched them up were drawn to the stops along the way. Military and civilian women veterans came wearing t-shirts saying, "I Served, Too." Connections were made. Hearts opened. Healing begun.

In San Antonio, it rained buckets but the money box for donations was stuffed full of wet, soggy ones, fives, tens, and twenties.

In Wichita, Kansas, bad traffic and driving rain slowed the convoy's journey. By the time the truck arrived—with a state police escort—it was dark. David wondered if anyone would have hung around for their arrival. Then, in the headlights he saw a scene that sent shivers down his spine: more than a thousand people were huddled in rain slickers and beneath umbrellas. When the lights popped on in the back of the truck and the side panels removed, the crowd pressed toward the statue as if moths to a flame.

I wasn't there for every stop. Though I was in touch with David every day to get updates on our progress, I only joined the journey at a handful of places. But, later, regarding the Wichita scene, David told me: "You couldn't see much, but you could see the tears." He said it was hard to describe but there was something spiritual about those moments.

At the Mall of America in Bloomington, Minnesota, the statue was removed from the Federal Express truck, the only time that happened. (Management insisted and we acquiesced, anticipating a huge turnout at the largest mall in the U.S. and knowing the Mall's owner had been a huge benefactor to our efforts.) A man dressed in fatigues pushed his wheelchair to the sculpture and grasped one of the bronze figures, then bowed his head. While I spoke, a Medal of Honor recipient came and stood by my side, at attention. Women veterans circled the statue holding hands without holding back their tears.

In Baltimore, a Navy chaplain was preparing to give an invocation for the unveiling of the traveling statue. "Something told me to turn around and look at the statue," he later said. "I hadn't seen it before, and when I did, I felt a hot, white light move all the way down my spine. I saw my son up there. That soldier, that wounded soldier, that was my Buddy. That was my son. He never came home."

In Pentagon City, Virginia, a Red Cross volunteer, saw it for the first time and later wrote: "The memorial has given me a sense of peace…a sense of great joy. It also gives me the incentive to continue to reach out to my sisters and brothers who have not quite reached that place of peace."

The journey had many such moments. Not that all went smoothly. Some states and cities were miffed that we weren't stopping for them. It was simply impossible to stop too often, otherwise we wouldn't get the statue to D.C. on time. But how could I say no when Jeff "Doc" Dentice, a former medic in Vietnam, called to ask for a stop in his home state of Wisconsin? Those Wisconsin veterans had been in the forefront of helping me get started. I owed them a debt of gratitude, and this was a way to show it.

Sometimes tempers flared, even between David and me; we were both strong-minded people and wanted the same outcome: a safe arrival for our statue. But we were bonded by our pasts in Vietnam and our present task of honoring the women who had served there. Together, we made it work.

Even the statue's arrival in Washington, D.C., came with unforeseen complications, like who was going to be in charge of security for the statue after it arrived but before it was dedicated in just over a month. Until President Clinton signed a "Memorandum of Conveyance" November 10 to accept the statue for the federal government on behalf of the American people, the National Park Service informed us it had no authority, nor responsibility, to provide such security. Technically, it didn't belong yet to the federal government—or, more precisely, the American people. But by now I'd seen the people-having-our-back scenario play out enough to know we'd find some sort of solution.

Glenna and I waited anxiously on the afternoon of September 19 for the statue to arrive. David had called an hour before to give us his ETA and we purposely didn't tell anyone about its arrival, lest a crowd complicate the challenge of getting a large statue into a small opening in a grove of trees. A sprinkling of people showed up anyway, including joggers and reporters.

At the site three hundred feet behind the apex of the Wall, a crane awaited, poised for the lift and place. Most of the landscaping was in place, including yellowwood trees, viburnum, shadblow, and cotoneaster. The pavers, a Carnelian red granite from Minnesota, surrounded the foundation on which the statue would be eased into place.

"There it is!" I said, "The truck!"

My heart beat double time. Glenna, I assumed, was no less anxious. She had patiently waited for a year while we guided the statue through the final political hoops, then spent another year designing and sculpting it. Amid that, she'd begun to feel a certain sanctity to her work, a level of reverence that she told us she'd never felt on any project she'd created. Now, her creation was here.

As it was being lowered from the crane, the expression on the bronze skyward-looking woman's face seemed not to be "looking for a chopper in Vietnam" but "looking to the heavens for a safe landing."

"It's beautiful," I said to Glenna. "So very beautiful."

She nodded, eyes misty. As the one-ton statue swung from a crane near its placement, she began happily instructing the crane operator. As if a NASA controller instructing the pilot of a lunar module onto the moon, she worked with the crane operator and a man holding a tether so the four holes in the statue's base slid through the four well-epoxied bolts that awaited—and the memorial was facing the proper way. She twisted and turned the swinging monument until the "nurse and wounded soldier" figures perfectly faced the apex of the Wall.

When the statue settled on its stone perch, my knees nearly buckled from relief. And, bolted in place, it spoke of permanence. No one could take it away now. No more hearings. No more approvals. Our memorial was finally home.

"Well, don't that beat all?" said Glenna in her Texas drawl.

"What?"

"See the African-American woman figure lookin' skyward?"

"Yes."

"She's facing the Lincoln Memorial."

I looked. It was uncanny, this serendipitous connection to history.

"Did you plan that?"

"No, but it was obviously meant to be."

We slowly circled the statue for minutes that became an hour, one hour that became two, looking at it from every angle, seeing how the evening's fading light played on the bronzed faces of the women representing us all.

We were almost ready to hail a cab for our hotel when we saw them—our solutions to the security problem: the Native Americans who'd arrived after their "Walk for the Women." The Park Service had initially bristled when, weeks ago, I'd suggested the solution; this could be a public relations disaster, they said.

"These men and women," I said, "have walked from New Mexico and Arizona in honor of the veterans this statue represents. And every one of them served their country in Vietnam. I believe they are more than worthy of the task."

The National Park Service officer looked down and around, as if suddenly ashamed to look me in the eye. Within a few days, I had assurance the park folks wouldn't give them any trouble as they stayed to guard our statue. Many of these Native Americans had watched each other's backs in the jungles of Vietnam and had "walked point"—the leading soldier advancing through hostile territory. I was confident they could handle Washington, D.C.

As we left, I glanced back one last time and smiled. More than two dozen Native Americans, each packing a sleeping bag, water, and food, had fanned out around the statue like Christmas presents around a tree.

21

At Last

November 1993

The big dedication day was coming. We parceled out responsibilities to each board member: fundraising, identifying invitees, publicity, and the innumerable details of such a major event. We hired the Wabasha Group out of Minnesota to be our event planners, doing all the behind-the-scenes work: security, a headquarters hotel, busses to transfer attendees to the memorial, getting a JumboTron screen in place, the works.

I was in charge of the ceremonies. I invited a handful of historians to write chapters for the *Celebration of Patriotism and Courage* commemorative program that would be given to all women veterans who attended. Collaborating with board members, we decided on our speakers. And decided who would sit where.

"Yes, how's that going to work?" a Wabasha contact asked me.

"Simple. There will be two kinds of seating: VIP and non-VIP. The VIP area is for all the women veterans. The non-VIP area is for everyone else."

The laughter from the Wabasha representative had a nervous edge to it.

"Uh, really?"

"Well, I suppose we'll give VIP status to a few of those who went above and beyond to support us—members of Congress, VSOs, major contributors, Vice President Gore, you know—but you get the idea: this is an event for our female veterans. They are the priority. They are the VIPs."

"Roger."

Paying attention to details, I printed two exact indexed notebooks outlining the activities and ceremonies of the three-day dedication event I was to emcee—and including my speeches, word-for-word. I made one for me to hand carry and mailed one to Diana Hellinger, our executive director, just in case my plane crashed. With or without me, the event would go on.

In some ways, planning for the dedication was similar to what we'd been doing for nearly ten years: organizing, lobbying and fundraising. But what differed was this: this time, we, the women who served, would be recipients, as well. We were giving this gift to America. America's gift to us was, "Welcome Home." Without thousands of Americans who helped build this memorial, we wouldn't be celebrating this historic dedication.

On the night before the unveiling of the memorial, I lay awake in my Washington, D.C., hotel and thought back to something Judge Dan Foley had told me a decade ago when we'd started the quest for honor. "Diane," he said, "success has a thousand fathers. Failure is an orphan."

Earlier that day, I'd stood beside President Bill Clinton and watched him sign the Memorandum of Conveyance to turn the statue over to the American people. When he lifted his pen after that final *n* on "Clinton," four inches below and to the right of my own signature, it seemed as if my entire body sighed in relief. The anxiety waned, replaced by a rare sense of peace. This made it "officially official."

Whether history would remember me as a failure or success, I knew I'd done whatever I could to make this happen, including help raise more than $5 million to pay for it—well, most of it. (We still owed $350,000 on the construction loan.). That was my peace: to look in the mirror and know I'd given my best for a worthy cause with so many admirable people by my side.

Mike's love and patience, my family's flexibility, my mother's babysitting, my board's support, my sister veterans' perseverance, my brother veterans having my back—they kept me going. They helped me get up off the ground when I'd been knocked down. They restored my faith in the belief that someday we were going to actually *have* this dedication.

Already, as if to fulfill Foley's "thousand fathers" reference, we'd seen people coming out of the woodwork, suddenly anxious to be part of the team, to be up on the stage, to grab their moment in the spotlight—even if they didn't particularly deserve it.

For the "failure is an orphan" part, I'd already experienced that ordeal numerous times in the last decade: the non-spotlight moments when we'd lost; the snubs from Scruggs and Doubek; the initial "no" vote at the VFW conference in Dallas; the four-to-one turndown by the Commission of Fine Arts; the betrayal from people who'd once linked arms with me and our core allies; the initial refusal of Congress to guarantee us a spot at the Vietnam Veterans Memorial itself—the list goes on.

At times, I was criticized for not accepting what I thought were watered-down offers for the memorial, specifically one from Congress that would have allowed us a memorial, but not at the Vietnam Veterans Memorial site. But our crusade, I felt, required waiting, working harder, working longer, and taking risks to get exactly what we wanted. I regretted losing some friends amid this crusade, people who still weren't talking to me. Yet as I had told our board repeatedly: we had to think about not what felt good right now but what was going to be satisfying a decade from now and beyond, when we were gone and our daughters and granddaughters were carrying on the mantle for us. It's these women of the future who made our decade-long task worth it.

Within that decade, my lined notebooks in which I kept my "to-do" and "done" list doubled in price. Our office began with typewriters and finished up on computers. The country went through three presidents: Ronald Reagan, George H.W. Bush, and Bill Clinton. Our children, all under ten or younger when I first talked to their dad about a statue, now were in high school and college.

For the "haters," those who left death threats on our phone, who called me a "feminazi," who wrote angry editorials claiming that our memorial was nothing but a political ploy for women's liberation, who, just recently, had vaguely threatened violence at the next day's ceremony, I had no energy. Not that they deserved it anyway. People will always disagree. But as Mike had recently reminded me, "Diane, it's time to forget all of that and remember all those fine people you met, your new friendships, and the people who stuck their necks out to help." He was right.

Not that the criticism of our venture ended. A week before the dedication, the *Los Angeles Times*' art critic, Christopher Knight, wrote a scathing column saying our goal in having the statue was misguided, that we were trying to "declare from the heart of Washington that the Vietnam War was a good and noble cause." I could only shake my head in disbelief. The statue no more condoned war than the plaque in Dallas for John F. Kennedy condones assassinations. There is war and there are the warriors. If Vietnam taught me anything, it was to never confuse the two.

Somewhere along the way someone told me: "Diane, you will lose your sleep, you will lose your friends. But you will win justice—for your daughters." That was good enough for me.

Yes, there had been costs. Was it worth the literal months and months of time, over ten years that I gave up with my family? Was it worth building strong friendships and, after seven years, seeing circumstances beyond our control sever those friendships? Was it worth the day-to-day stress of always worrying about this and that?

No, probably not. In the days leading up to the dedication, I was asked if, knowing what I knew now, I'd do it again. "If you're talking about Vietnam, I'd repeat that experience in a heartbeat," I said. "The memorial? I'm not so sure."

That said, I can hear Mike, forever my champion, saying: "Diane, think of how many lives will be changed because of that statue."

For him, the glass was always full. Even when I'd lose sight of our ultimate goal, he'd quietly nudge me back to believing in reaching that goal—and believing in myself. Beyond the obvious benefit of the memorial itself for women who served as part of the Vietnam War, I personally grew in ways I'm not sure I otherwise would have.

I had not intended to ever cry in public and I did. I had not intended on ever sharing my experiences in Vietnam—my fears, guilt, mistakes, vulnerabilities—and, instead, I had left them strewn behind me like Hansel and Gretel's crumbs. I hadn't known I had something burning inside of me—a latent courage, steeled in Vietnam—that would conquer false stereotypes, misogyny, sexism, mean-spirited antagonists, and a powerful political machine in Washington, D.C., but I found it. Finally, I had not thought myself capable of *feeling* again, but I did.

In the ten-year period, the cost of the project had skyrocketed from the $1.3 million we originally estimated to $5.5 million. And the resistance had been much stronger on every front than I'd ever imagined. It came in the form of sexism (see scout dogs), class (see the Commission of Fine Arts's and the *Washington Post*'s Benjamin Forgey's clear sense that our memorial would lead to a "ghettoization" of the grounds), resentment (see VFW women of World War II vintage and the founders of the Vietnam Veterans Memorial), and more.

Not that I thought it was going to be a cakewalk. But early on, our board had decided on a goal to dedicate the memorial in November 1988; our dedication to be held the next day would come five years after that original goal. (The Vietnam Veterans Memorial Wall took less than three.) We'd dreamed big, and perhaps big dreams are the ones worth dreaming and fighting for. It had taken seven years of testimony before Veterans Service Organizations, three federal commissions, and two congressional bills for us to succeed. And yet here we were, about to celebrate the victory.

You could float dozens of reasons why we ultimately were able to succeed. Among them, ironically, was J. Carter Brown's comment comparing women to scout dogs. That inspired *60 Minutes* to produce a story that put Congress's feet to the proverbial fire, and, keeping with the canine theme, wound up biting Brown's Commission of Fine Arts in the behind.

In the spirit of letting bygones be bygones, however, I appreciated that Brown, with Congressional approval on our side, ultimately lent his support. Asked to contribute an assessment of our statue for our commemorative program, he wrote: "Glenna Goodacre has created a dramatic and moving work. Rather than drawing on a single moment in time, her sculpture provides a metaphor for war as experienced by those whose heroic contributions have been so often ignored. This bronze brings to life the urgency and pathos of the field, as well the searing introspection that continues long, long after."

Another intriguing irony that I reflected upon in the days before the dedication: had the Wall simply been left alone, no women's memorial would likely have ever been built. After all, it was the addition of the Three Service*men*—added to resolve a dispute over the design of the Wall—that triggered my sense that women had been left out. And, for that, I would be forever grateful.

Beneath beautiful blue skies, I marveled at the hordes of people who flocked to the Mall on Veterans Day, November 11, 1993. Later, National Park officials would estimate we drew more than twenty-five thousand people for the dedication of the memorial, the second day of our three-day Vietnam Women's Memorial Project's Celebration of Patriotism and Courage.

Among them were many family members and friends, first and foremost Mike and our four children.

"Well, Mom, you did it!" said Luke, our nineteen-year-old son, at breakfast.

"You summited, Mom!" said Guy, almost twenty-one.

Both were at the University of Minnesota Duluth. Together, they climbed Lake Superior's rock and ice bluffs and had already summited mountain peaks in the Rocky Mountains.

"You'll have a lot of thank-you letters to write after this!" said Carrie, now sixteen.

Jon-Erik, at fourteen, was in awe of his first trip to the nation's capital, grinning with anticipation of what was about to unfold.

It was only eight in the morning, and my kids had already made my day. I would never stop feeling guilty for being away from my children so much from 1983 to 1993, but remarks like these helped ease the pain.

My father's health precluded him from coming, but my seventy-eight-year-old mother was there, along with my Aunt Ruth, who'd served in the Women's Army Corps in World War II. Mom was never one to lather me in praise but when I looked in her eyes on this day, I could see the pride, the "job-well-done" glint in her eye. It was from her, of course, that I'd learned to not be deterred; dig the hole, plant the seed, water... and to stay calm in the middle of a crisis.

My sister, Nola, came, as did my brother Ronnie, an army veteran; my one and only grade school classmate—literally—Jimmy Anderson; fellow veterans and friends from when I'd lived in River Falls, Wisconsin, and Northfield, Minnesota; and many others.

But the people I loved seeing most on that day were the faces of the women vets. Because this day was about them. I'd never seen so many women veterans together in the same place. In my perfect world, of course, I'd imagined all 265,000 women who'd served as part of the Vietnam campaign—or at least those who were still alive—attending. But seeing more than 10,000 parading down Constitutional Avenue—Americans, Canadians, Australians—was a sight to behold.

During the parade and at the Vietnam Women's Memorial, what moved me most was seeing connections between people: Red Cross women finding each other with t-shirts saying: "A Touch of Home in the Combat Zone," nurses connecting with other nurses, civilians connecting with veterans, disabled veterans connecting with nurses. And, of course, Mike and our four beaming children. I looked at them with pride; how wonderful to have all six of us together.

Amid this, plain-clothed Secret Service agents, along with a few police officers with dogs, did a bomb sweep. What would an event like this be without a couple of loonies threatening to blow up the statue—and me? Nearby, someone burned Jane Fonda in effigy, as they had at the dedication of the Vietnam Veterans Memorial in 1982. I could have done without that. Regardless of our views on the war and its many players, today was a day of healing and reconciliation.

Sue Rowe, a fifty-something woman from Phoenix who'd been a nurse in Vietnam, saw a woman she thought to be familiar. "Sue. Sue Rowe," she said to Virginia Willard. "We worked together in the OR in Pleiku!" Willard screeched and wrapped her arms around Rowe. They laughed aloud then began to cry.

Cameras from all the major networks—including CSPAN, which covered the entire ceremony live—adjusted their lenses as the ceremony neared. At 2:00 p.m., we began. The ceremony lasted more than two hours but it seemed like two minutes. It was bathed in so much sunshine, joy, hope, healing, and reconnection that experiencing it was like trying to take a drink out of a magnificent waterfall: overwhelming.

When our board members, Glenna Goodacre, and a handful of other key people circled the statue and pulled away its nylon cloak, I experienced a moment that I'd played hundreds of times in my mind but honestly wondered if ever would become real. I shed joyful tears and hugged those who'd been in the trenches with me. I looked out at the sea of people, thousands of men and women who had served, many in their Army, Navy, Air Force, Coast Guard, and Marine Corps uniforms, and with the symbol of the Red Cross everywhere.

Soon it was time for my remarks. How many speeches had I given since that day in 1984 when I made my first to the American Legion Post of River Falls, Wisconsin, when my nerves would hardly allow my mouth to move? If only one per week—and that might be on the low end—that would make five hundred. But I would enjoy none more than the one on this day.

"The sun," I began, "is shining on us! We have just unveiled the first monument in the history of the United States of America dedicated in our nation's capital to American women who served during wartime. Welcome home, daughters of America! Welcome home, my sister veterans! Allow the love and pride that fills this hallowed space to enter your hearts and souls today and forever as we continue on our journey in life! Today, for the first time in more than twenty years since returning from the war, we are together again!"

As I scanned the looks of appreciation on the women's faces, I wish I could have bottled that scene and kept it forever. To one side of me sat some of the board members who'd worked beside me in eager anticipation of this day. To the other stood Glenna's statue. And all of it was across from the Wall chiseled with the names of more than fifty-eight thousand souls who'd lost their lives in Vietnam. At last, we were all together in one place.

I honored those who had lost loved ones in Vietnam. I honored my brother veterans who served in the war. Then it seemed right to challenge women vets to *not* do what too many of us had done for far too long: allow the nation's silence or subtle shunning of us to define who we were.

"Let no one ever again mistake who you are. Let no one ever again forget what a difference you made. Don't ever hide the fact that you are a veteran of the Vietnam War. It's been a long journey from Vietnam and wherever else you might have served in the war. But the journey for most is not over. Many are only beginning to heal, but this is our place to start.

"We have waited for this day and we feared it might not happen. We feared we'd never find a monument that would meet the approval of the agencies in this town. We feared that those who said this was an impossible dream might be right. Some have feared to come to this Wall. But today we need to set aside our fears. We veterans have prevailed. We have come together in love and a celebration of patriotism and courage of Vietnam women's vets and all vets."

At one point while I was speaking, a man from the crowd yelled, "How dare you celebrate war!" And left in a huff. I wished he hadn't. I would have told him this wasn't about celebrating war, but about honoring women who chose to serve their country when they didn't have to. Who voluntarily sacrificed their time and talents in support of our nation while the men who were summoned to the draft had little choice but to serve.

The remarks by the others were heartfelt, hopeful, and focused on the act of healing that had underscored our ten-year effort.

Adm. William J. Crowe Jr., USN (Ret.), one of our most steadfast champions, choked back tears when he opened his remarks—sharing one of his own explicit memories from his service in Vietnam. He recalled watching nurses, as they jumped from a landing helicopter, run to skillfully take charge of wounded soldiers. In that moment, he reflected having thought, "I have just seen an angel of the Lord." He continued his remarks to share about our memorial, "What a magnificent legacy for the women who served during the Vietnam War to leave our great Republic.... This moving monument finally completes the Vietnam circle by honoring the spirit and achievement of the women who participated in that effort. But more important, it will serve as a shining beacon for future generations of American women."

Harry G. Robinson, a Vietnam vet and Howard University professor, stunned me by calling me "the woman who brought our nation to this high moment—a hero's hero. If it weren't for her, we wouldn't be here. She's the most tenacious, determined, ferocious, singled-minded woman I have ever known."

Glenna Goodacre's remarks triggered my tears (not the first time of the day). "That my hands can shape the clay which might touch the hearts and heal the wounds of those who served fills me with humility and deep satisfaction," she said.

After Goodacre's son-in-law, Harry Connick Jr., sang "America," Col. Jane Carson, a board member who never gave up on our mission, talked of how we kept hoping "next year" we'd have a statue but, for whatever reason, "next year" wouldn't come. Now it had. "From this day forward, may this be a place of healing and hope for those who suffered the invisible and silent wounds of war. May it stand as a symbol for all generations of the enduring legacies of strength, courage, compassion, and caring by millions of military and civilian women at home and abroad in this difficult time for our nation."

Vice President Al Gore, himself a Vietnam vet, offered an exuberant exclamation mark to it all. "Let the healing spirit of this place join with the healing spirit of many millions of Americans...and flow to the west, the north, the east, the south, and through countries around the world."

Afterward, the formality gave way to unbridled, unscripted joy. People pressed toward me, Glenna, and others on our team, wanting to say thank you. In particular, I'd underestimated how meaningful the memorial was to men who had served in Vietnam. They shook my hand, gave me hugs, and told me of how their souls had been touched by nurses twenty to thirty years ago in Vietnam and now had been touched again.

"It's as if you and the others were the only ones who truly understood," one told me.

Women veterans came to me with almost replicated words: "I just need to touch you," they'd say. "You made this real for *us*."

Meanwhile, I thanked them—because they're the ones who served and, in many cases, who helped support our fight for the memorial.

Some veterans tried to speak but could not, so overcome were they by emotion. But in their silence, I heard them.

"The Potomac is higher today for all the tears shed," one woman said.

Florence Johnson, of Massachusetts, showed up in the all-white Gold Star Mothers uniform that marked her as the parent of a soldier killed in battle. "They took care of our kids," she told the *Washington Post*. "Maybe somebody here today took care of my boy before he died."

Tim Davis, a Marine, had lost both legs on Hill 55 in Vietnam in 1968. He came to pay his respects to the nurses who helped him. And to be reminded of the connection between the nurses and those who died. "These women were the last people those guys saw or talked to before they died."

When David Chung approached me, my emotions let loose. He had spent over a month guarding and driving the monument on its way to Washington D.C. I knew how much he had sacrificed and how much he had put up with in terms of ugly racism. I'd also sparred with him a bit here and there. Anyway, in that moment, the tears flowed as we wrapped our arms around each other.

"You know, you taught me more about leadership in the last few years than I'd learned in my entire life," he said. "If it wasn't for you, I don't know where I'd be or what I'd be doing, but it wouldn't be good.

Somehow, you always managed to take the moral high ground, and I admire you for that."

I was honored by his comments, even if I'd stumbled plenty of times on our journey.

Military and civilian women veterans, and Donut Dollies, the affectionate term for the Red Cross women who had served in Vietnam, sensed the need to touch the statue itself. I'd see them wait, off to the side, until the crowd had cleared a bit and then timidly walk forward and, most often, touch the wounded soldier. And I knew where they were at that moment: back in Vietnam, touching the soldier who they'd never forgotten. Next, they'd look into the eyes of the standing woman, almost certainly hearing the thrum of those blades, seeing the orange dirt swirl into the air as the ground below was whipped by the chopper.

My family, rather than feeling like people in a choir who don't know the words, were embraced by veterans as soon as they were identified as having connections to me. Hugs. High-fives. *Thank-yous*. People took them under their wings, making them feel honored and appreciated. It not only caught them by surprise, but it helped them understand what this meant to these women and men. Remember, from their perspective, Mom made phone calls and hopped on airplanes and wrote letters for ten years—but they never got to see what this was all for. Never got to see the results. Until today. It was so affirming to see them finally *understand*.

Mike felt great relief. He wrapped his arms around me.

"Now, maybe I can get back to normal," I said.

"Honey, there is no normal. You don't know what normal is."

He was right, of course.

Three women in bronze weren't going to wipe away decades of personal grief, nor pay off the $350,000 we still had to raise to pay off the construction loan. But it was a great start.

After the memorial found its permanent place, some despised it. "The nurses' memorial became a political thing," a prestigious Washington, D.C., architect told the Associated Press. "Who could be against nurses? And so, a dumb memorial got built." *Who could be against nurses?* For a decade, it seemed like a lot of people.

An art critic from Denver said, "it's nothing but a bronze wet dream for the American GI." What? Had she just insulted every veteran, male and female? But most of the letter-writing response from people who were there, and who watched the event on TV, was warm, wide, and deep.

"Never have I been so proud to say that I am a nurse (or will be in five weeks)," wrote Gloria Fancher Pruitt. "I can only hope that I can someday have some effect on another nursing student as you and Jane Carson have had on me."

"I knew it was going to be an 'emotional week' but no words can describe my feelings adequately as to what it meant for me to be there," wrote Colleen Helmstetter, a nurse from Gresham, Oregon, who served in Vietnam. "I've never cried so many tears of joy and sorrow all at the same time. I guess that's what 'cleansing tears' are all about. I've never hugged so many people—fellow nurses, some I had worked with, some I was just meeting for the first time, but there was a bond of friendship and understanding so strong between all of us. Then there were the guys. I never dreamt there would be so many guys there to say thank you and to be celebrating our homecoming with us!"

"I felt so honored to march in the parade. It was the first time since coming back to the states over twenty years ago that I can say I felt proud of myself for serving in Vietnam," wrote a woman from Arkansas. "I know I will never feel ashamed about it again."

"I am a male soldier stationed at Fort Ritchie, Maryland," wrote a young man. "I wanted to thank you from the bottom of my heart for the Vietnam Women's Memorial. The tribute, so symbolic of the *mercy* to which all nurses are so devoted, is a national debt of conscience we have owed the 'angels of the battlefield' for twenty years. We vets of Desert Storm had our angels, too. Welcome home, ma'am."

"My husband was a chopper pilot in the Marines during Vietnam," wrote Lynne Morris of Seattle. "When I see the statue, I can't help thinking that the nurse looking skyward is searching for signs of him—or one of his chopper pilots—*thwopping* in to bring out the living, and the dead. So the memorial represents one person's interpretation of one particular moment in one particular battlefield. But it also speaks for all moments, throughout history, when people quietly (or at the top of their lungs) bravely (or scared beyond description) did what needed to be done. I hope the memorial continues to teach, and to heal. I know it honors people long overdue for recognition, and for our gratitude."

These were the people the memorial had been built for: people touched by the war in all sorts of ways. The Red Cross workers who encouraged soldiers when encouragement was hard to find. The WACs who counted caskets as they arrived in San Francisco. The medics who unloaded endless casualties in Japan, soldiers too sick to come home. And, yes, the nurses like Maggie Arriola who wouldn't give up on a guy without any arms and legs, and who, decades later, realized he'd lived, made a life for himself—in part, perhaps, because she refused to let him die.

The night after the dedication, sculptor Glenna Goodacre and I went together to see the statue without all the crowds. Close to midnight there were still people there, standing or circling the four figures as the lighting glimmered downward on the newly polished bronze.

Among them was a group of veterans, including a woman wearing a Vietnam field jacket who apparently knew who Glenna and I were. She stepped toward us, her face wet with tears. She reached out her hands for ours.

"Thank you," she said. "Now, I can come home."

That's it, I thought. That's why the memorial is so much more than simply a well-sculpted piece of art. That's why we fought for ten years for that statue in this place: So women like her could feel what she felt and say what she said and take away the sense of hope she took away. So American women involved in that horrific war could feel—after much too long—as if we were finally home.

EPILOGUE

The 25th Anniversary Commemoration of the Dedication was held November 11, 2018, during the Veteran's Day Observance at the Wall and at the Vietnam Women's Memorial. Col. Jane Carson, the featured speaker, had also spoken in 1993 during the dedication. We'd come full circle. It was a glorious weekend—a crowd of three thousand showed up—and, just like in 1993, I was blessed to have my entire family with me—this time with grandchildren!

Following the dedication of the memorial in 1993, the Vietnam Women's Memorial Project's board of directors renamed the non-profit corporation to the Vietnam Women's Memorial *Foundation* (VWMF) to more accurately reflect the organization's remaining mission.

Shortly thereafter, the VWMF instituted Storytelling: In Their Own Words, a program held on site at the Vietnam Women's Memorial every Veterans Day and Memorial Day that gives veterans and others a forum to share their stories with the public. Since 1994, hundreds of individuals have participated.

Just as the fight to get the memorial had its bumps, our time since the original dedication hasn't always been smooth. Though we made clear to the Vietnam Veterans Memorial Fund (VVMF), the stewards of the Wall, that a woman speaker would participate during every Memorial Day and Veteran's Day official ceremony staged near the Wall, we got resistance. I received a letter from the VVMF President Jan Scruggs saying, "There was simply not enough time to allow a woman speaker." I contested this with the National Park Service, which overruled Scruggs and upheld our right to participate based upon stipulations in the Vietnam Women's Memorial Memorandum of Conveyance. Finally, after fifteen years, the right of women to participate in the ceremony was no longer contested.

At the time the memorial was dedicated, we were $350,000 in debt. But there were still champions of women veterans out there. Paul DelRossi, the Chairman and CEO of General Cinema Theaters in Boston— and the brother of a Vietnam vet—had heard me speak in Stoneham, Massachusetts, and when learning of our shortfall told me, "Diane, this is not your debt. This is America's debt. I will raise that money." During the Fifth Anniversary Commemoration of the Dedication of the Vietnam Women's Memorial, DelRossi presented a check for $350,000—money he'd made by holding a sneak preview of a movie in his theaters. Pepsi-Cola—CEO Roger Enrico was a Vietnam vet—donated its money from drink sales. Our debt was paid.

For twenty-two years following the dedication, our VWMF executive director and members of our board sustained the mission. We responded to hundreds of inquiries from the press, scholars, researchers, students in the U.S. and from around the world. We facilitated research on women veterans with the Department of Veterans Affairs and private entities. We identified sister veterans and connected veterans when possible. We identified women veterans for interviews requested for radio, TV, panel discussion, events, documentaries.

By 2015, I had led the Vietnam Women's Memorial Foundation (formerly "Project") for thirty-two years. It was time to secure the stewardship of the Vietnam Women's Memorial into the future. Eastern National, an association recognized by Congress to promote the educational and interpretive mission of the National Park Service, assumed the assets and operating mission of the Vietnam Women's Memorial Foundation to honor the legacy of women veterans from the Vietnam era. Upon the dissolution of the Foundation, we donated thirteen thousand names of women veterans registered in our Sister Search data base to WIMSA, *The Women's Memorial*, located at the entrance to Arlington

Cemetery. And yes, *The Women's Memorial* includes and also honors the Vietnam veteran generation of women.

Sadly, Rodger Brodin passed away in November 1995, leaving a legacy of magnificent bronze artwork. He was fifty-five. One of the four statues of "the Nurse" stands proudly at the Highground Veterans Memorial Park in Neillsville, Wisconsin.

Sculptor Glenna Goodacre announced her retirement in September 2016. She created nearly six hundred sculptural works, including the Irish Memorial in Philadelphia, and a circulating U.S. coin, the Sacagawea Dollar. Glenna says that the most meaningful piece she created was the Vietnam Women's Memorial.

Ann Cunningham, my friend who lost a fiancé in Vietnam, died unexpectedly of a cerebral hemorrhage on September 2, 2007, while attending the Wolfhound 25th Infantry Reunion in Lexington, Kentucky, surrounded by the men and women she loved and who loved her so dearly.

Charley Streiff survived his injury and completed his active duty commitment stateside, then returned to Minnesota to farm with his father. He later became an agricultural lender for thirty-five years.

Edie McCoy Meeks, a hootchmate in Pleiku, lives in New York and is still working as an operating room nurse. She radiates her cheer and love to everyone she knows in the nursing profession and while advocating for her sister and brother veterans on the local and state level.

David Chung, who did so much to move the statue from New Mexico to Washington, D.C., worked at Federal Express for twenty-five years and retired in 2000. Today he lives in Bozeman, Montana, where he serves as the Senior Vice Commander for the Military Order of the Purple Heart, Department of Montana.

Following their service, many Vietnam women veterans went on to higher education and advanced their careers as nurses, dentists, physicians, judges, attorneys, professors, artists, teachers, psychologists, licensed clinical social workers, and pilots, to name a few. Many of them stayed in the military and helped change the course of history for women in service to our nation. Some achieved "firsts," including Army Nurse Brig. Gen. Anna Mae Violet McCabe Hays who was the first woman in the U.S. Armed Forces to be promoted to a General Officer rank in 1970. Hays paved the way for equal treatment of women, countering occupational sexism and made numerous recommendations advancing the role of women into military policy. She died in 2018.

Women in uniform have faced challenges wherever they serve and have proven they are not "shrinking violets" on the battlefield and in war zones. They demonstrated courage in Vietnam and around the world, just as women in previous wars had and women in the military continue to do. They paved the way for us. And Vietnam veteran women paved the way for opening up every specialty women warriors serve in today. Each generation inspires and leads into the next era, opening the doors for advancement and leaving legacies of inspiration.

While building the Vietnam Women's Memorial, veteran women sliced through decades of silence and transformed images and conversation about Vietnam, affirming that women, too, share the crucible of war.

AUTHOR'S NOTE

Life for me changed after the dedication of the Vietnam Women's Memorial. I had more time for my family. I started sleeping through the night. I exchanged letters with new friends and reacquainted with old friends. But as life relaxed, I was fighting my own old demons. I no longer fought dreams of failing the Vietnam Women's Memorial Foundation or what I must say the next day at an agency hearing. But Vietnam would not go away.

I went to the VA for help. And found it. I was not ashamed to be diagnosed with PTSD. For me, healing has meant remembering and honoring not just human beings but also memories. I look at them now without fear but a quiet reverence; they are a part of me and are what inspired me to continue to serve my country as an advocate for veterans.

It helped me to return to Vietnam; for the first time, I saw it as a country, not a war. In 1998, I had the opportunity to join World TEAM Sports for an international event bringing disabled and able-bodied athletes together to bicycle 1,200 miles from Hanoi down Highway One to Vũng Tàu and finishing at Ho Chi Minh City (Saigon). Its mission was reconciliation with the enemy.

Led by world-class road racing cyclist Greg Lemond and champion long-distance swimmer athlete Diana Nyad, more than fifty of us U.S. veterans, some blind on tandem bikes and many amputees, bicycled for fourteen days with veterans of the former North Vietnamese Army; in the evenings we had conversations with the help of translators.

We saw the North Vietnamese as people, not as the enemy. We shared stories, and we shared the pain of a war few of us wanted. Along the way we visited hospitals, clinics, and schools. We had raised enough money to donate thousands of dollars to help rebuild the Bach Mai Hospital in Hanoi, which our stray bombs had destroyed in 1972. I am grateful to Vietnam Veterans of America, one of my sponsors, for its contribution to the Bach Mai Hospital. I came home with new memories, new friends, and an understanding of the ways the people of Vietnam had forged ahead in shaping their lives and their country after the war.

The dedication of the Vietnam Women's Memorial was a culmination of my life's work. But my work was not over. It was a privilege to chair the board of directors of the VWMF for twenty-two additional years following the dedication in 1993; together we advanced our educational, research, and sister-search mission. The connections I had made over the years, along with the experience and confidence I had gained, gave me a platform to advocate for veteran's health and benefits on the local, state, and national levels.

Through presidential appointments, I served under six Secretaries of Veterans Affairs on the VA Advisory Committee on the Readjustment of Veterans in Washington, D.C. In that role, I joined my committee colleagues in advocating strongly to fund the expansion of the Vet Center program to more than three hundred centers across the United States. I accepted numerous invitations to present commencement addresses at high schools and universities across the country. I spoke at veterans' reunions and lectured at schools of nursing, at numerous U.S. Army ROTC (Reserve Officer Training Corps) programs, and to U.S. Military Academies.

Among others, my audiences have been students in grade school through graduate school, historical societies, civic organizations, VA Medical Centers, the Library of Congress, StoryCorps, the Veterans History Project, and the National Archives. I served as a consultant on many projects and participated in documentaries about the Vietnam War and about women veterans. I continue to work with researchers, authors, and journalists, facilitating their efforts to tell the stories and history of women who served, concentrating on a wide range of their experiences during and post-Vietnam. These activities have been highly rewarding.

In Montana, my home now, the mountains, trails, lakes, and rivers offer me boundless opportunities in the natural world. My ultimate therapy is spending time outdoors, which helps to keep me healthy both physically and emotionally.

I don't understand the word "closure." I had tried that with denial and "compartmentalizing" by putting memories away in boxes, like the footlocker—*DO NOT OPEN*—those subconsciously tucked away in the recesses of our minds. I closed off Vietnam. It didn't work. I am a survivor. And to save myself, I needed to help others. I am gratified with my journey and the work accomplished, in partnership with so many exceptional people and allies along the way.

Today, I feel peace. The grace I used to pray for when the casualties came in has been showing up more frequently. Prayers have been answered. Faith restored. Joy permitted. Guilt quieted.

My greatest joy is spending time with our seven grandchildren. Is there a wartime veteran alive who doesn't realize that every day on earth is an extra day afforded by some miracle to us and one not to those who didn't come home?

By another miracle, Mike and I have been married for forty-eight years. When I met the man I was to love more than any other, I had no idea he would lead me out of the depths of grief and loss and be my quiet sentry while shepherding me through ten years of work to honor the women of the Vietnam War. If not for him, I might not have been around to fight that fight.

AFTERWORD

A DAUGHTER'S REFLECTION
BY CARRIE EVANS

My mom's work on the Vietnam Women's Memorial Project infused and deeply shaped my childhood and who I am today. I was six when she founded the project and have few memories of her before it. I called her the "midnight activist." At night, I often woke to find my mom at a small, antique desk in our living room. She was usually writing thank you letters to volunteers or appeals to potential supporters. As Dad worked a demanding job, she didn't have enough hours in the day to manage the project, raise my brothers and me, and juggle the many details and complexities of a life with so many responsibilities and commitments. So, she often went without a full night's sleep to tackle what there hadn't been enough time for in the day. She gave herself so fully, sacrificing any time for herself to the project and to motherhood.

My mom is exceedingly industrious and a masterful multitasker. She was always busy working on the project while both preparing and insisting that everyone be home at six o'clock for the meal she somehow made while fielding phone calls and working on the project all day. Our house was a busy hangout spot for my brothers' friends and mine. To keep our fridge full while feeding us and a neighborhood crowd, she and I would make a weekly trip to the grocery store, often filling two carts. Despite my brothers' best efforts, we kept the cookie jar full and I gained a lifelong love of baking, inspired by many of her childhood recipes from the farm. She called me her shadow because I went everywhere with her.

During those years, my mom traveled frequently to Washington, D.C., and across the country, expanding the roster of the project's supporters and navigating layers of regulatory approvals. She made huge meals ahead of time and ensured we all had what we needed. She may not have attended all our school events or our extracurricular activities, but her sacrifices and example instilled other strengths in my brothers and me. Out of her journey, the four of us emerged independent, industrious, and with tremendous pride in our mom's accomplishments.

Watching my mom shaped my life. As her "shadow," I would spend my time reading or doing homework in her office, listening to her calls and her clacking away on the keyboard. At times, I traveled with her to hearings and veterans' events. From my otherwise comfortable and privileged childhood, I witnessed firsthand the significant challenges women face in the public space and in leadership roles. But I was also exposed to the exceptional diversity of our country. I watched my mom interact with thousands of vets with love and openness—greeting almost everyone with a hug. From the hardscrabble to professionals, vets of every race, religion, and background, urban and rural—she saw them all as the eighteen-year-old boys she treated.

As a mom myself now, and a professional in higher education, I think often about the development of young people and our future generations of leaders. I reflect upon the relentless obstacles my mom faced in mounting a national effort to dedicate a memorial recognizing women. Aspiring to, and actually accomplishing, big things generally requires one to sacrifice; she certainly did. How she navigated and overcame failure and hardships is a cornerstone of her success story.

On leadership

I've learned a tremendous amount about leadership, persistence, resilience, industriousness, and the value of gratitude from my mother. Her story imparts a richness of leadership lessons.

First and foremost: resilience. My mom has it in spades. Despite so many stumbles and setbacks, she kept going. There would not be a Vietnam Women's Memorial without her resolute persistence and resilience in the face of moments of defeat, insults, fatigue, and uncertainty of the path forward. This book touches upon only a fraction of the challenges she endured. When I remind her now of incidents or moments that I can recall, I see the recognition dawn on her face as she acknowledges these challenges. She moved on, buried them and—in not dwelling on or lamenting what couldn't be changed—stayed focused on her vision and the next steps to achieve it.

My mom is exceptionally generous in sharing praise and gratitude. Whether someone volunteered for an hour to stuff newsletters into envelopes or for month after month on the project's efforts, she expressed her thanks and made them feel uniquely valuable for their contributions. She made everyone involved, even those in minor roles, feel like a key contributor to the project's efforts. When I've attended Memorial Day and Veterans Day ceremonies, I know much of the profound love and respect Vietnam veterans showed my mom stems from the generosity of her appreciation and attention to them.

For many male Vietnam veterans, she represents the nurse who may have cared for them, whom they never had a chance to thank. She brings an authenticity and profoundly deep compassion for her fellow veterans. As her profile on the national stage of veterans' advocacy grew, she stayed true to her roots and—unlike some others I watched around her as their power and influence grew—didn't have an ego that got in the way.

Her achievements are also testament to the importance of surrounding oneself with trusted allies and supporters. Testing her grit and resilience, there were many moments she may have stopped had it not been for someone stepping in to provide support, help, comfort, or inspiration: my amazing Grandma Dorothy, for watching my brothers and me, cooking huge farm-style meals to feed us all and laundering mountains of clothes; my dad, for being her steadfast rock of support; and the countless friends, volunteers, board members and exceptional allies who she drew around her and the project. The network of people around her was, and is, essential.

Her resiliency, her gratitude, her support network, and her ability and willingness to forge alliances even with those who had previously put up roadblocks or had been condescending, cruel, or otherwise less than supportive at some point earlier along the way. All are trademarks of my mother. She doesn't hold grudges. With her signature compassionate tenacity, she seeks opportunities to find common ground and would repeatedly try a new approach if the first, second, or third tactic didn't work. She'd find a way.

Her legacy

When in Washington, D.C., I like to sit quietly on the benches at the Vietnam Women's Memorial, observing the visitors: school groups, families, children, veterans, travelers from across the world. Filled with joy, I watch and listen to their comments. With pride in my mom's and her supporters' remarkable achievement, I feel tremendously fortunate to have witnessed this history. Sitting there, I just absorb. The children who say, "Mommy, is this a nurse? Is she caring for someone who is hurt?" or visitors' reflections on women who served in wartime. Veterans who leave a rose in the hand of the wounded soldier. Women who look into the eyes of the standing woman or bend down to gently touch the face of the kneeling woman.

The Wall—Maya Lin's extraordinary design—is devastatingly moving and perhaps among the most memorable of any war memorial ever built. But I know, as an adult watching the visitors to the memorial, that my mom was right: the addition of the Three Servicemen statue left a void at this site. The Vietnam Women's Memorial filled that. It created a space for healing and hope, as it aimed to do. It also has been part of our country's education and movement towards recognizing the "men *and women*" in uniform and, specifically, the roles of women in wartime.

For a long time, my mom wanted to write her story to document the remarkable ten-year effort that led to the memorial's dedication in 1993. I am grateful to author Bob Welch for helping give her the structure and guidance to share her leadership journey. And I am immensely grateful to my mom. Her courage not only left a mark on the world but has been an inspiration for me and countless others. On behalf of my family, and all who have found solace at the memorial, we're so glad she persevered through this journey.

Welcome home, Mom.

Carrie Evans is Senior Assistant Dean of Student Affairs and Executive Education at the Daniel J. Evans School of Public Policy & Governance at the University of Washington in Seattle.

ACKNOWLEDGMENTS

My warmest and grateful thanks are due to those many people who helped in ways large and small to shape this book. I wish to thank everyone who has been on my life's journey from family to friend, mentor, colleague, cheerleader, and devoted helper whilst navigating the long footpath to realize my dream. I can only begin to name those who have walked beside me since my youth. Your name may not be here but you are not forgotten.

My foremost thanks to co-author Bob Welch for his passionate commitment: though reluctant at first, he came to believe wholeheartedly in my story even though he had already written *American Nightingale*, what he felt was the ultimate story of a military nurse, Frances Slanger, a World War II heroine killed the night after she'd written a poignant letter honoring American GIs. *Thank you, Frances, for whispering in Bob's ear that he needed to do another one.* And a heartfelt thank you to Beck McLaughlin, whose mother Marion McLaughlin—a nurse—had urged her to share the book with me. It inspired me to contact Bob. Journalist David Halberstam, before his untimely death in 2007, told me, "a good book should burn inside of you." When I told Bob my story burned inside of me, it was that phrase—and knowing this nurse was alive—that convinced him to partner with me on it.

I would also like to thank Sally Welch for her generous heart and support to her husband Bob for enduring his time away writing—and for providing us with cinnamon twists as we met on the Oregon Coast for interviewing. A very special thanks to his sister-in-law, Ann Petersen, for her keen editing of the first look of our script.

I am indebted to John Toensing, a Vietnam veteran helicopter pilot, who kept urging me to write this story. He was so committed that he bribed Bob—whose son was a high school friend of John's son—with fresh fish he'd caught in the Pacific Ocean. It worked! And thanks to John's lovely wife, Lynn, who encouraged the project.

I am ever grateful to my literary agent, Greg Johnson, for his unwavering enthusiasm and commitment to this story. Writing and publishing a book is not a solitary endeavor and I am deeply indebted to my publisher, Permuted Press and Anthony Ziccardi who saw value in this story from the very beginning. I cannot thank their editors enough—CT Ferrell and Kiera Hufford—whose critiques and suggestions enormously improved the manuscript. It has been a great pleasure to work with Heather King, my managing editor, whose clarity and proficiency kept us on track with the numerous moving parts in publishing a book.

Thanks, also, to Vietnam veterans: Col. Amelia Jane Carson, USA, (Ret.), Lt. Col. John Westerlund, USA, (Ret.), and Lt. Col. Justin (Jerry) Martin, USMC, (Ret.) who reviewed the manuscript and offered helpful suggestions toward its improvement. Any mistakes are my own.

Thank you to my sister veterans who needled and pushed me to write my story and provide endless encouragement over many years: Col. Amelia Jane Carson, USA, (Ret.), Col. Cindy Gurney, USA, (Ret.), Edie McCoy Meeks, Dottie Beatty, Karen King-Johnson, Lynn Kohl, Diane Jaeger, Pam Lovell, Barb Lilly, Capt. Kay Bauer, USN, (Ret.), Col. Lennie Enzel, USA (Ret.), Carolyn Tanaka, Maj. Laureen Otto, USA, (Ret.) and Col. Eily Pat Gorman, USA (Ret.).

The completion of my memoir is tinged with sadness, as several of those dearest of friends who heroically supported the memorial effort through good times and bad, didn't live to see it published: Lt. Col. P. Evangeline Jamison, USA (Ret.), Rear Adm. Frances Shea Buckley, USN, (Ret), Ann Cunningham, Diana Hellinger, Cheryl Nicol, Charlotte Nicol, Emily Strange, The Honorable Daniel Foley, Adm. William J. Crowe, USN, (Ret.) and his wife Shirley Crowe, John Geiger, Gerald

C. Bender, Ted Fetting, Ernie DiRocco, Terry Babler, Lane Evans, B.T. Collins, and Jill Ker Conway.

Heartfelt gratitude to my dearest brother veterans who provided unfailing encouragement, wisdom, and guidance: Richard Timmerman, Lorin Sather, Marv Freedman, Robert Brudno, Dick DelRossi, Lt. Col. John Black, USA, (Ret.), Robert Spanogle, John Sommer, John Hanson, Tom Haynes, Dud Hendrick, David O. Chung, Allen Hoe, Jeff "Doc" Dentice, Brig. Gen. George Price, USA, (Ret.), Harry Robinson, Maj. Gen. William Roosma, USA, (Ret.), Gen. Colin Powell, USA, (Ret.), Col. Douglas E. Moore, USA, (Ret.), Richard (Dick) Marbes, Rick Schultz, Bob Wallace, Paul Masi, Joe Belardo, Col. Thomas Chisholm, USA, (Ret.), Leon Cotton, Francis Whitebird (Lakota Nation), Col. Don Bishop, USA (Ret.), Paul Critchlow, Charles T. Hagel, Billy Ray Cameron, Phil Yeager, Jake Singer (Navajo Nation), Milton Chee (Navajo Nation), Col. Ray Read, USA (Ret.), Tom Cory, Ron Young, Maj. Gen. Gene Prendergast, USA, (Ret.), Bryce Gregerson, Larry Turner, Charlie Wells, Medal of Honor Recipients Sammy Davis Jr., and Gary Wetzel.

I owe a debt of gratitude and deepest appreciation to Paul Mahon, for his tireless assistance and invaluable legal guidance to the Vietnam Women's Memorial Project Foundation's board of directors and for me personally. And to those people whose talents, expertise, and encouragement were immeasurable: George Dickie, Dana Delany, Jeff Stoffer, Gary Gilson, Paul DelRossi, Dan and Ruth Daly, Wilma Blakeman, Judith Helein, Sheldon Smith, Raquel Ramati, Kara Dixon Vuic, Marsha Guenzler-Stevens, Karen Spears Zacharias, Lt. Col. Sharon "Sam" Alden, USA (Ret.), Arlene Adams-Cataldo, Comdr. Anne M. Devney, USN, (Ret.), Mary Beth Newkumet, Stephen McKinnon, Diane Brady, Nancy Mayger, Judy Leavitt, Janis Nark, Kim Heikkila, Karen Kleeman, Nancy Chisholm, Mary Ruedisilli, and Malayna Evans.

I am indebted to Laura Palmer and Jurate Kazickas, reporters who covered the war in Vietnam and who supported the memorial from day one and urged me to write about what I saw and felt in the war and why I fought for the Vietnam Women's Memorial. And to Joe Galloway and the late Morley Safer of CBS's *60 Minutes*, who both had reported from Vietnam and believed women deserved their place at the Vietnam Veterans Memorial, inspiring me to never give up telling my story.

I cannot express enough gratitude to the late Rodger Brodin for his belief in a monument to women and for his generosity in time, effort, and kindred spirit as he helped forge the vision to its strong start. I salute him here, and acknowledge the extraordinary importance of his contribution.

And abiding eternal thanks to the insightful and gifted woman who sculpted the bronze Vietnam Women's Memorial statue, Glenna Goodacre, who was always asking, "Now Diane, when are you going to write that book? What are you waiting for?" And to her talented manager, Dan Anthony, whose considerate and cheerful attention to every detail made our work together a great pleasure.

I am indebted to those early trailblazers and mentors who helped me to wage a battle in Washington, D.C., and ultimately be able to write this story: Mary Stout, past president of Vietnam Veterans of America, including those who have passed on but will never to be forgotten: Brig. Gen. Lillian Dunlap, USA, Brig. Gen. Hazel-Johnson Brown, USA, and Maj. Gen. Jeanne M. Holm, USAF. There are so many more women who fit this category; I am only sorry I cannot list them all.

Special recognition to the women veterans and VWMP board members whose groundwork during those early days in the Project's history made a difference: Doris (Dee) Troth Lippman, Cathie Solomonson, Mary Ann Attebury, Linda Schwartz, and Margaret Hodge.

There aren't enough words to express the appreciation of the late Rod McBrien, a singer-songwriter who, with John Linde, wrote the theme song *Til The White Dove Flies Alone*, sung by Crystal Gayle at the dedication, and to the talented Kera O'Bryon for performing this tribute at every anniversary hence.

I would like to thank the good people at the Vet Centers I have frequented who have no idea how they have contributed to this book. They helped me find strength and hope. More than once, they saved my life.

My gratitude is not complete without thanking those who contributed to the success of the Vietnam Women's Memorial mission post dedication. Jim Knott, president of the Vietnam Veterans Memorial Fund, and members of its board of directors chaired by John Dibble, have validated that women, too, belong at the sacred place entrusted to their stewardship, along with those good people at the National Park Service who never wavered in their support for a memorial to women.

I have enormous appreciation for the National Park Service's "Volunteers at the Wall," who have helped me over the years to find precious names and keep me hydrated on those searing hot D.C. days sitting up on the stage or standing at the Wall while the wreaths are presented on Memorial and Veterans days. And for teaching millions of visitors about the women whose names are on the Wall.

I would be remiss if I didn't mention how important the women in the Philanthropic Education Organization (PEO) have been for me since joining them the year after the dedication. I thank them for their loving concern and opportunity to expand my interests outside of the veteran's community and their push to get this memoir written.

My greatest primary source is from living memory and the thirty-two years' worth of archival materials covering the memorial effort from 1983–2015. I was a saver of most every scrap of paper including calendar entries. I am grateful to former executive directors, and staff, of the Vietnam Women's Memorial Foundation (formerly "Project") for also being savers. This was a time before email notes and letters disappeared into the thin air with a click of a mouse. I have originals/copies of letters, notes, testimony, and transactions with Congress and the federal agencies in Washington, D.C. I extend gratitude to the Library of Congress for housing them.

The memorial wouldn't have happened without the strong support of the VSOs (veterans service organizations): The American Legion, Veterans of Foreign Wars, Disabled American Veterans, Vietnam Veterans of America, Paralyzed Veterans of America, VietNow, Military Order of the Purple Heart, AMVETS, and Jewish War Veterans. I am grateful for their commitment to lobbying Congress and campaigns to their posts throughout America for financial support.

I acknowledge the invaluable assistance of the National Association of State Directors of Veterans Affairs, The American Nurses Association, and that of every major nursing and civic association who passed resolutions in support of honoring women Vietnam veterans. Artie Muller and Rolling Thunder National, walked, if not rode on this journey with us by strongly advocating for their sister veterans.

Thank you to every volunteer and donor who stepped up, with $1 or $500,000, for giving of your time and treasure; you can be proud to know that you helped create an historic tribute in the healing journey for veterans and for all of America. I wish I could list every name here.

I am grateful to my daughters-in-law, Grace Evans and Jennifer Evans, and son-in-law Jika Gqiba-Knight for their love and support.

My eternal gratitude for my dear parents, Newell and Dorothy, who gave me a lifetime of love and support; my older brothers Chester and Ronald, who have both passed on, and who inspired me into service; and younger brothers Maynard and Ward, who are waiting to hear my story. Very special thanks to my dearest sister, Nola, always there for me, but when I returned from Vietnam was too young to understand what I was going through. I hope this book answers the questions I never adequately answered back then.

Guy, Luke, Carrie, and Jon-Erik, I love you so much and thank you for providing endless trust and good humor while keeping my feet firmly planted on the ground—knowing that Vietnam was as much a part of me as you are—and for your patience and boundless affection. I am so proud of you. You have blessed my life beyond measure.

In particular, I thank my wise daughter Carrie, who never doubted me, who provides daily joy in my life, and who added editorial suggestions that were invaluable, if not entertaining at times. My children each have kept me true to myself and helped me find my way home through writing this final Vietnam chapter.

At long last, I record here my deepest appreciation and abiding love to my husband Mike for his infinite patience and devotion, for standing by me through difficult and frightening times. He was, and will always be, my hero. I so wish that his late mother, Beulah, and father, Ruel, could read this book and understand the role their son played in service to our nation, and in helping to realize a national memorial honoring his sister veterans. Thank you, Mike for your love, loyalty, and unwavering faith that sustained me.

GLOSSARY AND ABBREVIATIONS

Article #15: Uniform Code of Military Justice provides commanders with a non-judicial, administrative tool to maintain discipline for relatively minor infractions involving enlisted soldiers. For officers, it is often a career-ending punishment.

ARVN: Army Republic of Vietnam.

AWOL: Absent Without Leave.

BAMC: Brooke Army Medical Center, Fort Sam Houston, Texas.

Boonie Hat: Slang for a military issue hat for wear in the jungle, or South Vietnam.

Bouncing Betty: A mine with two charges: one to propel the explosive charge upward and the other set to explode at about waist level.

BOQ: Bachelor Officers' Quarters.

Charlie: Slang for Viet Cong.

Chinook: The official name of the CH-47 tandem rotor transport helicopter. Also known as a "Hook."

CFA: Commission of Fine Arts.

Chopper: Helicopter.

Corpsman: Medical aid serviceman or woman—usually in a hospital setting.

CWA: Commemorative Works Act.

DAV: Disabled American Veterans.

DEROS: Date of Estimated Return from overseas.

DMZ: Demilitarized Zone; created by Geneva Convention along 17th parallel.

DPC: Delayed Primary Closure—surgical procedure to close wounds after two to three days.

Dustoff: Radio call sign for medical evacuation helicopters; the term refers to the great amount of dust thrown up by the rotors as the medevacs come in to land.

ER: Emergency Room.

ETA: Estimated time of arrival.

Fire Base: An artillery battery set up to give fire support to surrounding units.

GI: Government Issue. Often a reference to men drafted for military service and called a "GI."

Green Beret: Popular name for the Special Forces, taken from the color of their distinctive headgear.

Grunt: A non-offensive term used to designate the guys on the ground. Originally slang for a Marine fighting on the battlegrounds of Vietnam, but later applied to any infantryman fighting there.

Gurney: A flat transport often of canvas stretched on a frame for carrying the sick, wounded, or dead.

Hootch: A building housing military personnel in the combat theater.

Huey: HU-1, the utility helicopter that was the workhorse of Vietnam.

ICU: Intensive Care Unit in a hospital.

IV: Intravenous injection for administering fluids and medication.

KIA: Killed in action.

Litter: A flat transport, often of canvas stretched on a frame, for carrying the sick, wounded, or dead.

LZ: Landing zone.

LOH: Pronounced "loach"—light observation helicopter.

M16: American 5.56mm infantry rifle.

Mama San: Term used in Vietnam to describe an older woman.

MARS: Military Auxiliary Radio System.

Med Cap: Medical Civil Assistance Program sponsored by the U.S. for Vietnamese civilians.

Medevac: Term used for aerial medical evacuation.

Medic: Medical aid serviceman or woman on the battlefield or in a hospital unit.

MP: Military Police.

Napalm: Jellied gasoline used in air strikes.

NPS: National Park Service.

NVA: North Vietnamese Army or generic term for any soldier or group of soldiers from the North.

NCPC: National Capital Planning Commission.

NCMC: National Capital Memorial Commission.

Point: The lead man in a patrol.

POW: Prisoner of War.

Pseudomonas: Bacillus resistant to most antibiotics.

Push: Mass casualties.

PVA: Paralyzed Veterans of America.

Quonset Hut: A multiuse lightweight prefabricated structure of corrugate galvanize steel having a semicircular cross-section. Used in Vietnam for hospital wards and storage.

R&R: Rest and Recuperation: reference to time off for military personnel.

ROTC: Reserve Officer Training Corps.

Sapper: Enemy soldier trained to attack fortifications.

Stretcher: A flat transport, often of canvas stretched on a frame, for carrying the sick, wounded, or dead.

Three Servicemen: Statue at the Vietnam Veterans Memorial in Washington, D.C. Designed by Frederick Hart.

The Wall: The Vietnam Veterans Memorial in Washington, D.C.

Triage: The sorting out of patients according to the criticalness of their needs, i.e., those who need immediate surgery versus those who need only minimal care or less urgent care.

VC: Viet Cong; also known as "Victor Charlie."

Vet Center: Community-based counseling center that provides a wide range of social and psychological services to military veterans and active duty personnel.

Viet Cong: Also known as the National Liberation Front—a mass political organization in South Vietnam and Cambodia with its own army that fought against the United States and South Vietnamese governments.

VSI: Very seriously ill. Army designation for those patients who may die without immediate and definitive medical care.

VVA: Vietnam Veterans of America.

VVMF: Vietnam Veterans Memorial Fund.

VWMP: Vietnam Women's Memorial Project.

VWMF: Vietnam Women's Memorial Foundation.

WIA: Wounded in Action.

FOR MORE INFORMATION

To learn more about the memorial effort, its education programs, and research on women who served during the Vietnam era visit: www.vietnamwomensmemorial.org

Or visit Diane Carlson Evans' web site: www.dianecarlsonevans.com

SHARON ANN LANE

1st Lieutenant Sharon Ann Lane, U.S. Army was killed by a rocket explosion on June 8, 1969, less than 10 weeks after she arrived in Vietnam. Assigned to the 312th Evacuation Hospital, 1LT Lane was working in the Vietnamese ward of the hospital when the rocket exploded, killing her and her patients. She was from Ohio and her name can be found on Panel 23W, Line 112.

HEDWIG DIANE ORLOWSKI

1st Lieutenant Hedwig Diane Orlowski, U.S. Army was onboard with Capt. Alexander when their plane crashed on its return trip to Qui Nhon. She was assigned to the 67th Evacuation Hospital. 1LT Orlowski was from Michigan. She is remembered on Panel 31E, Line 15.

WOMEN ON THE WALL

VIETNAM VETERANS MEMORIAL FUND

FOUNDERS OF THE WALL

ELEANOR GRACE ALEXANDER

Captain Eleanor Grace Alexander, U.S. Army had been working in a hospital in Pleiku to help out during mass casualties from Dak To when her plane crashed on the return trip to Qui Nhon on November 30, 1967. She was with the 85th Evacuation Hospital. She was from New Jersey and is remembered on Panel 31E, Line 8.

PAMELA DOROTHY DONOVAN

2nd Lieutenant Pamela Dorothy Donovan, U.S. Army died of a rare Southeast Asian virus on July 8, 1968. Born in Ireland, she was assigned to the 85th Evacuation Hospital in Qui Nhon. 2LT Donovan is remembered on Panel 53W, Line 43.

CAROL ANN ELIZABETH DRAZBA

2nd Lieutenant Carol Ann Elizabeth Drazba, U.S. Army was killed in a helicopter crash near Saigon on February 18, 1966. Born and raised in Pennsylvania, she is remembered on Panel 5E, Line 46

ANNIE RUTH GRAHAM

Lieutenant Colonel Annie Ruth Graham, U.S. Army suffered a stroke on August 14, 1968. She was from North Carolina and was the Chief Nurse with the 91st Evacuation Hospital in Tuy Hoa. Her name can be found on Panel 48W, Line 12

ELIZABETH ANN JONES

2nd Lieutenant Elizabeth Ann Jones, U.S. Army was flying with 2LT Drazba and was killed in the same helicopter crash near Saigon. She was assigned to the 3rd Field Hospital. 2LT Jones was from South Carolina and is remembered on Panel 5E, Line 47.

MARY THERESE KLINKER

Captain Mary Therese Klinker, U.S. Air Force was part of an on-board medical team during Operation Babylift. Her flight was carrying 243 infants and children when it developed pressure problems and crashed while attempting to return to the airport. Captain Klinker was killed on April 4, 1975, just three weeks before the Fall of Saigon. A native of Indiana, she is remembered on Panel 1W, Line 122.

Women who died in Vietnam.
Seven Army Nurses. One Air Force Nurse.
(Courtesy Vietnam Veterans Memorial Fund, Washington D.C.)